MW01070810

MUSTANG:
the story
FROM ZERO TO $1 BILLION

written by:
BILL HIGGS

Inspired by Paul Redmon, Felix Covington and a legion of Mustangers

PEOPLE ORIENTED, PROJECT DRIVEN™

For more information and resources on Mustang: The Story please visit: www.mustangthestory.com

ISBN 978-1-4951-9876-5 (hardcover)

ISBN 978-1-4951-9876-2 (softcover)

Layout and design by:
HAVEN CREATIVE
www.thehavencreative.com

COMPLIANT PILED TOWER

[THANKS]

Dena Lee would not let the idea of a book on Mustang die. She arranged for Paul, Felix, me, our wives, and herself to meet at Constance Goodwin's home in Martha's Vineyard, Massachusetts. Constance had been consulting at Mustang for a few years, helping us prepare the second generation leadership team to take over. While our wives went shopping and exploring, Dena, Constance and the three of us worked on the vision and objectives for this book. We also relived those first years and our personal history as that background became the foundation on which Mustang grew. Paul and Felix are the best partners anyone could hope for and towards the end of the weekend they gave me carte-blanche to take their thoughts and the Mustang history and just run with it. They will read it for the first time as you do!

I enlisted the help of Bob Mahlstedt who, as a consultant, had helped me develop the Mustang message since 1988. Lisa Buckner who helped develop the "heart of Mustang" campaign, found much of the materials needed to flesh out the stories. Jeni Bukolt provided graphic design, formatting, editorial assistance and a social media campaign. Kim McClusky read the manuscript from her perspective as a structural engineer who grew into a major management role over twenty years. Jom Kirkland exhibited great patience and tenacity while pulling the pictures and pieces together. These people and all of the Mustangers who gave of themselves over the years to create a unique culture deserve our heartfelt thanks.

**MUSTANG founders
Bill, Felix and Paul
circa 2000**

[DEDICATION]

We would like to dedicate this book to all of the clients, vendors and Mustangers who put projects ahead of politics and personal gain... in an effort to create a win-win environment. Together we created a new heroic space in the petroleum industry.

We're thinking of this book as our proposal to the world on how to treat people, take care of business and make heroes. I wrote this book in similar fashion to how we pursued work at Mustang. I would work to establish a relationship with the client and bring in the experience of our team to expand that connection and move them to a new place.

We want this book to show why and how we started Mustang. Then, as the history of Mustang unfolds, show how our concept of being care-takers rather than owners facilitated the development of a strong culture that set the organization up to overachieve. This book relates how I personally reacted to things and what I perceived were the drivers for actions in order to better engage the reader. We wanted to show failures as well as successes. These experiences shaped our decision-making and risk tolerance as we grew and transitioned through various phases of company growth. Key themes will come through that are applicable to; startup businesses, project people (everything is a project in business), workers, leaders, managers and CEOs of any size business or organization.

MUSTANG founders Felix, Paul and Bill on "move-in" day, 1987

"It was the best of times, it was the worst of times."

Charles Dickens,
A Tale of Two Cities

[TABLE OF CONTENTS]

Prologue

Three men in motion. That's all we were in the beginning in 1985. Three men were moving toward each other through discussions of values, beliefs, family, and work environment. And then in the summer of 1987, we were moving drafting tables, desks, chairs, etc., out of three engineering firms that were closing up shop. It was hot in those shut down buildings in three different parts of the city, and hot outside loading pickup trucks. 98 degrees in the shade and, with the humidity, what is called the "misery index" in Houston was pegged at 107!!

Houston...an Industry under Stress

Misery index seemed an apt term for Houston in those days. After a tremendous oil boom in the seventies, when prices went from $3.00 to $30.00 per barrel, the oil patch and Houston in particular, fell on hard times starting in 1982, when oil plummeted to $15.00 per barrel over a short five year period. The misery index climbed as oil companies reduced staff by 35-40 percent and their vendors and contractors cut even deeper. As companies consolidated for survival, the brunt of this contraction was absorbed by individuals and their families.

There were home foreclosures on every street as families moved to other cities for work. Even the "Luv Ya Blue" Oilers of the National Football League had fallen off the radar screen, as there appeared to be nothing to stop the downward spiral of companies, banks, and attitudes.

The catch phrase became "Stay alive 'til '85"...a far cry from "Drive fast and freeze a Yankee!"... which had been the motto just a few years earlier. But in 1985, companies cut another 20-35 percent and continued to consolidate. When you finished a project at an engineering firm, you were let go if you couldn't find another project on which to bill your time. In some measure, this was "turnabout is fair play" as engineers and drafters had jumped companies regularly in the boom times for small pay increases as low as 25 cents an hour.

"Three men in motion. That's all we were in the beginning in 1985. Three men were moving toward each other through discussions of values, beliefs, family, and work environment. "

Think about being an oil company project manager going through this boom and bust cycle. During the boom, the engineering company you hired had trouble keeping a team together as people changed companies. During the bust, the engineering firm you hired could not get a job to complete as people procrastinated for job security. At the same time, if your project doesn't meet super aggressive cost and schedule criteria, you will lose your job in the oil company because the cuts and consolidations continue.

The environment was rank with injustices. Companies disappeared out from under good, hard-working people. People were let go in November and hired back at a reduced salary in January by the same company. Companies did this to avoid paying for downtime, and to reduce labor costs for a competitive edge. They did this because they felt it was a requirement for survival.

Oil companies also pushed vendors and contractors into survival mode by bidding unmercifully to obtain below cost proposals. They did this because they knew suppliers were hungry and the clients felt they had to bring in low cost solutions in order to keep their own jobs.

NO SECURITY

Companies and individuals looked out for themselves in reaction to an oil price they could not control. Then, as now, even the largest U.S. Oil Companies were just marginal players compared to the resources and market clout of the Organization of Petroleum Exporting Countries (OPEC) and the National Oil Companies (NOCs). It seemed reasonable, in a world where it felt as if you had no control or impact over the situation, that you would take care of number one.

FINDING ANOTHER WAY

We decided in 1985 that we needed to do something different and met periodically to discuss what was possible. Our wives came to most of the meetings because there were three quality marriages, kids and mortgages that could all be ground up in the effort to create a company diametrically opposed to the industry's traditional practices.

Having watched about 30 engineering firms start during the '70s and '80s and having known the owners of a number of them, there was a wide selection of do's and don'ts available for us to pull from. We added to this industry experience our lists of likes and dislikes from being employees in small engineering firms that had started during the boom cycle. All of this was filtered through our past experiences of growing up as wage earners from a young age, varsity sports, religious beliefs, Boy Scouts, engineering training in the Texas A&M (Aggie) culture and for me, intense West Point and Army Ranger training.

What came through our filters were PEOPLE, and beyond that, TEAMS to do projects. We loved people and teams in similar proportion to disliking company interferences with project execution. Our first priority was to create a company that functioned like a super project team: with clear focus, clean lines of communication and an execution mentality.

DECISION TIME

Then reality hit in February of 1987. Joyce Covington came to the kitchen table delivering freshly baked Toll House® cookies and ice cold milk. With a PhD, Joyce was the department head of communications at St. Thomas University and did not mince words. She had a message from our wives, Kay Redmon, Ann Higgs and herself. She said these were the last cookies...either decide to start this company or not - there had been enough talk over the last 15 months!

Felix, her husband of 20 years, understood the message best and picked a date. He felt July 20th, the day America landed a man on the moon, would be a fitting launch date for such an ambitious endeavor.

Paul Redmon and I loved the idea of July 20th, as it gave us time to get our act together on some major projects. The date also worked as an objective and galvanized us into action.

Finally, we were three men moving with purpose, prayer and hope that we could effect a change to improve peoples' lives in an industry we enjoyed.

THROUGH-CYCLE RESULTS

Now it is more than 30 years and 7.5 boom or bust cycles later. The original business plan of 35-85 employees would have made us very successful compared to the 30 companies we had seen. However, the 6,500 people now working on 15 billion dollars-worth of annual spend on global projects at an exceptional value-driven profit margin, feel that we should relate some of the Mustang story. These people proudly call themselves "Mustangers" and they want other companies, organizations, and just plain folks, to build similar hero-making cultures. They have seen the benefits to themselves, their families, their communities, and the industry.

This company has seen it all. From hyper growth to busts that happened industry-wide in a matter of weeks. From the drive to "offshore" engineering services to low cost centers in India to being valued for our expertise. From being discovered by *Fortune Magazine* in 1990 to being the fastest growing engineering firm in America as ranked by *Inc. Magazine* in 1992. The frenetic pace continued unabated.

You will see how we implemented an Employee Stock Ownership Plan in 1996 and then sold the company through an "Adopt a Parent" program in 2000. We worked through a transition process to second generation leadership, completed in 2006, and they took the company to 1 Billion dollars of revenue in 2008! All of this was accomplished while sustaining double digit growth and staying true to all that is encompassed in Mustang's mantra of "People Oriented...Project Driven ™."

We have been recognized by our industry as "Kings of Culture" for building a company where loyalty and taking care of people reigned supreme in the intensely competitive cauldron of the energy industry. This industry, comprised of owners, engineers and suppliers, selected us to receive their 2004 Lifetime Achievement Award for "Visionary Leadership in the Process Industries," which we felt was a huge pat on the back for our people.

YOU CAN DO IT

As we like to say, "there is a pony in here somewhere" that can help others - let's find it. Take this journey to see how "cannots" were turned into "coulds" and finally into "cans." Come see how the same challenges you face were addressed by people with a just-do-it mentality. You will move from the feeling that this team was just lucky to understanding how their unwavering focus on delivering their value proposition created much of their own luck and moved an industry. As you become absorbed into the heroic win-win environment created by Mustang, your world of possibility will expand in figuring out how to take care of *PEOPLE*.

[KEY THEMES]

- We took care of each other no matter what happened.

- We put the Golden Rule into business practice.

- What a company does or makes is not as important as how it conducts business.

- We learned better project management techniques and want to share them.

- If you beat the drum long enough with a "win-win" proposition, eventually people will dance to that drumbeat.

- We learned how to build teams and a culture.

- We grew slower than we could have in order to consistently deliver our value proposition.

We want people to start identifying with Mustang's methods, such that while reading they feel that they can think and act like a Mustanger...and want to act on that thought!!

[VALUE PROPOSITION]

We will deliver your entire project, not just the engineering, for 25% less than you could get it done elsewhere due to our people, team building, execution focus, industry relationships and contracting strategies. This cost reduction stays in your pocket, so every fifth project is free.

[POSSIBLE MARKETS]

- Oil industry
- Businesses / Entrepreneurs
- Military services
- Engineering and business schools
- Aggies and West Pointers
- Boy Scouts
- Church groups
- Gung-ho Employees

"We have nothing to fear, but fear itself."

Franklin D. Roosevelt,
President, USA

PART 1:

MUSTANG 1985-1987
FEELING OUR WAY
Luck...where preparation meets opportunity.
End of the beginning.

We're not totally sure why Mustang was started; other than it sounded like a good idea at the time. Why do soldiers "take that hill" at serious risk to life and limb? They do not "take the hill" due to orders from above, patriotic altruism, or because they want to. They take the hill because they do not want to let their buddy down - knowing their mutual courage will protect each other's flanks.

Once you have been through enough together, the attitude and commitment of all for one and one for all creates a potentially dominating force. At this point, you may not know what is coming, but you are comfortable that you can react and handle any combination of situations.

We knew that we were out-of-the-box thinkers who had been able to effect positive change on projects. We felt that this ability could build a company.

They Must Have Had Us In Mind

When Ford introduced the Mustang almost 40 years ago, they used the slogan "Total Performance". It epitomized responsiveness, ingenuity, quality and price competitiveness -- all in a small package.

They could have been talking about Mustang Engineering instead if they had only added "experience". We are known worldwide for providing super-ior offshore pipeline services. Now we offer total performance capability for onshore pipeline work as well -- from project surveying and right-of-way engineering to inspection and complete project management, utilizing sophisticated AutoCAD® and Intergraph® systems.

Our organization has the experienced people needed to get the job done sooner and on budget. That's why we are working on today's major pipeline projects, compressor stations and gas storage facilities.

To find out more about our total performance capabilities and our list of repeat clients, call Dave Edgar or Bill Higgs TODAY.

MUSTANG ENGINEERING, INC.

First ad

> "There is nothing new under the sun."
> Ecclesiastes 1:9

1: RECOGNIZING THE PIECES

Felix Covington and I would come in early to work and frequently sit down to visit, since our offices were next to each other at CBS Engineering. I found him interesting because he had gone from working in the field on pipelines to being a big-time project manager at Ford Bacon and Davis, a hundred year old pipeline company in Monroe, Louisiana. The intense pressures and long hours inherent in project management took a toll on his health and family, so he just packed everyone up and moved to Houston in 1982. He signed on at CBS Engineering, Inc. as a contract electrical engineer, which gave him a very manageable job considering his skills.

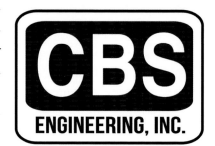

FELIX PUSHES THE BUTTON

At West Point, we would have affectionately labeled Felix Covington as part of the "soft underbelly." These were cadets who had the talent to be at the top of the class but were content to be in the top 200 and "have a life!" Felix skipped the second semester of his senior year in high school when he found out that he could enter Texas A&I University early with the credits he had already earned. No sense being bored, so he moved on. He picked engineering by looking to see which area of study paid the most after graduation and figured he would end up in the booming aerospace industry. He was good at figuring out what needed to be done, cutting the frills and making it happen.

I wondered if Felix smiled inwardly as he watched me strive to move from mechanical engineer to project engineer and then to project manager. Five years older than me, Felix had done it all and now had good balance in his life between work, a family with two teenage daughters, and a furniture shop he and his wife Joyce had started. Our talks allowed me to see deeper into the talent Felix possessed while he had fun making observations about the company, projects, and people we worked with every day.

One of my key interests had always been the study of leadership, management, and the psychology of teams. This interest had started in the Boy Scouts where I moved from patrol leader to senior patrol leader to Assistant Scout Master of a start-up troop while in high school. Broad study in the intense leadership courses at West Point just whetted my appetite to get out into the "real world" of accomplishing missions in the Army.

In the Army, I completed the Engineer Officer Advanced Course at night by correspondence as a First Lieutenant. Since combat engineers are normally limited in their career path, my plan was to attend the Infantry Officer Advanced Course in residence to meet my Infantry peers, switch to that branch, and allow my career to go all the way to the top of the Army. Having the Engineer Advanced Course completed, allowed me to command a 220 man Combat Engineer Company in the First Cavalry Division, which was normally a Captain's job. I was a Company Commander for two years; earning many commendations before leaving the Army after five years.

My Army leadership and team building experiences were enhanced and broadened through discussions with Felix in a four year old 100 person engineering firm. No subject was safe as we talked about the owners, our boss, different team dynamics, administrative staff, industry trends and clients.

Being the only electrical engineer, Felix had the advantage of working on every project in the company, while I was limited to the few under my direct control.

Leadership progression

In 1985, direct employees took a big pay cut of 20-25% as the industry continued a precipitous downward spiral that started in 1982. Large engineering houses like Earl & Wright and Bechtel and Fluor closed up shop in Houston as the major oil companies went through massive cuts in people and projects. Of course, hundreds of smaller companies just vanished as Houston was economically hammered. That fall, some key hard workers were laid off at CBS, and no one felt any job security. At the same time, I did not feel I could go anywhere else as I might end up "last in...first out" if that company started going down.

Felix must have sensed my trapped feeling when one morning he said, "Bill, we should go start an engineering firm, all it takes is a pad and a pencil." That was typical Felix...no sense making something bigger than it needed to be! After a moment's thought, my response was "Yes we should, but I would not do it without Paul, as he is an Engineer's engineer." Felix totally agreed and since he did electrical design on both Paul Redmon's and my projects, said he would visit with Paul.

COULD WE DO IT?

As Felix left, I thought a little about the magnitude of what we were contemplating. My mind wandered to my parents and what they had done. Mom had remarried in 1962 after moving three kids and a cat from Colorado to Ohio, when I was eight. By the mid '60s both mom and my step-dad had started their own businesses…sort of the American Dream. Dad pulled out of corporate America due to high blood pressure and started a construction company building small commercial buildings and custom homes in Cleveland, Ohio. Mom was fed up with the lack of opportunity for women in the workplace and started a yarn shop that became a three store chain. They invested in themselves, their robust work ethic, and retired at age forty-eight to follow other dreams.

I had always felt that I would start a company someday but not something as technical as an engineering firm. My first investment attempt was a real estate venture that flopped due to the prolonged downturn in the Houston housing market. Perhaps this was the way to go…invest in a business where I knew most of the pieces, and trust in my unfailing energy to fill in the gaps. I knew I did not want to be 50 years old someday and wish that I had tried.

Then, some realistic thoughts came to me. I'd left the Army six years earlier despite being at the top of my year group, because I wanted to be in a smaller organization where I could make an impact without playing politics. Larry Weir had been my company commander and was now in Houston. He worked for Petro Marine Engineering (PME) where he recommended I interview. With the mini-boom in the industry, I was very quickly hired by PME, a 130 man company doing offshore oil platforms. Larry had described offshore platform work as intense Army missions. These platforms required managing men and materials on a tight schedule in a harsh environment...what more could an Airborne Ranger ask for? That company spiraled down to 30 people in my first seven months and I thought I might need to go back into the Army.

My wife, Ann, provided us with a good financial cushion since she was an RN from Texas Woman's University working full time. Due to this stability, I decided to follow the three guys that left PME to start CBS Engineering because I respected Murray Burns, who had hired me out of the military, and I wanted to work for him. Unfortunately, after four months, I spent a year in radiation and cutting-edge chemotherapy, successfully fighting an awfully aggressive Stage IV cancer with an 11 percent survival rate at The MD Anderson Cancer Center. Luckily for me Dr. Melvin Samuels was "Making Cancer History ®." Back in the saddle, I then watched CBS follow the incredibly tough market fluctuations in the offshore oil and gas industry.

In 1983 I asked Murray to put me in sales since I was between projects. He took me on a few sales calls and then turned me loose. I found that I enjoyed helping clients solve their problems during the six months I was in sales before Murray pulled me to manage the design and construction of two big offshore platforms.

Sales showed me how harsh this industry was when there wasn't enough work to go around. Engineering was cut-throat competitive due to the number of small shops. At one point I told Murray that we should combine our prime competitor Omega Marine with CBS and we would be unbeatable. This was from hearing clients talk good about Omega's platform structural capability and CBS's facilities or production equipment capability. I was always trying to put the right combination in front of clients to make their decision to use us obvious and easy...and this sounded good if not doable.

To me, sales was not so much work, as it was fun trying to put all the pieces together in real time for a client...connecting the dots and solving complex problems. Similarly, counting the money was fun for Felix and project execution was fun for Paul. From my experiences, I felt that Felix and I could do and also felt that Paul and Felix could do ok starting a company, due to the skills and passions each of those combinations would possess. If all three of us would team up, I had much more confidence that we could turn some heads. Paul would be essential for me to get out of my comfort zone and help start an engineering business.

PAUL IS THE KEY

Paul and Felix had both grown up in rural towns of south Texas. Their parents worked hard and raised sons that earned their own way from a young age. Both played varsity football...of course...this was Texas!!.. and went to Texas colleges.

 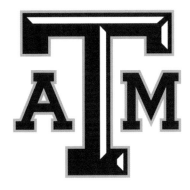

Paul was two years younger than me and graduated magna cum laude in Civil Engineering from Texas A&M in 1976. He smashed his ankle in flag football just before marrying Kay, his high school sweetheart, and ended up in a full leg cast on their honeymoon. That seemed like it would put a damper on the honeymoon but he said being an engineer, he figured things out just fine.

He took his first job with PME in New Orleans since the Houston office was just starting. He worked as a structural design engineer in the booming offshore platform market. After a few years, he was sent to help the London office on some world class offshore platforms in the North Sea. Just prior to my leaving PME, there was a buzz about this "water-walker" structural engineer that was coming to the Houston office from London.

Paul had feelers out (this would become his trademark), and knew the morale was very poor at PME, Houston. The most recent development had been someone's "bright idea" to conserve electricity by removing every other bank of flores-cent lights in the hallways. This "savings" heightened the feel-ing of gloom and doom, driving attitudes even lower as people continued to leave.

Paul knew that he would be an impact player wherever he went and felt being in a small, troubled satellite office of New Orleans would not be the best investment of his talent, attitude and energy. He interviewed with Ken Caldwell, the owner of a two year old startup engineering company called Omega Marine, and was offered a stock position to join them. However, Paul had a lot of respect for Sam Carruba's structural expertise and decided to go to CBS Engineering, arriving about six weeks after me in 1980.

"Knowledge rooted in experience."
Bell Hooks, Author

2: TRANSCO

Due to limited space in the CBS offices, Paul and I were put together in the small conference room for a few weeks. Although we shared an office, we had different technical backgrounds and were on separate projects. He was doing structural and I was doing mechanical or what is called production facilities engineering in the offshore industry. Soon we were separated and pursuing separate career paths as CBS grew.

OFFSHORE PLATFORM SCHEMATIC

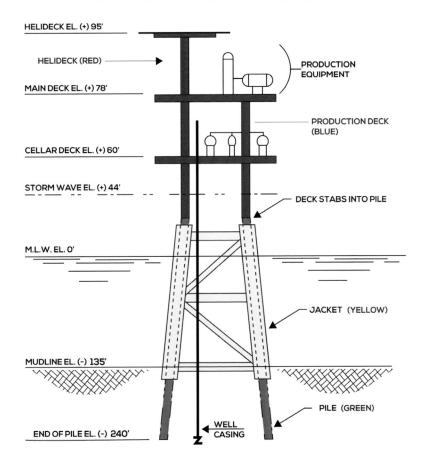

HELIDECK EL. (+) 95'

HELIDECK (RED)

PRODUCTION EQUIPMENT

MAIN DECK EL. (+) 78'

PRODUCTION DECK (BLUE)

CELLAR DECK EL. (+) 60'

STORM WAVE EL. (+) 44'

DECK STABS INTO PILE

M.L.W. EL. 0'

JACKET (YELLOW)

MUDLINE EL. (-) 135'

PILE (GREEN)

WELL CASING

END OF PILE EL. (-) 240'

The offshore platform schematic on page 17 covered about 98 percent of the platforms in the Gulf of Mexico (Gulf) up through 1988. They were simple, located in 150 feet of water or less on the Outer Continental Shelf, and produced natural gas. The jacket was essentially a steel space frame through which the piling was driven into the sea floor for support. The deck was outfitted with production equipment onshore and lifted into place, where it was welded to the top of the piles.

Basic criteria that drove the design and development of an offshore platform project included:

- Deck size and load – determined by drilling and production equipment, the number of wells, and the operating requirements.
- Environmental conditions – the "100 year storm" for wind & wave...essentially a hurricane. The wind pressure was applied to everything above the water line and from different directions to determine lateral forces on the platform. The wave pressure was applied from different directions to everything that pierced the waterline up to the height of the hundred year storm wave plus five feet of "safety factor".
- Soil condition – determined piling diameter, wall thickness and depth based on deck weight, wind and wave forces.

An example of how this criteria was interrelated can be seen in how the deck is supported about 60 feet above the waterline. This height puts the deck above the 100 year wave, thus reducing the wave load that must be absorbed by the piles, reducing their diameter and the cost to install them. Just looking at the picture and understanding the number of trade-offs that had to be worked through, it is easy to understand why structural engineering ruled the roost in offshore platform development.

Up through the early '80s, structural design was done using punched cards that fed a timeshare Cray™ supercomputer. This was necessary due to the large number of calculations required to optimize the structure for all the forces and fatigue (repetitive forces) it might see in the typical 20 year design life. Structural design criteria and installation techniques were all in constant flux as the industry learned more and moved toward deeper water.

STRUCTURAL RULES

Most of the concept development work for offshore was done by the major oil companies using their in-house engineering departments. Detailed design was then done by the major engineering and construction companies. As designs and techniques were proven, along came the "fast followers." Fast followers were the independent oil companies and small engineering firms that were started by people who had left the major oil companies for niche opportunities during the boom period of the '70s. They could quickly take new, proven concepts and pare down the design for application to smaller reservoirs that the major oil companies did not feel could be developed economically.

Structural designs and concepts were evolving rapidly because the structure and installation represented about 70% of the cost of a platform. Since clients wanted the cost saving innovations but "did not want their platform to fall over... period," structural engineers normally started up or headed the new engineering firms. Generally an engineering company was picked by the client for their structural capability and the project was kicked off. Later, the client would give the production facility design to the company and facility engineering would work for the structural project manager. Paul was well on his way to being one of the top structural engineers considering his fast pace, attention to detail, and ability to innovate.

THE BIG SHIFT FOR PAUL

Like Felix moving to Houston and my leaving the Army, Paul was not comfortable with his success to date and the obvious path in front of him. He saw platform decks getting bigger as clients found bigger reservoirs and needed more production equipment. In the North Sea, he had worked on huge oil platforms the size of small towns with 300 people living on them in a specially designed offshore hotel called the living quarters. He decided that he needed to learn more about drilling and production facilities if he was going to be the best at optimizing a structural design.

In 1980 Paul started night classes to earn his Master's Degree in Petroleum Engineering from the University of Houston, which was about a 45 minute drive from his house in Katy, Texas. His wife Kay was also busy during this period, raising a son and two daughters born between 1980 and 1984. While learning the details of designing production equipment at night school, Paul fell in love with the broader array of challenges he encountered in designing production equipment compared to what he was doing in structural design only.

Paul asked Sam and Murray to move him into facilities engineering and he was put on a new project I was just kicking off for Transco. The project was unusual for the Gulf at that time, in that it had both a gas train and an oil train. Each production train cleaned the water, sand, and "junk" out of the flow from the wells and then compressed the gas or pumped the oil into separate pipelines going to shore. Due to Paul's capability and drive, Murray suggested I give him a good chunk of the job to put his arms around, while at the same time providing my knowledge and systems experience.

In the following picture, Transco's competitor is in the background. Both companies would be pulling oil and gas out of the same reservoir, so whomever came on line first would get more out of the reservoir...now THAT is real competition!!! As soon as both companies were producing, they negotiated to unitize the field and produce it prudently.

WEST CAMERON BLOCK 215

Two offshore platforms, bridge connected with two Jack-Up drilling rigs working. Design, purchasing and construction management were done for Al Daniels of Transco Exploration by Paul, Felix and Bill while at CBS Engineering, Inc.

Paul took on the oil train and I fed him all the things I'd been doing to optimize the design, procurement and construction of facilities for Transco platforms. We came up with a new optimization due to Paul's structural design experience.

We fixed both ends of the bridge connecting the platforms in order to eliminate large "flex-loops" in the piping that were required if one end was allowed to slide. Allowing one end of the bridge to slide let the structures move independently. The loops would have taken up a lot of space and been very expensive to install. The additional steel required in the bridge due to this innovation was minimal.

Paul really threw himself into developing Transco's "Oil Train" on a tight schedule. Using go-bys from past work and understanding the requirements of Transco's production people, we had reduced engineering from $800,000 to $400,000 and shortened the schedule by four months. Four months earlier cash flow from oil production was a big shot in the arm for the oil company, to the tune of $20,000,000. Like a duck to water, Paul took off and soon was doing back-to-back projects for Cities Service, which became Occidental Petroleum (Oxy). His obvious intelligence, common sense and technical competence allowed him to form close bonds with multiple clients. Paul knew, without a doubt, that if he ever started an engineering firm, these clients would award him projects.

COMIN' TOGETHER

Felix found the opportunity to ask Paul about starting an engineering company while in Paul's office discussing an Oxy project. Paul had been thinking along these lines and said he thought they could do it- but not without Bill, "he can sell ice to Eskimos… and he actually likes selling." Felix told Paul I was interested and they decided to come and talk to me…four doors down the hall.

There was some cautious excitement when Paul and Felix came in and sat down. Felix said Paul definitely agreed with the team and felt it was time for us to visit. Just then, for the first time in three months, Murray stuck his head in my door and asked me to come see him when I had a minute. Whew!

That felt weird because we all liked and respected Murray.

We had all the technical knowledge to design and project manage offshore platforms. Structural and electrical were covered by Paul and Felix respectively. All three of us could do the chemical, mechanical, instrument, scheduling and procurement aspects of an offshore platform. We knew how to deliver good projects and costs from vendors consistently. All of us had clients that held us in high regard. We decided to meet at Felix's house for further discussion.

We had chosen each other out of mutual respect garnered from working together. We really did not know each other outside of work. Our value systems seemed similar based on the way we worked with our teams, the vendors, and clients. The success of the next stage of our careers however, would depend on our core values and ability to support each other through the severe pressures of a startup. We needed to meet and dig a little deeper into how we would mesh as a team. All the pieces however, seemed to fit.

"Keep your eyes on the stars and your feet on the ground."
Kasey Kasum, Disc jockey

3: CAN WE BE DIFFERENT?

Paul, Felix and I were bothered by the treatment of project people in Houston. Top management at engineering and construction companies seemed comfortable with a "plug and play" mentality towards engineers, drafters and support people on their projects.

They felt the ebb and flow of project people was mandated by the vagaries of winning bids, compounded by capricious industry cycles. There was nothing they could do to create continuity of work for more than a core team.

We had seen the piping design group at CBS go up to 35 people, then down to 5, then up to 37 and down to 6. Each time we moved a project into drafting, we had new players. We saw the same mistakes being made in design, and many were not caught until they were seen in fabrication. This frustrated us and our clients, who expected us to get better with each project.

CHECKLISTS...A PATCH

Eugene Island Block 10 was my first big project for Transco while at CBS. The final product was great and produced well for Transco for many years. Designing, buying the equipment, fabrication, installation, hookup, and commissioning, however, felt like a very messy sausage making process. There was no written guide on how to design, procure, and build offshore platforms. Being a self-professed "efficiency guru," I felt out of control due to the magnitude of the problems encountered on this project. Also, knowing that I loved the challenge of this work, I took detailed notes on mistakes, oversights, and resource or schedule conflicts. By the time we started gas production on the platform, I had over 200 comprehensive items in my notes that could streamline the next project.

Then I spent two days offshore walking the platform with Transco's veteran operations people ...and was totally flayed, skewered, and cooked. They doubled my list as they commented in detail on everything from the platform crane, to the sewage treatment unit, to valve placement and foot stools to read meters. I furiously took notes as we walked and think they had a good time blowing my hair back.

> **"Checklists... let's mess up something new on this project."**

I turned all of the collected data into checklists for the various engineering disciplines, from design through purchasing, fabrication and startup. On the next project, I gave the lists to the team and said, "Let's mess up something new on this project...everything on these lists must be double checked as we know what the client wants!"

A year and a half after being flayed, I walked through the new platform, West Cameron Block 215, where Paul, Felix and I used the checklists. The same operations folks could do nothing but pat us on the back. For an even more complex platform than the first one, the overall schedule had been reduced by four months, engineering cost cut in half, installation time cut in half, hookup and commissioning offshore reduced from 98 days to 32 days and...best of all...no comments by operations!!

Of course, now that we had the formula, it was almost impossible for another engineering firm to win work from that client. Paul, Felix, and I loved this feeling of "locking up a client" due to superior performance. We continued to improve our use of previous project work or "go-bys" and checklists as we worked for other clients at CBS. These methods were our "lessons learned," and helped us guarantee delivery of top performance as our team members continued to change.

TAKING CARE OF PEOPLE

We were using our industry "pull" to try and keep top per-formers billable to projects. Felix kept LD Cunningham, who did his drafting, fed with work. Paul and I both used Paul Post, who single-handedly could carry the piping design due to his

LD Cunningham   Paul Post

speed...manual drafting back then...and accuracy. Then there was Glen "give me a mile marker on that truck!!" Damashek in procurement, who could expedite and get anything delivered. We started to feel responsible for the livelihoods of the people who were taking care of our work. At the same time, we had very limited capability to deliver any job security for them. We were ready to change this feeling of inadequacy when we first met at Felix's house.

WHO ARE THESE GUYS?

Meeting at Felix's house was a great idea, but once there, we were not sure how to start. This idea was very different from starting and doing projects. We bounced around a little by discussing how we had come together and our general feel-ing that, at first blush, we had the capability between us to make a go of having our own company.

We realized that we needed a name for the company to make the conversation easier. CBS and other companies had used the owners' initials. Others picked an easy name to remember, like Omega, Paragon, or Olympia. We played with this for a while, as it gave us something real to talk about and some of our personal philosophies started to come out. Our initials did not sound like a good idea because we wanted the company to easily be able to grow beyond us.

Picking a name out of the blue was a non-starter for us as we just drew blanks while thinking about the idea. Finally, we talked about using parts of our last names to create a word that could stand alone in the future. We came up with Recoh Engineering, Inc. (REI): Redmon, Covington and the "H" is silent which we got a kick out of, since it is hard to shut me up! Felix said that he would submit this name for approval in Texas.

This took us into a discussion of our general lack of understanding the business side of running an engineering firm. I was tasked to arrange for us to attend a Small Business Administration seminar on starting a business. We talked a little about ways to identify a lawyer to craft corporate documents. Felix had two friends he could line up to be our insurance agent and a CPA. Everything seemed to become more relaxed as we talked and enumerated some action items.

EMPLOYEE PERSPECTIVE

Owners Change Attitude

We talked for a while about what we liked and didn't like in the companies where we had worked. We had already discussed that it seemed owners of startup engineering firms became thick skinned after a few years and removed themselves from the employees and day-to-day action. We knew these people were top-notch and surely started out just as idealistic as we were. Something must have crept in as time passed and moved these folks to a place they had not planned to go. Maybe, if we could write things down now, while we were still employees, we could periodically review the list and catch ourselves if we were incrementing to a place we would not like. This became a very lively discussion as Paul and Felix were keenly observant when it came to people and organizational interactions. Our discussion ranged from the puny to the sublime as we realized our discussion could be the foundation of a new type of company.

Employees See Everything

Some of the puny items showed how little things were important to employees. For example, people on our company softball team could not get a new baseball cap, while a client could get as many as they wanted. We would go years without using a sick day while it was obvious others used their sick days every year as a "right." Company cars for some and plush owner's offices made obvious differences between people.

We felt that there were many things that interfered with building a tighter team mentality. Structural and facilities groups were in different hallways, despite needing close communication to optimize designs. Paychecks were not handed out by the owners, giving implied power to the person who did hand them out. There were very few team building activities to pull people closer together. Bonuses were more of a "duty" at the end of the year instead of a "thank you" as the year progressed. Why couldn't they sell outside of the platform market to keep teams together?

What we liked and wanted

We also talked about the things we liked in the companies we were familiar with. We loved the people and the "can do" attitude towards any challenge thrown in front of them. The feeling of accomplishing a tough mission when everything finally comes together through the team's efforts was a great adrenalin rush. We enjoyed the small company feel and being around good technical people.

Organizationally, we liked the identifying, interviewing and hiring being done by whomever would have to use the person hired. We liked having close relationships with vendors, such that we felt we were delivering as a team for the client once they had won a bid. Most of all, we liked working a project from concept through startup, so we could learn from mistakes firsthand out in the field.

The list we generated seemed like pretty obvious things at the time. We added that we would like to be an Employee Stock Ownership Plan (ESOP) company so people would be rewarded automatically for growing the enterprise.

INDUSTRY IS CHANGING

Our industry was changing due to layoffs and consolidations. One notable change was the dismantling of the "good old boy" network that used to award projects over three martini lunches. With the industry tightening, projects were being bid and awarded to the best technical and execution answer. Awarding based on ability should give us a more level playing field in which to win work.

The industry was also changing its focus towards larger reservoirs. These larger reservoirs required more substantial facilities to produce the higher flow rates of oil and natural gas.

> **Production facility would become the project driver.**

We saw this change as moving the project emphasis away from the structural jacket and deck. The production facility and utility equipment would have to become the prime project driver and this would play into our decision to build a facilities oriented company.

PREPARATION

Each of us had things we would need to do individually in preparation for the startup. One was to clear out as much personal debt as possible to relieve personal financial pressures. Another was to save some money for initial company expenditures and to hold us over for the first six months. We felt we would need to go without pay as we developed "sweat equity" in the business.

In order to be an owner of a firm with "Engineering" in the name, you had to be a Registered Professional Engineer. Both Paul and Felix were registered, but I was not. West Point, while being the oldest engineering school in America, was not accredited in engineering when I graduated in 1974. This meant that I would have to study and take the eight hour Principles and Practices test to earn my Professional Engineer's License in Mechanical Engineering.

It was late in 1985 and we decided that we would start to meet regularly in order to stay connected and advance the "Recoh Project." We also decided to meet with our wives the next time and bring them up to speed with our thoughts so far. We set up the next meeting at Felix's house.

As we left, knowing that we had set up another meeting became very significant to me. Although we had seemed to gel as a team and had some direction, the hill we were planning to climb just seemed way too big for us. Plus, there was the inertia of having a good job and family responsibilities to overcome in deciding to start at the bottom. It seemed more likely that we would fall apart and just keep working, rather than jump into the unknown abyss of starting an engineering firm. At the same time, I had bonded with Paul and Felix and would not hold them back if they continued to have energy for this significant undertaking.

WHAT COULD BE?

We knew we were good at technical execution of projects and had a formula that would "lock up" clients if we could get the opportunity to do just one project for them. We knew we had strong sales and presentation capability along with client relationships that should generate the opportunities we needed.

Our drivers for jumping into the abyss were primarily "other oriented": providing job security to keep our teams together, assembling good teams to take care of the client's work, creating flexibility to stay ahead of industry changes, and generating continuous profitable work so the company would not disappear out from under people and clients.

If we could pull all of this off, we would have a great place to work and have more fun doing projects...lots of possibility in all of this!

A focus on people and projects.

"Learn by doing."
Aristotle, Philosopher

4: SAMEDAN

Two years out of West Point, I went and asked the Battalion Commander for a Combat Engineer Company Command job that was coming open...denied. Instead, I became a company executive officer, where I could see everything a company commander did for seven months. Then I did a special project directly for the Battalion Commander, reorganizing the battalion from an air mobile Vietnam era Division to heavy armor support. I worked with all six company commanders to plan and execute this significant change in personnel and equipment. Three months after becoming a company commander, I knew I was much better at the job due to the additional time I had to observe others.

NO RUSH... STILL LEARNING

BP Bid

We met twice during 1985 as the industry just seemed to be getting worse. A ray of hope at the end of 1985 was a large British Petroleum (BP) proposal for a 20,000 barrels of oil per day platform in Ewing Bank 826, which was the "block" name in the Gulf. The Gulf had a grid overlay and companies purchased the rights to drill on blocks at auctions conducted by the Minerals Management Service of the US Government. The proposal came out around the 10th of December and was due on the 2nd of January. This was pretty typical for the oil company to have us working while their people were off on vacation, in order to maximize their people's productive time.

Our daughter, Stephanie, was born December 23rd, so I had a busy holiday as the proposal manager at CBS and as a new father...two birthing processes!! The good thing for Ann was that since I was going to be up all night working on the proposal, I could watch the baby between feedings and stretch the time frame as long as possible. I worked in the dining room and rocked her with my foot under the table. Our chances of winning the project seemed small though, as all the "big boys" were chasing this large project hard. It was the only project of any significance on the street and everyone wanted it for the start of 1986.

BP Presentation

We were short listed for the project and scheduled for a presentation at the CBS Engineering offices. Murray approved for me to "pull out the stops" and wow BP with our presentation. We set up a large open space with tables, white table cloths, name cards and a mocked up platform model made out of display board material.

The model came from my experience in Ranger School of doing a terrain map in the dirt to brief the platoon on the mission. Getting around the terrain map allowed everyone to have input and visualize actions, escape routes and rally points to get back together.

Everyone was briefed and rehearsed on the overall project and their responsibilities. Using name cards on tables allowed us to intersperse our people to sit with their counterpart from BP and hopefully gain some rapport. I was trying to prevent an "us and them" presentation flavor. Each person used the cardboard model as they discussed how their part of the project would flow and interact with others.

Being engineers, the BP personnel did not sit silently in their seats and came up at various times to provide their input by pointing out things in the rough model. The BP team learned each other's concerns and preferences due to the detailed nature of the discussions over the model and we felt like the catalyst for the interactions.

Frame Five

One of the most telling moments was when Dick West-brook was discussing the compression and power generation requirements. BP asked if he was a "Frame Five" man. Now, Dick is broad in the shoulders, but stands a skosh under 5'-8", so I was not sure if he was Frame Five! Luckily, Dick had refinery experience and knew they were talking about using turbines for power. Turbines were talked about in terms of frame sizes instead of model numbers. This one conversation showed me how much of a stretch this project would be for a company that was used to doing small natural gas platforms with small power generation requirements.

Three weeks later the project was cancelled as BP decided they needed more drilling to firm up the estimate of recoverable reserves in the block. However, we had learned many things about BP's decision criteria and our own capability through this bid process. The discussions had positioned CBS higher in BP's eyes for future projects.

WHAT'S IN A NAME

Felix had told us the company name of Recoh Engineering, Inc. had been taken in Texas, so we would have to come up with something else. I brought a list of car names to our next meeting. My wife, Ann, had written down names of cars while stuck in traffic on the way to work. Her thinking was that car manufacturers make a huge investment in coming up with names that have broad appeal, so we might as well use that research to our benefit...gotta love a girl that thinks globally and economically! Given a list of twelve names, the three of us could definitely pick one. Mustang sort of jumped out at us, due to its history of changing the automotive industry under the legendary leadership of Lee Iacocca. The Mustang had been his baby and propelled his career to the top. We always joked that we could have been Yugo or Pinto Engineering, but those names really were not on the list as Ann knew better. Felix had a new name to try and register...Mustang Engineering, Inc.

TIME TO INNOVATE

Minimum Structures

Canceling Ewing Bank Block 826 did not bode well for project work in 1986. Workload in the Gulf was determined more by the natural gas price than the oil price since oil companies were primarily finding gas under the continental shelf. Natural gas had gone from $5.15/ million British Thermal Units to $1.10/mbtu. Competitors were finding a way to make projects go at these gas prices by developing minimal platform concepts with innovative drilling support systems and "cookbook" facilities equipment. Engineering had to be minimized in order to win projects and the new "minimal platform" concepts seemed to be winning the day.

Not wanting to miss these projects, I sent out a memo to top people at CBS, including the owners, to schedule an after-hours meeting that would be unpaid due to the tight times. I wanted to see if we could come up with a minimal concept to compete with designs that others were patenting. We had good attendance, including Murray and Sam, two of the owners. We talked about the various concepts other companies had developed. In discussing the pros and cons for each concept, we started to feel like a pretty focused team.

As the discussion went on, I could see a light bulb go off in Paul's mind and he started sketching and talking to the structural engineer next to him. I asked him to come up and draw his concept for everyone to see. His innovative sketch withstood the test of everyone trying to poke holes in it. Toward the end of the meeting, Sam said that he had a name for it; the Minimum Offshore Support Structure or MOSS. Sam was excited and took on the job of selling one to a client and getting a patent. I took on the job of putting together a marketing campaign to get the MOSS concept considered whenever a client had a minimal structural application.

Sam was able to sell the first application to an independent oil company named Samedan Oil Corporation and we were at least in the game when a client had a project. We were finding ways to make projects go with a $1.10 natural gas price...unthinkable just a few years earlier. And, Paul and I had worked together now as "intrapreneurs" within CBS.

Small Projects

Paul, Felix and I stayed in scramble mode all year, working on many small projects with tight budgets and schedules. Competing for these projects definitely "turned our brains on" to figure out how to reduce the engineering required in meeting the needs of construction.

We learned through experimentation and asking questions in the field that many of the drawings we had been doing were not needed by construction superintendents. During the boom times, money was not a problem and engineering over-killed the problem by detailing way more than what was needed to get the job done. Since the scope of the work to be done was directly related to the manhours required to do the work, we found a way to legitimately reduce our manhours and still give the client a quality job. There was resistance from engineers and drafters as we reduced drawings, because more manhours equaled job security.

> "Drawings are a means to an end...not the end."

We saw the bigger picture of being able to bid lower as the real job security and continued to find ways to reduce the engineering scope. The prolonged slump in the industry was honing our skills at doing projects in the leanest fashion possible.

HELIDECK
WELL DRIVE PIPE
TWO LEG JACKET
DECK SUPPORT FRAME
PRODUCTION & WELLHEAD DECK

The CBS Engineering MOSS structure.
Sketched by Paul Redmon and patented by Sam Carruba.
Finding a way to "get in the game" of minimal structures.

"What's in a name?"
William Shakespeare, Poet and Playwright

5: PREPARATION

Getting a professional engineer's license in mechanical engineering twelve years after college was going to be tough. I signed up for a year-long correspondence course and advanced all the work such that I could complete it between February and September of 1986 - eight months. In the first packet there was a Fluid Dynamics problem I would have sworn that I had never seen before. However, after reviewing my fluids notebook from school, I found a similar problem worked in my own handwriting! This was going to be much tougher than I had anticipated. I had been a Starman at West Point, meaning that I wore stars on my collar to signify that I was in the top 5% of the class academically, but this was going to be a real challenge.

PROFESSIONAL ENGINEERING LICENSE

Mechanical engineering covered a very broad range of topics. The only engineering I had done in the Army was civil for roads, structural for bridges, and the real fun stuff - demolition using explosives. The test would be on a Saturday in October and consist of two four hour sessions broken by lunch. In each session I would have to do four problems out of the eight offered. Each problem had many parts, which made sequencing my thought process very important. It was also very important to pick the right problems so that I did not get stymied part way through and have to start another problem. The test was open book, but there would not be time for searching around in the reference manuals. My understanding was that getting the correct answer was weighted less than showing all of your work and analytical capability. In the real world there would be checks and balances on getting the right answer.

One week before the test I was down at The Brown Bookstore in Houston looking at technical books. I found a book specifically designed for the Mechanical Engineer's P.E. test. After reviewing it, I bought the book as it was a gold mine. The next week I just worked on learning how to use the book as a reference while re-working sample problems. I took the Friday before the test off to unwind from project work and rest for the test.

The test was as hard as could be imagined. Essentially I had one hour for each problem and working very hard I was finishing them in 56 or 57 minutes each! There was no time for quality checking, although I did quickly run through the math to find any glaring errors. I was brain dead after the test and decided that if I did not pass, I would be content to not be an owner and just work for Paul and Felix. Only 20% of the test covered topics we used in the oil patch.

That night I laid out each problem on paper from memory and reviewed how I had progressed to the answers for the various sub-problems. I graded my efforts in a strict fashion and felt I had scored a 93, which was a great relief. 70 was a passing score, so I was feeling pretty good, but they were very complicated word problems with pages of calculations each, so there would be some subjectivity in the grading.

In January of 1987, notice came that I had passed and was a Professional Engineer in Texas...yeah!!

Our Engineering Seals

FEELING BETTER... BP AND OXY

Deja' vu, all over again as Yogi Berra would say. December of '86 BP came out for bid again on Ewing Bank Block 826, which was now named Amberjack.

At the same time, Paul was bidding a major project of similar size for Oxy. We'd been able to keep people billable by working tons of hours on a plethora of small projects. The hard work resulted in a payoff as CBS won both large projects and had to staff up. On these projects Paul and I worked through the billing rates for people and worked the contracts, enabling us to learn more facets of running an engineering firm.

EB 826 Production Drilling & Quarters platform.

These projects were three times the size of what we had considered big projects up to that time, significantly stretching Paul's and my management capability and spreading Felix very thin. Bidding and winning these 30,000 manhour projects toward the end of 1986 gave us the feeling that we could kick off Mustang in 1987 due to the increase in work.

MUSTANG IT IS

Felix received approval of the name Mustang Engineering, Inc. We met and decided to get things rolling by having corporate documents drawn up. There was some discussion on who should be president. Felix and I felt it should be Paul because he would be the driving force within the company. He would be creating the teams, systems, and organizational structure to produce quality work. With his technical ability and hard work, Paul would easily earn the respect of any engineer and be able to motivate them. Paul was also a Texas A&M "Aggie" which had a significant worldwide network in the hydrocarbon industry...very similar to West Point in the Army. Felix and I would essentially support his efforts with good sales and administration, when we were not working on projects with him.

Paul pushed for all three of us to share the title or rotate it every six months. This discussion told volumes about how "other oriented" the three of us were. My push back was from my Army background where there needed to be one person in charge for good order and discipline when things heated up. In sales, I felt it would be confusing to the industry if the position rotated. Clients wanted to know who the final decision maker was, in case they needed action. Behind the scenes we could be all for one and one for all, but to the public there needed to be a top dog. Felix agreed, so I smiled and said let's vote!! Paul won the job by a landslide!

We went to meet with our lawyer and CPA on Friday the 13th of February, 1987 to provide information for preparation of corporate documents and our buy/sell agreement. The buy/sell was essentially a divorce document lining out how the corporation would be valued and split if things did not work out. The lawyer coached us that this was hard to talk about at this time, but was best done while we were still friends and optimistic. We truly felt that we could settle things ourselves but worked diligently to understand the document and tailor it to our thinking. When we were done adjusting it, the buy/sell seemed airtight and very black and white on the company valuation method. The other documentation was pretty much just form work for the lawyer.

> "The buy/sell was essentially a divorce document."

Out in the parking lot after meeting with the lawyer we all agreed that divorce was not an option. We felt that we were of a like mind and could use our focus on the work to keep us together. We also talked about making sure Mustang did not mess up our real marriages. This was a very heart felt discussion and commitment among the three of us.

One month later on Friday the 13th of March we met again at the lawyer's office to sign the papers establishing Mustang.

OTHER OPTIONS

We met at my house with four other engineers who were planning to start an engineering firm doing offshore platforms. Both teams wanted to see if it made sense to combine our talents, resources and client relationships for a better startup.

The meeting was good as everyone worked to figure out how we might work together. We covered enough ground for the teams to go their separate ways for internal discussions.

These discussions were important for us in our development as a team. By looking at these other very talented people and evaluating their strengths and weaknesses, we learned more about ourselves.

We realized that the three of us really had our egos in check and were looking to give... in a true win-win environment. It would be virtually impossible to get that comfortable with this other team without meaningful time together. From the short time we had been together in discussion, and what we knew about them, it did not feel like they would be as giving as we planned to be. We decided to wish them all the best, but we would go on our own.

We also talked a little about our fall back plans if Mustang did not survive. All of us could go to an oil company and make a difference. Our other option was to return to CBS or go to Omega and work on combining the capabilities of the two companies. We would not be out of work for very long if Mustang failed.

We had definitely pulled together as a team over the past year and learned more about how to run Mustang. The delay in starting was setting us up to have more confidence in our abilities. Felix picked July 20th, the day America landed a man on the moon as the launch date for Mustang. We had a date and the corporate papers, now we needed a plan to track against.

JULY 20, 1987

"Planning is the result...not the plan."
Peter F. Drucker, Educator

6: GETTING ORGANIZED

Yo!! California!!!...I called to my neighbor Mark Sutton across the street. We had moved in four months earlier and become good friends. He was pretty high in the BP organization and had a very diverse background in our target market of upstream offshore projects. I met him in the middle of the street to tell him I was quitting CBS to start an engineering firm with two other guys. He said he hoped it was not going to be in the offshore oil and gas industry. When I said it was, he asked me to come tell him about it, so we went and sat on the curb in front of his house for half an hour as I related our plans.

NOT A GOOD IDEA

Mark told me later he went into his house after our conversation out on the curb and told his wife Gail that the neighbor across the street was "certifiable" to a mental institution. Mark was much more familiar with the awful state of the industry.

He had been in strategic planning sessions at BP that gave him a worldwide view. He was "wired" into many top people in other oil companies and all of the principal support contractors from engineering to construction. He knew beyond a doubt that starting Mustang in July of 1987 was a poorly conceived idea, with little chance of surviving.

In our curbside talk though, Mark just asked questions and was supportive because he could feel the energy and dedication I had for jumping into Mustang with Paul and Felix.

BUSINESS PLAN

We attended a two night Small Business Association forum on starting a business and came away with two things. One was to pay the employee withholding tax to the government ASAP, so there is no temptation to use it to help cash flow... the government can be a harsh master. The other was to do a plan.

To Paul and Felix, a business plan seemed like selling Mustang, so writing it fell to me! I purchased a book on writing business plans to make sure that all the key areas would be addressed.

The original business plan.

Our business plan Table of Contents read as follows:
1. The Market.
2. The Management Team & Organization.
3. The Financial Plan.
4. Cash Management.
5. Potential Risks and Problems.
6. Corporate Documents.

MARKET

Felix, Paul and I had been in the industry for 16, 10 and 6 years respectively and had a feel for the market. We would be targeting small modification and revamp projects from companies for whom we had done work in the past. We knew who we would be competing against and their billing rate structure.

Small projects were identified, budgeted, bid and awarded in a matter of weeks, so we could not identify specific projects to chase. The larger "named" projects were beyond our reach as a startup company. Being realistic about our ability to win named projects saved us a lot of sales time, proposal time and aggravation. We would work to identify projects we could win due to reputation or that would be bid and awarded in a matter of days.

We identified two major oil companies, four large independent oil companies, and eight small independents as targets for work. All of these companies potentially had small modification projects. These smaller projects are generally hard to control and make a profit on but were real work and below the radar screen of most competitors. We had decided that we would be making a clean break from CBS Engineering, without taking a project with us. This was an unusual tactic for engineering startups. Our ethical decision would make the startup very stressful. At the same time, it would be exciting to see who would be first to entrust us with their work!

While the market for projects was poor, the market for people was pretty good. Companies had cut fat, muscle, and recently had started cutting bone out of their organizations. Absolutely top-quality people were now sitting at the house, moving to a new city, or working in other industries. If we could get work, there were great resources available to execute in a quality manner.

One of the things we learned from watching other startup companies was not to "farm" ourselves out as contract engineers working in someone else's office. Others had done this and while they had made good short term money, they did not have an "officed" nucleus to build a company around. Although it would hurt us financially, our vision centered on building a sustainable company that would be viable long term.

The market strategy of doing our own sales based on our personal engineering capability and relationships was a good way to control growth as there would be no time to sell if we were busy. Doing the sales and the work ourselves would also insure quality, save money, and provide the personal touch.

We would not do any advertising as we only wanted to chase very real things that were screened by how we found them. This, along with low overhead pricing, would give the client a "good deal" and high value-added efforts from a top-notch team. Part of the low overhead was due to the fact that we were not planning to pay ourselves for the first six months, while working unbelievable hours to build Mustang's nest egg.

ORGANIZATION

Blend of outside and inside

Our organization plan was built around the three of us with support of a lawyer, a CPA and an insurance provider on an as needed basis. This would be the entire management team. We created a matrix of skills (see next page) needed in the company and rated each person's capability from 1 to 3, with 3 being the most qualified. In every category we had at least two people that were top rated, giving us good balance.

ITEM	REDMON	COVINGTON	HIGGS	LAWYER	CPA
ENGR/PROJECT MGMT.	3	3	3		
LEGAL/LEASE NEGOTIATIONS	2	3	2	3	
INSURANCE PLANNING	2	3	2	3	
FINANCIAL PLAN/ACCOUNTING	2	3	2		3
SALES/MARKET PLANNING	3	2	3		

Model

According to our strengths, each of us had one leg of the following organizational model.

This upside down pyramid was reflective of our thinking. We wanted administration and sales "supporting" operations both visually and in actuality. Operations would concentrate on delivering our value proposition internally to Mustang and externally to clients.

This organization enabled each of us to work in our area of strength, while at the same time helping the other aspects of running a business. We wanted to keep the business aspects streamlined and very supportive of project requirements. My primary leg in the organization was sales; however, I did projects to help with operations and did the payroll and monthly financial statements to help with administration. The overlaps at the apexes of the equilateral triangle made this base organization unbelievably strong when coupled with each of us wanting to support the other two in any way possible. We each believed the person in each leg was the best in the industry, but we wanted to do anything we could to help ease their load.

Paul headed the operations leg, with primary responsibility for organizational development, hiring, and execution excellence in projects. Felix headed the administration leg, with responsibility for invoicing, contracts, insurance, bills and keeping us healthy. I headed the sales leg, focused on sales, marketing and providing continuous work. Paul and Felix were 70% and 90% respectively focused internally to Mustang, while I was 80% focused externally.

Time sheets Critical

Everyone in the company, both billable and overhead personnel, would do time sheets and expense reports twice a month as we had done at CBS. These time sheets and expense reports were reviewed and approved by Paul or Felix, depending on the person's primary job. All of these were given a final review by Felix and consolidated for payroll. I input the time sheets and expense reports into the ADP® payroll system along with any other changes to the payroll fields.

Thus, without talking, all three legs of the triangle-organization knew who was working for Mustang, what jobs they were on, how billable they were, and where they went if they had to travel. This was a huge amount of information that gave each of us a good gut feel for what was happening and where assistance was needed. Then, without discussion, we just moved to fill the gaps as we saw them.

"After you've wrestled, everything else in life is easy."
Dan Gable, Olympic wrestler and coach

7: FINANCIAL INNOVATION

One gap we anticipated was in the cash flow. The plan stated that "Upon winning the first project of any size, it is anticipated that the company will become a nine person office. We anticipate the company will stay this size three to four months–then gradually increase to 20 personnel by the end of the first full year." From these estimates, we built up our billing schedules of rates, our costs and net income projections for the first three years. We anticipated being at 30 people in the third year. Our analysis showed that "In order to allow flexibility in growth of the company and allowing that some clients will be slower to pay, Mustang needs a line of credit of $300,000 for payroll financing."

LINE OF CREDIT

Bank Financing

We took our business plan to a number of banks to brief them and secure the payroll financing. The fact we had bought our furniture at ten cents on the dollar from engineering firms just like ours that were closing, never entered our minds. It did however enter the minds of the bankers who were polite, tried not to laugh and related some of the huge losses they were writing off in the energy industry and related businesses in Houston. They listed huge engineering houses as well as smaller firms that had moved out of Houston, or closed in the past three years. Having much better data than us, they saw the oil money moving overseas where discovery costs for big reservoirs were much less. The bankers were not pleased with the oil patch.

But then they said the one thing that stuck with us. They said engineers do not run companies like a business. Engineers do OK initially on their first projects but get in trouble trying to do the projects "right" and not getting paid for the effort. Engineers also would not push their clients for prompt payment, resulting in cash flow problems. Engineers just like to do projects, so the business aspects of the company suffer. Wow, this gave us something to think about.

> "But then they said one thing that stuck with us. They said engineers do not run companies like a business.."

For financing, we ended up working with Preferred Savings & Loan. They provided financing to a competing firm called Omega, which had been around for ten years. They knew our business model.

The deal we worked was to each put $5,000 into Certificates of Deposit at the S&L and we could borrow that amount back at a charge of only 2%. We would issue monthly financial statements and keep our loan officer, Mike Campbell, apprised of Mustang's progress. Then, down the road, he might be able to finance payroll to some percentage of receivables. We took this deal and set up another more innovative approach.

Vendor Financing

We knew that initially we did not want to have direct-hire employees because we would not know our viability of having work week to week. So, we went to "job shops" that we knew in Houston and explained our need. We said we would exclusively lock into three job shops to get contract employees, if they would let us pay their invoices when we were paid by the client.

These job shops were intimately familiar with the energy industry in Houston. They agreed to our terms and did not charge more than their normal markup! Job shops ended up financing $5-35,000 per month for us on projects where they approved of the client. We expedited invoices with our clients and normally paid the job shops in less than 45 days...their normal requirement.

We developed tight relationships with these shops, to the point where they would call us when they had a "Mustang type person" coming free. By our seventh year, some of these job shops were doing one million dollars a quarter from Mustang and being paid in thirty days or less. The early win-win deal developed into a long term major win for both sides...good people for us and good income for them.

CASH MANAGEMENT

Managing cash was a very simple section of our business plan. We essentially wanted to plug all holes in the bucket and not let any cash leave the company. This was clearly intoned in "Disbursements from any of the accounts that exceed $3,000 will require the signature of any two of the corporate officers."

During the startup it seemed like there were just continuous required costs for things that were not anticipated. It made us feel that new companies cannot make it because all the existing companies bleed them dry with startup charges.

At this time, Felix became known as Mikey, like the cereal advertisement at the time..."Will Mikey eat it?" For example, I brought in quotes for a phone system. Felix multiplied the bid numbers by 0.2 and said "Let's find it for that"... and we did!!

RISKS

Our key risks centered on our capability and ability to get work. The industry was at rock bottom. Finding small projects would be extremely difficult. Also, it would take time and convincing to be added to a client's approved vendors list in order to be considered for work. This realization, that obtaining work was our real challenge, also drove us to "keep permanent staff and overhead to an absolute minimum" as stated in the plan.

By choosing clients carefully, we did not antiicpate any risk of not being paid for our services.

FINAL STEPS

My roommate and wrestling buddy from West Point, Fred Stellar, visited for the 4th of July weekend in 1987. He went with me to meet Paul and sign the lease for Mustang's first office. Fred liked putting a face with Paul's name. He watched us interact and said he enjoyed seeing the high energy we had for getting Mustang started.

Paul and I had been working like crazy to get our projects in shape for our departure. These were the largest projects ever done by CBS and for clients we hoped to work for in the future...BP and Oxy. We planned to see Murray right after the weekend and turn in our notice. In reality, we needed another two weeks, but we did not know if CBS would let us stay or ask us to leave the office right away.

Going in together to see Murray was very tough because he was such a good man. His initial comment was "all three of you?" We discussed the status of our projects, and he agreed that the best thing was for us to stay two more weeks. He wanted us to not tell others what was going on in order to keep the disruption down. He felt we had done a good job of keeping this startup quiet and wanted to stay very professional as we split off.

Later that day, Murray came and told me I could tell my best friend in Houston and at CBS, Jack Gatewood, what we were planning. I told Murray that I appreciated his thinking of our friendship and giving me time to visit with Jack before anything leaked out. Years earlier when I was diagnosed with cancer, I went first into Jack's office and told him that I might be in some big trouble. He was always there for me and I wanted our friendship to continue past the initiation of Mustang.

RESULTS

We had all of our legal documents in place and had a business plan. The key objective of the plan had been to obtain accounts receivable financing, which it failed in doing. The plan met the requirements of bankers, our lawyer and CPA. It had all the pieces, and caused us to think through many of the mechanics of running the business side of Mustang. This was very important, because we did not want to be great engineers, yet have the company fail due to business issues.

We saw ourselves as caretakers of Mustang and knew we had to become very smart at the business end to make Mustang a viable and desirable place to work.

8: DARE TO BE DIFFERENT

We wanted a logo to go with the Mustang name in order to help develop a visually recognizable brand. Hopefully the logo could help imply that we were always going to be moving and changing, with a lot of energy and innovation to match a very dynamic industry. I went to a print shop close to the office to get some business cards made and looked through their catalogs to find a suitable image. None of the cars excited me at all, so I started looking at horses.

THE HORSE

I found a horse that was rearing up, ready to jump out there, and decided to go with it. The horse was on one foot, so it had to be moving! I picked a solid, forward slanting font for Mustang to show strength and stability, while implying motion. Felix wanted blue...true blue... for the company color and I picked "process" blue as that color. I'm color blind and it still looked blue! We put our home phone numbers on the cards to show that we were serious about taking care of our clients... call us anytime with whatever problem you have!

BREAK-NECK SPEED

We had been going 120 miles per hour during our final two weeks at CBS in an effort to get our projects in good shape for us to leave. My team had over 100 purchase orders for equipment that needed to be specified, bid, and awarded between March and July. We were in the final throes of that effort and were able to get everything awarded by Friday July 17, 1987. It was a crazy amount of work to get done by the team without them knowing I had my own deadline for leaving CBS. Over the weekend we finished moving the second-hand furniture we had stored in Felix's living room to our first office in the Park Ten office complex and were pretty well exhausted.

PHOTOS A-D: Moving into the first office.
PHOTO E: Owners and wives gathered around a drafting table.
"If we could just fill ten drafing seats, we would be doing well."
PHOTO F: "All for one!" under the Mustang.

MOON SHOT

We opened on Monday July 20, 1987. Paul and I were in the same office and the rest of the space was empty. Felix was back working full time at CBS in a contract role on the huge projects Paul and I had left, since he was the only electrical engineer. Our first checks coming into Mustang were from CBS for Felix's work.

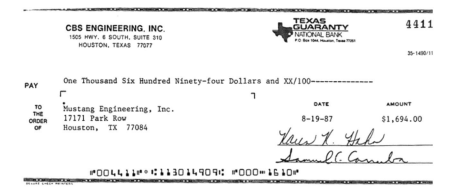

"First check" - Mustang's first income...we're "real"!

It was a funny-weird feeling to have no project work to do after the hectic pace of the first six months of 1987 and the super hectic pace of the previous two weeks. The phone was not ringing...not even with questions from the projects we had left. We decided to de-pressure a little and just do some organizing before jumping in to start calling clients.

Paul's initials "PR" actually stand for Pack Rat from my experience. He had collected an amazing amount of stuff from past projects. Some of the material I had given to him knowing that I could always go ask him and he could put his fingers on it. My favorite was a non-sparking hand pump that could be used offshore to transfer diesel from a 55 gallon drum to a platform crane. It was a simple and effective solution to a tough problem...Paul could always come up with that pamphlet! He had some fun putting all of his material into filing cabinets and labeling the folders. Paul figured that once things heated up, he would be back to business as usual, with lots of stacks, but at least this material would be searchable.

I started working on a qualifications package and decided not to call on clients until the next week. I wanted to have a package to flip through and a business card to leave with the client. Sales calls always seemed easier to me if I could engage the client over a drawing or picture of a project and then free flow from the client's comments.

Paul called a few clients that first week, and they were very positive in saying they would try to find something for him. Felmont Oil gave him a ten hour job to do that first week!

In the second week I had business cards and a qualification package that laid out the philosophy of Mustang along with experience based on Paul, Felix, and me. The qualification package had been pulled from the business plan and updated. I was already thinking differently and keener now that we were actually developing Mustang for real. It was subtle, but the words meant more and they had to get our message across.

DESIGNING MUSTANG

We wanted to stay out of the fixed price contracting "game," which was generally win-lose, and rather work on a reimbursable time and material basis for our clients. We wanted the focus to be squarely on project execution, such that we both could "win." We would have to design a company that could be profitable on industry competitive manhour rates, and structure project execution to foster a buildup of trust. The design of Mustang would have to evolve as our knowledge grew. However, we wanted everything to be about people and projects.

We liked people and genuinely wanted to help them be successful. For Mustangers, this meant providing challenging work, quality folks around them and a supportive and empowering environment with a constant push for innovation. For vendors, this meant well defined bid packages in a transparent bid process that pulled them in as a valued member of the team if they won. For clients, this meant defining their needs, helping to control their wants and insuring that engineering was removed from the schedule's critical path as soon as possible. For us, this meant removing energy "drains" from the business day so people would have energy to put into their families and then their communities.

We liked projects and genuinely wanted every project to be successful. For Mustangers, this meant using good project execution processes and systems, being innovative and communicating well. For vendors, this meant turning their brains on to provide the best solution in support of the team. Clients needed to define success and be a protective umbrella over the team to reduce changes. Somehow, we had to set up a company where the project manager was responsible for client and project success with little or no regard to Mustang's business success. Mustang would become successful through repeat work generated from good projects and satisfied clients.

Designing a company focused on people and projects would build strong trust bridges between us and Mustangers, between us and clients and between us and the vendors. Then we could start cross-connecting the trust bridges based on repeatable top performance. The cross-connecting would build a project execution methodology and teaming mentality across companies in the industry on a very strong foundation of trust.

9: REIMBURSABLE CONTRACTING

One bedrock philosophy was driven by our understanding of manhours and the type of relationship we wanted to build with our clients. Our business model would be built around signing reimbursable engineering contracts. Under this type of contract, the client would pay for services through the use of a schedule of rates for labor, computer time, car mileage, client offices, copies, etc. The contract would include a detailed scope of work to be performed and an estimate of costs prepared by the engineer.

SCHEDULE OF RATES

Clients would pay for engineering services in accordance with the schedule of rates. Costs for oil production equipment and construction of the offshore platform would be bid out by us on the client's behalf and become a direct cost to the client.

Generally, the reimbursable engineering and project management was 12-15% of the project's total installed cost. Production equipment and construction were awarded through lump sum or fixed price type of contracts based on the drawings, specifications and scope of work provided in the bid documents. These equipment and construction expenditures made up the other 85-88% of a project's cost.

$2.75 per billable hour. That was the business answer. $2.75 was the bottom line profit, or Earnings, Before Interest and Taxes (EBIT) as we would learn in year seven. Our average cost per manhour was the $17.00 base pay times a multiplier of 1.55 to cover statutory and overhead costs, giving $26.35 as our total cost. Analysis of these numbers made our world very simple...every hour of overhead ate up the profit from ten billable hours. A 10:1 "break even" was planted in our brains as a stark reality that had to be met head-on every day.

We could not afford to take our eyes off of this break even measurement for a moment, because it would be hard to recover overhead monies spent at the ratio of 10:1. Our accountability toward the labor overhead reality would drive many of our actions from behind the scenes.

TAKE MONEY OUT OF THE EQUATION

Reimbursable contracting "took money out from being a wedge between the client and the engineer." Both sides could work together, essentially on the same side of the table, to figure out the best way to deliver the project in the current industry environment. A relationship like this was important because the capabilities of contractors and the availability of materials changed dramatically in short periods of time and the team had to react swiftly to control cost, quality and schedule.

The upstream oil environment contributed to making project definition elusive. Part way through the project a new exploratory well might be tested and change many design parameters, impacting the project deliverables. The new design criteria had to be incorporated and equipment revised for the facility to match what was now going to come out of the ground. Reimbursable engineering, with timely fixed price contracting, appeared to be the win-win strategy for a free-flowing environment like the upstream oil patch, except for one missing ingredient...trust.

TRUST

Trust between clients and engineering contractors had dissolved due to poor behaviors on both sides during the '70s boom and '80s bust cycles. Clients wanted lump sum contracting to put the risks for project unknowns on the contractor. They wanted the contractor to have "skin in the game," such that both sides were aligned on cost over-runs hurting their respective businesses. Contractors wanted lump sum contracting because they could push the client out of the decision making process, control the risks and "use their smarts" to make a good profit.

Clients began to give less and less project scope definition in order to "give the contractors freedom" in execution methodology. Less definition also provided less room for contractors to claim an extra cost for scope change, because everything was included by the general terms used in project definition. Clients also did not have adequate staff in either the boom or the bust cycle to define projects in detail. Generally clients would award a reimbursable engineering contract to help with project definition and develop bid documents. The client would then revert to lump sum for detailed design engineering.

CONVENTIONAL WISDOM

Throughout the boom and bust cycle, a belief developed that engineering rates were not profitable because clients knew costs and knew how to squeeze them. The only way to come out ahead was to do lump sum engineering and take on additional scope, like the production equipment or construction on a lump sum basis. Once you had the contract, you pushed some of the engineering to the vendors and contractors, while also pinching their estimates down through bidding. All of this "gamesmanship" should produce a profit for the engineering company.

The real price of this "gamesmanship" was eliminating trust between clients, engineers, vendors and contractors. Each company had to diligently configure their scope, cost, pricing, and execution strategy to remain viable in the industry. The mentality was definitely that the game was "win-lose" and you wanted to be the winner.

Problems with this contracting situation became very clear during the bust cycle, when there were not enough projects to go around. Contractors started cutting the risk and contingency money in their bids due to more competition for the work. Clients learned how to control cost growth with tighter contracts. More projects started going to litigation due to finger pointing over who had to absorb the cost of a change.

Clients had the ability to recoup costs from twenty years of production, while contractors only had the current project to earn from. Contractors and clients lost huge sums on the one out of five "bad" projects, resulting in bankruptcy protection, layoffs and management personnel turnover.

THE DIFFERENCE

Mustang wanted to be built on reimbursable Engineering, Purchasing and Construction Management (EPCM) contracts and trusting relationships developed through performance. We would have less overhead manhours for a number of reasons:

- Contracts would go into a drawer and there would be no litigation initiated by Mustang, which would be savings for clients and vendors.
- Minimal bid effort would be required as teams did re-

peat work for clients whose systems they understood.

- Separate sets of accounting books to track company profitability versus project costs would not be needed.
- The client would not push scope of work activities on us that he should keep, thus reducing the need for some groups of people altogether.

A reimbursable philosophy would create a differentiation in overhead labor cost, relieving some of the pressure from the 10:1 break even reality.

The big risk in taking this approach was that a company set up from its core to do reimbursable work could not do lump sum work very well. The mind-set was too different. Once we decided to go reimbursable, we set up a work ethic and approach that we had to stay true to. If we wavered, the industry would eat us up due to inconsistency in approach...we would probably lose money on both reimbursable and lump sum work. The die was cast as we wanted to do only reimbursable work and generate the ability to eventually get into "win-win" contracting long term.

MUSTANG MOTION

We had to embody everything the blue horse logo and Mustang Engineering font implied in order to stay true to a reimbursable contracting philosophy. We would have to be constantly moving and pushing for projects, people, performance and passion. We would let the industry's clients and vendors discover the difference we were creating by delivering significant improvement to their bottom line.

"A penny saved is a penny earned."
Mom

10: THE ALBATROSS

Our 1200 square feet of space was getting a little crowded in October of 1987. We met with the leasing agent to look at the space next to us. It turned out that on the other side of a partition in one of our hallways was a coffee bar area!! We currently had to haul water from the bathrooms for coffee. Although this cut down the coffee drinking, because no one wanted to take the last cup and make the run, it was also a waste of time. We went back to tell everyone that we had a new short term company goal...grow enough to punch through the partition and get to the coffee bar.

REAL ESTATE

Real estate was the next big overhead cost after labor. As we loaded furniture from engineering firms that were closing, we asked the owners a lot of questions. A common thread in the responses was that leases were unmanageable as their head count shrank. "Like an albatross around their neck" was heard more than once from these owners. They had negotiated five or seven year leases to lock in lower rates, resulting in a cost of about $1.50 per billable manhour. Once they went to one third or one fourth the size in head count, the lease cost per manhour became untenable.

Finding a space and leasing it for our first office fell to me. Felix felt we should do the cheapest solution available because clients rarely went to the engineering office. Trying to be innovative, I did a layout for putting Mustang into a 1200 sq. ft. home we used to live in and were now renting out for $550 per month, which covered our mortgage cost of $450. Using the garage and living room for drafting, and parking at a nearby school, we could make it work. $450 per month was a super low cost and would let us see if Mustang was viable before we went and signed a lease for office space. Of course using the house for office space would violate neighborhood deed restrictions. I felt that with all the foreclosures, we could dodge around the community association for awhile with only six or eight people working. The house was quite a drive for Paul and me, but worth it in order to have no long term commitment. I also went to look at office space for cost comparison.

Doing a map recon, I picked an area called Park Ten for a few reasons. The area was just west of the "energy corridor" in west Houston, where most of the oil companies had offices. Leasing was half the cost of space in the energy corridor due to it being built with class "C" instead of class "B" buildings. It provided good access to the oil companies and was half way between Felix's and Paul's houses. I lived just a few miles north of Park Ten.

Our leasing solution for a startup company began with hiring a real estate agent who was willing to help us meet our criteria of matching leased space to our head count. Again, we wanted to be innovative in order to reduce the chance of a lease commitment causing us to go out of business. We needed to find a building owner who was hungry enough to do almost anything to get us in their building and not charge us extra due to the "perceived risk" they were taking with a startup company. Our agent was able to find three such buildings in Park Ten due to the softest office space market in Houston in 18 years.

We considered the three buildings and noted each had space with room for us to grow. The cheapest was a two story building with no parking garage and minimal amenities on Park Row. We could get 1200 square feet for $5.50 a square foot per year, or $550 per month. Our agent showed us that the rate was barely above the operating cost for the building.

This cost per month was only $100 more than using the house, eliminated the possible community association pressure and shortened our drive. Additionally, there was room to grow above the 10 people we could accommodate with the inefficient layout of the house.

We decided to take the office in Park Ten and signed a lease for 1,200 square feet for six months. Our agent negotiated a few other things for us in that first lease, while we had the attention of the building owner. With two months of notice, we could extend the lease by a month with no rate change through the first twelve months. Additionally, we could add space with short 45 day back out clauses. This lease would allow us to grow but also would limit the downward drag on finances that could result if we hit a slump in work. We did not need to sign a long term lease as a way to reduce costs because the real estate market was so poor that leases were dirt cheap.

JUGGLING = PROFIT

Controlling lease space was a tough juggling act. Our workload would have natural peaks and valleys that could not be controlled due to the short duration of the projects. We planned to hire minimal personnel direct as employees, figuring we could "load and unload" the staff with contract personnel. Once people started in the office, however, we immediately became attached to them and did not want to "unload" them if possible.

In order to shave the peaks, we worked some people part time from their homes, or had them use offices at night in a true moonlighting fashion. Pushing work to homes or evenings was a tremendous effort and put a lot of stress on Paul, but helped manage a large overhead cost.

The initials for the drafter on many drawings was "MLP," which Paul Post used for "Moon Light Person," since he was still at CBS Engineering.

Although we could not put our finger on costs per project and calculate profit, we knew that we had to be running at close to the absolute bottom for the industry in cost per manhour.

Paul and I shared an office initially, which was deja' vu since we had shared an office when we first met in 1980 at CBS. It was good for communications but distracting due to the intensity with which we worked. During the day, I was always on the phone and Paul had a continuous stream of people coming in to work technical problems. We had put a banner up on the wall across from our desks that said "Strong to the Hoop" to encourage everyone to finish things.

We had obtained swivel desk chairs for $5.00 each; Paul's was brown and mine was burnt orange. We always tried to trick Paul into sitting in my chair but, being a Texas Aggie and maroon to the core, it never worked due to burnt orange representing the University of Texas color.

I had learned to freehand Old English lettering in high school and enjoyed doodling with it for relaxation. I made our first "shingle" for the front door and taped it up.

First "shingle"

Someone from CBS came by and taped up a bucking mustang horse with its rear hoofs looking at you and the caption of "Twice as good as Omega"...one of our potentially prime competitors.

People were talking about us and having some fun in the industry. Lease space restrictions and minimizing office furniture costs were pulling us together and creating some lasting memories.

SHORT TERM GOAL

Lease space had created the first short term company goal...get to that coffee pot and sink!! In December of 1987, we signed the short term lease for five more offices and put a fist through the partition that had been separating us from the coffee bar! Everyone enjoyed the feeling of accomplishment as we celebrated meeting an obvious short term goal. At the same time, it meant that we were growing beyond the ten drafting tables we had set up...pretty amazing.

OFFICE MOVES

My office had been moved a month earlier in the original space to allow engineering to be co-located. I went in Christmas morning of 1987, when the family had gone down for a nap and moved Paul's office into the new area. He felt others should have the new offices, but we knew that he wanted to be in the middle of the project area, so this was a good Christmas present for him.

> "No one could get comfortable and 'settled' and turf could not be built."

Lease space optimization combined with putting project teams together meant everyone seemed to be constantly moving, even the three of us. This movement helped create motion and newness continuously. No one could get comfortable and "settled" and turf could not be built. Everyone was in the position of taking care of people and projects while they personally just tried to keep up with the perpetual motion of Mustang. This feeling of movement created by actual movement became a modus operandi that new people had to get used to.

Juggling lease space, like juggling people was crucial for controlling costs in our move toward profitability. The third big piece of juggling came from our strategy to win "below the radar screen" small projects.

Loyalty and trust are built on performance.

11: SMALL PROJECTS

For the first three years, 80% of the billable hours were on jobs that lasted less than eight weeks. Our "going out of business" curve...our other albatross...looked like this:

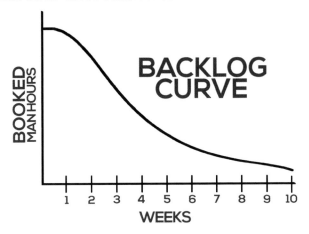

DEAL WITH THE MARGIN

Sometimes the curve was steeper. Being conservative, we always said our going out of business horizon was six weeks. Combine this with controlling overhead hours and lease space and something had to give. The easiest solution at the time, and common in the industry, was to hire and fire technical people to limit overhead and match job requirements.

Loyalty and trust, however, are built on performance. We wanted to build loyalty and trust, so we had to find another way. Our attention had to be squarely on filling the backlog curve with work. We would always be dealing with the margin...the half or full person about to go on overhead. Hiring people who were flexible and able to do many types of work helped. But the reality was that we needed to continuously fill the backlog to create loyalty and trust with our people.

JOB ON THE CORNER OF THE DESK

Job One

My challenge became to put a job on the corner of the designer's desk and say "please hurry up and finish, so you can get onto this project." If we could do this, then the people would not have to be worried about their job and could put all of their energy into doing good efficient work. "Job on the corner of the desk" became a mantra for me in sales and had some far reaching consequences.

In addition to relieving the stress people had for finding a new job, this philosophy increased efficiency. Normally it is hard to finish projects as they have a tendency to drag out. Now people found ways to push for completion and get onto the new hot project.

Push Efficiency

Small projects on the corner of the desk made us very efficient at starting and finishing projects. This efficiency reduced the manhours it took for us to do a project, making our cost per project competitive even at fully loaded manhour rates. Thus, we could pay the going rate for people and still have a lower estimated cost in our bids.

> "Sales had to close and projects had to close."

Job on the corner of the desk also meant that we did not have to include as much downtime in our overhead. This led to increased profitability within the existing industry standard rates. This efficiency was where we were able to squeeze out bonus money for everyone who was working so hard.

Job on the corner of the desk forced a sales discipline and a completion discipline. Sales had to close and projects had to close.

"SAME SENTENCE SALES"

There were about 20 competitors and 40 clients in exploration & production or what is commonly referred to as the "upstream" oil business, working on offshore platforms. Due to Paul's client relationships, we had 12 designers working in our sixth week. Our design group was in the Houston "network" that shared information on where projects were and how companies were faring. This network was the designer's lifeline for the next job. They "heard it through the grapevine" that a prime competitor, Omega, had four salesmen and three less designers working. This piece of information had such an impact on us that we did not hire a salesman in upstream until our eighth year. A salesman just did not fit with our control of overhead labor, lease space and general expenses.

Instead, we developed our relationships with 17 vendor salesmen. Valve salesmen, control panel salesmen, equipment salesmen, etc. were shaking the bushes hard, looking for work. They all had certain strong relationships with clients based on past performance. Each had trust relationships where the client would ask their opinion on which engineering firm could do a good job for them. We asked these salesmen to put our name in the same sentence with known companies like CBS and Omega that they trusted. This was our "same sentence" sales goal of the first few years.

The vendors knew we would take good care of the client and they had no problem working Mustang's name into conversations. Generally they called us if there was work at a given client's office, and we shared what bids were coming out of Mustang or other work we had heard about. In this manner, we stayed super-wired into the industry. The sales calls we made as a result of this network were "rifle shots" targeted toward a specific project and the person who could award the work. We also knew the client's concerns and how to win from the conversations with vendors, who were trying to put together a winning sales strategy.

The juggling was intense as we worked to create trust and loyalty between Mustangers, vendors and clients. Paul, Felix and I worked unbelievable hours putting ourselves in the gaps to minimize overhead labor hours and handle excess work on projects. Paul lost 30 pounds, Felix chewed Nicorette® gum like there was no tomorrow and I had salt stains on my shoes from sweating through them pounding the pavement for work in Houston. This was a very humbling experience as we saw how tenuous Mustang's grip was on surviving.

DESIGNING THE DREAM

We all had ideas of what we wanted Mustang to become. My dream was a company called Hudson Engineering that had been at the top in Houston in the late '70s. The blue Hudson name on top of a 20 story white building was known as the place to go for the best people, engineering, project management and execution for any project: upstream, downstream, pipeline or midstream. Understanding how to achieve this dream was something we were learning piece by piece.

> **The only reason for Mustang to exist was to do projects for clients.**

The realities of our situation made us realize, quite simply, that the only reason for Mustang to exist was to do projects for clients. Anything that did not support getting projects done was an un-needed luxury. We were starting to design a company without fat and were scared enough to keep it that way.

We knew we could work within the constraints of $2.75 profit per billable hour. After all, the industry set the labor rates and billing rates and others were somehow making ends meet. Some competitors had special relationships where their value insured a profit. Others came out ahead enough times on lump sum projects to stay in business.

No one felt a viable, growing company could be built on purely reimbursable work, but that was the direction we felt we had to go in order to create trust. We needed to prove to clients the value of using us in a reimbursable manner through above average performance.

This was our world and pretty typical for a start-up company. We needed good people to demonstrate that we had credible capability to get work. We needed projects in order to minimize overhead labor and pay the business costs. And, we needed all of this synchronized to some extent to match the early stages of cash flow. In addition, we wanted to put the heart in the Mustang, so we would have to continue being innovative as we designed the company to be better and different.

Like my favorite process engineer back then, Mark Valerius, used to say "this is no step for a stepper," let's get after it!

Original patch for baseball caps and sticker for hard hats.

"Great vision without great people, is irrelevant."
James C. Collins, Good to Great

12: OCCIDENTAL PETROLEUM

Hi! We're your piping design group. It's Wednesday July 22nd, day three of Mustang. Rocky Lawrence and Tom Nordyke showed up at our office-two guys we had never met before.

We called them our "Stork Basket" designers. They had bookcases, reference material, drafting tools, and a computer, (which was unusual at the time) in their pickup trucks and started moving into our ten table drafting room. We told them we had no work, therefore no cash flow, and we could not pay them. They said "no problem, we know your reputations and know that you will get work. In the meantime, we'll get things set up to handle the first projects."

Well, there was a vote of confidence. This event also put a lot of pressure on us to find work. These men had families and we felt we needed to start paying them soon.

Stork brings two designers and a computer to Mustang.

BUILDING A TEAM MENTALITY

Paul secured a small modification project on an offshore platform the second week after we opened the office from Win Thornton of Oxy. Win was a high energy guy who moved fast in building Oxy's offshore business. He needed solid engineering and project execution through startup in order to make sure he did not misstep. He totally trusted Paul but needed aggressive pricing and proof of full engineering and design capability in order to justify starting a small modification project at Mustang. Our two "stork basket" designers helped us win that first project just by being there with good resumes. Then, Win's business objectives changed and the modification job grew significantly until by mid-September, all three owners and twelve others were working to meet schedule on six small but related projects.

Paul's wife, Kay, brought in a home cooked lunch for the entire office every Friday to help with team building. Kay was very warm and gracious, evoking true southern hospitality. People enjoyed visiting with Kay. They asked about her children and how it was that she came to be driving a public school bus. They did not know that the owners were not getting paid for at least six months in order to build up a cash position in Mustang. In the eleventh week while on her way to the office to bring lunch, Kay had to stop quickly and the lunch of lasagna and salad went everywhere in the family van. The $120.00 tab for cleanup nixed the lunches, but by then we were communicating well and executing as a team.

Felix was the "old man" of the company and his wife, Joyce, invited the whole company to their house in October for his 40th birthday party. This was a great social event with everyone getting to know spouses. People enjoyed seeing pictures of Felix from age zero up and getting to know his wife.

Always one to speak her mind, Joyce was a hoot once people got to know her. She mingled easily with the Mustangers and ensured everyone enjoyed themselves.

Spouses of our new team members began to understand why everyone worked so hard, and they saw the obvious camaraderie in this team of Mustangers. Rocky had everyone doing his new Mustang horse dance in the driveway to the song "The Loco-motion" only he sang it as Mustang Motion. They were also a talkative bunch with lots of questions. Where did the name Mustang come from? How did the three of you get together? Is there going to be work through the winter? Do you want to meet a friend of mine who is a top talent and has the personality of a Mustanger? Can this feeling of being on a tight knit "A" team be maintained? Can we stay different?

> "Can this feeling of being on a tight knit "A" team be maintained?"

And, a number of comments were heard. "The owners and their wives are so nice and 'real'... hope they stay that way." "This is the first time I have ever been to a company owner's house." "This team sure has a lot of energy and enthusiasm." "The owners seem genuinely focused on our well-being."

Mustang came out of the blocks well and those moments in Felix's driveway captured everything that had been envisioned in preparation for the startup. We had work at a reasonable rate for our overhead situation. We had people who had selected each other based on technical capability, personal compatibility with the team, and work ethic. We were taking great care of our clients and treating vendors as part of the team. The people felt supported and empowered by the owners' hard work and attention toward giving them what they needed to be successful.

Typical offshore production equipment.

CREATING TECHNICAL COMPETENCE.... CAD

One of our technical goals when we started Mustang was to move into Computer Aided Design (CAD). CAD had been used for years, but the cost to set it up was prohibitive. CAD was run on large, climate controlled mainframe computers. Even timesharing on computers like these was very expensive. Additionally, there were training costs and significant programming required to tailor the software to your specific design requirements. However, over the previous five years, a number of personal computer (PC) based systems had been working their way into the industry as PCs became more powerful.

All of our drawings were done by hand with pencils, drawing templates and a new invention...the electric eraser. We kept the originals filed away and made blueprints for design reviews and to send to the field for fabrication. The smell of ammonia from the blueprinting process was always a problem back then.

Our "Stork" designers had been experimenting with one of these PC based CAD programs at home in the evenings to do schematic type drawings. Schematics are made up of lines with circles, squares, triangles and some text to depict the flow of a process. They showed us what they had done and how easy it was to revise the drawing as a project progressed. Projects in upstream oil and gas were essentially "progressive elaboration" over time as details became available, so easy revisions would be a money saver for the client. Easy revisions would also reduce our manhours and make us more responsive to client needs...all good things when your focus is on doing more projects per capita, rather than "milking" fewer projects for billable hours.

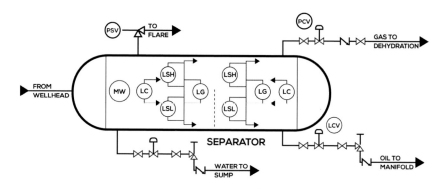

Early Separator Process & Instrument Diagram done on CAD.

We paid the guys to do a CAD schematic on one of our Oxy projects, tracked the time, and then tracked the time to do a revision. It was great! We took this data to the client and he opted for a full set of CAD schematics on the project. So, in our fourth week, we created Mustang's first, and the first of our collective careers, billable CAD drawing. This was huge, as it showed our commitment to being on the cutting edge of the available technology.

"CREATE" ON PROJECTS

This CAD experiment also set up our "modus operandi" for creating new efficiencies in executing work:

- Canvass people for efficiency or quality improvement ideas.
- Investigate enough to know the cost to develop the idea and the potential savings.
- Develop and implement the idea within a project.
- Develop the idea with the people who will use it, in order to keep it lean and efficient.
- Measure the results quantitatively and qualitatively.
- Set up a procedure for quality control.
- Implement across the company on all projects.

Best of all, the originals stayed in the computer, eliminating the need for large flat filing cabinets for schematics. Additionally, the schematics were printed on a copy machine with no ammonia smell...the industry would just have to get used to black and white drawings instead of blueprints.

Rocky Lawrence offshore sketching piping tie-ins for a modification.

"He who has begun, is half done."
Horace, Poet

13: CREATING NEW HABITS

Our principal challenge was obtaining computers that could handle the size and complexity of CAD programs with decent speed. Most of our designers had a one or two year old machine at home and were taking some CAD classes. At work, however, there were just a few personally owned computers to use. Essentially, it was faster to do drawings by hand at your drafting table than wait to get on a computer.

In order to change designer's habits, we needed them to have a computer right next to their drafting table to eliminate a major excuse for not doing CAD. Then we needed training, creation of design standards and increased ability to execute as a team within computer models. We knew where we needed to go, but the first step was hardware...computers...and they were expensive.

CAD CAPABILITY

Hardware

We made a proposal to our designers. Preferred Savings & Loan pre-approved each of them for a loan to buy a PC for use in their work. We provided them with minimum criteria for the PC's capability and encouraged them to buy one. We would pay them $150 per month for eighteen months for the use of the computer at Mustang. By the end of 18 months, they would:

- Have paid off the loan.
- Own a computer for the house.
- Become proficient at CAD.
- Have increased their earning power by 25%.

Software

We also committed to pay Rocky Lawrence and a consultant as required, to teach CAD classes two nights a week at Mustang. These classes would be voluntary, free, and eventually be taught 100% by Mustangers. In late September 1987, everyone took us up on the offer, resulting in $40,000 of computers coming into the office virtually overnight.

KEEPING IT LEAN

CAD Development

We were excited about the opportunities available with CAD, but had read enough stories about computer system development killing small businesses to be concerned. Since our only funding was from clients, computer system development was straightforward:

- Develop on a project.
- Develop to increase efficiency on a project.
- Develop only what was needed.
- Develop with billable people.

Develop Differently

While other firms hired computer programmers and hardware specialists to set up their design systems as an overhead project, we followed our lean philosophy as listed above. Our method was very difficult, because each piece had to be justified to a client on a project and pieces were being created on a number of different projects simultaneously. The evening CAD classes turned out to be a godsend. At these classes, our designers shared what they were doing and discussed the next step. At the same time, they learned each other's strengths, while welding themselves into a team.

They knew that they were creating something different from the ground up. They developed systems and methods for efficiency "from a designer's point-of-view." Systems were easy for anyone with some CAD experience to get into and be productive immediately. If there was a problem, the designers could quickly fix it because the programming was logical to their way of thinking and written by them. This was critical in the no overhead environment we had created. Billable designers also functioned as our Information Technology (IT) department.

> "Billable designers also functioned as our Information Technology department."

Clients liked our computer systems because they were not proprietary and were easy for the client's organization to use in updating drawings without having to come back to Mustang. The message here was that we would be happy to update drawings if the client wanted us to, but we were not forcing them to use us. Do what makes sense in your organization.

YOUNG PEOPLE

Our designers had 10-15 years of experience when they started learning CAD. We didn't understand how much of the transition was coming through word-of-mouth and experimentation until the summer of 1988.

We hired Kristen Peterson as a summer intern--our first "Young Gun." She was going to be a college junior in mechanical engineering and had good computer skills. We put her in the drafting room, figuring that when she went back to school, she could show drawings she had created over the summer. By the third week, we had 15 year veterans, with three years of CAD experience, lauding the tricks she showed them to save time in creating a design. The difference was that when she read the software program manual at night, she understood it better than the designers, and figured out how to apply the shortcuts in our design methods. This was a fun mental challenge for her and a boost to the team's capability.

We learned an important lesson about the ability to continuously improve efficiency...it requires someone's focus; a champion.

Across the 18 months of the computer-loan program, a number of things transpired:

- We developed a team-oriented CAD group.
- Mustangers learned they could trust the owners.
- The people and Mustang both profited financially and both improved their resume for future work.
- Mustang re-invested the funds earned from billing computer time into new higher speed PCs when people took their computer home.

Kristen showed us we needed to figure out how to bring young people into Mustang. The industry had already gone five years without bringing in youth due to their lack of experience. Not hiring young people because clients would not let us use them on their projects seemed short-sighted as there would be a severe age gap in providing and training future leaders. We saw the problem but did not have resources to invest in this area.

IT SEEMS TO BE WORKING

The owners and wives went above and beyond what was required to make sure each employee, their spouse and family knew they were important to us as individuals and important to the success of Mustang. We had found ways to insure Mustangers had the tools and training to be successful.

Designers knew we believed they were the backbone of the organization. They took input from engineering and the equipment vendor data to work out the details of a design. They were the quality system. Through their checking, all the conflicts were resolved before drawings went out the door. This was where the "rubber meets the road," where the heat and friction would be created in pushing to get all the details correct. This is where we built the company reputation.

The stimulus for our belief in designers was our experience and seeing the quality team that was built from our original "stork" designers. My Army experience had also taught me that Sergeants were the backbone and needed to be treated well for top performance. We worked with David Sneed, our lead piping designer and Ken Lipinski, our lead structural designer, to insure we took care of our designers.

We were building Mustang in a different way, with designers treated and valued as professionals who could make a project successful. In other companies, designers were "hire and fire" components of the engineering machine. Building trust and relationships with our designers put some of the heart into Mustang as our value proposition began to clarify itself.

Divakar Pathak (Piping) and Louis McGlory (Structural).

"QUALITY OUT THE DOOR"

"You only have one chance... to make a first impression."
Major Ed Ruff, 8th Engineer Battalion

14: THE SNICKERS™ STORY

Dick Westbrook called Mustang in August of 1987 from Houston's Metro bus transportation department. Metro was where Dick landed after being laid off from CBS. We had done a number of projects together and I considered him a top-rated project engineer. He wanted to know if I was serious about wanting to diversify from offshore oil platforms, like I had always been telling him at CBS. When I said yes, I could tell he was ready to tell me his brainstorm.

BUS MAINTENANCE FACILITIES?

With Dick, nothing was ever slow or partially thought through. He had a number of bus maintenance facilities that needed modification for safety issues. They had just damaged a tank and Dick found that the project drawings were lacking in details. These facilities had some high pressure piping, various pumps, pressure vessels, atmospheric tanks, and utility and electrical systems. Dick felt the methods we used on offshore platforms to design safe systems would save him three years of trying to teach the engineering firms that Metro was using.

We had some significant reservations about chasing government work, but it was very hard to say no to Dick. I told him I'd come over to meet his boss and look at drawings of the facilities he needed help with. My first concern from my Army experience was the type of paperwork that would be required. We were working very long hours with little overhead and could not handle a lot of bureaucratic red tape...we just needed to do projects.

Dick had been in the Army, and had been at Metro for seven months, so I had to trust his judgment that this work matched the type of company we were building.

WE COULD BRING VALUE

Dick definitely has what I called a "sales bone" in his body and was ready to reel me in at our first visit. First he showed me schematic drawings and went through the systems typical in a maintenance facility. Then he showed me some of the problems they had and guided the conversation to let me say what needed to be done from an engineering standpoint.

From there we looked at construction drawings. The problems were so obvious I knew we could make a huge difference in their safety, cost, schedule, and quality with our methods. Dick had me hooked, and we went to see his boss now that I could talk intelligently about the value Mustang could bring to their projects.

His boss had a good background in the oil industry and fully understood the difference that a Mustang could bring to the work. He asked if Dick had explained the use of DBEs and WBEs on the work. A quizzical look came to my face as I did not understand these abbreviations.

THE CHALLENGE

Dick jumped in to say that he had wanted to see how this meeting went before he laid out all of the challenges Mustang would have in obtaining the contract for general engineering services. In normal Dick fashion, he had a list of things we would need to do when we got back to his office. He knew I had never heard of these things and had solutions ready as he started talking about them. Key items he went through were:

- DBE is a Disadvantaged Business Enterprise. These companies had certificates showing that they were approved as a DBE. We had to insure that 5% of the revenue earned through the contract went to DBEs.
- WBE is a Woman owned Business Enterprise. Everything was similar to the DBE, except that the minimum percentage was 3%.
- Government form 254, giving relevant project experience.
- Government form 255, giving experience and data on each person proposed for the work.
- Presentation. Dick felt that we had a 75% chance of being short listed because we would be so different that the bid review board would want to hear about our offer in person. We needed to wow the board like we did in the BP presentation 18 months earlier (remember Dick being a Frame V?) if we were going to move from a curiosity for the board to the recommended company.

We talked about having some of our people walk through a bus maintenance facility with Dick to make sure we could do a good job for Metro.

RELATIONSHIPS MUST BE CHERISHED

We had a good discussion on the slim possibility of winning this work for Metro. We decided to pursue the work for one reason only...we all loved and respected Dick Westbrook. He had saved our projects numerous times at CBS and was indefatigable when it came to accomplishing a mission. If he felt he needed us, then we were going to give him our best shot as a thank you for all he had done. If nothing else, maybe we could shake up the status quo, allowing Dick to get better work out of the usual contractors. His professional reputation was at stake and he needed much better execution and attention to detail.

GET TO THE SHORT LIST

From interviews and some analysis, we picked two good companies to be our DBE and WBE. We explored what capability each of these companies had and figured out a way for them to start helping us immediately on offshore work. The goal in this effort was to be able to show the board that we had worked together and for these companies, who were known to the board, to vouch for the similarities in the work. We also wanted these companies to be able to describe in their own words why they felt Mustang would be a different and better solution for Metro since they had worked for all of the engineering firms with Metro experience.

The request for proposal came out in early September and we did a lot of late nights pulling it together. By choosing the right words, we showed our project experience in such a manner that the fact it was on offshore platforms was not very evident...it was piping, mechanical, structural and electrical work.

STAYING BUSY!!

We turned the proposal in and ignored its progress through the system. We were way too busy to waste time thinking about what might or might not happen with that proposal. I was checking the piping dimensions on an Oxy platform by yellowing them off with a highlighter to double check everything done by our designers. At the same time, I was chasing some compressor additions for Arco. Paul was hiring and moving people around between the six Oxy projects to deliver them at a good cost and excellent quality. Felix was chasing down the money, doing electrical design on everything, working insurance, and building the office infrastructure.

Our quick growth put us in a bind by mid October. I planned to take our three personal credit cards to the bank and secure the funds for payroll. Paul's dad had also volunteered to float us a loan if required. Just in the nick of time, Win Thornton of Oxy was able to walk a check through their system and we were solvent. We were going nuts... and Dick called all excited about us being short listed.

PRESENTATION.... WIN THE TIE

Dick called the next day to say that they were going to have four presentations in one morning starting at 8:00 a.m. and everything would wrap up by noon. We would be the last presenter.

As a young company, we did not have any transportable ability to give presentations using the computer. Down the hall from us was a Campbell's Soup™ marketing office that threw out some thick advertising posters of cans of soup. I picked up the posters and wrote the presentation on the back.

Our team walked in carrying an easel and the advertising boards – just hoping to get some attention. I then flipped the first board over to reveal the start of our presentation. Written in magic marker were the words:

"MUSTANG WILL SATISFY YOU"

I probably broke all of the protocol rules of Metro and walked over into their space. Starting with the first board member, I put a large Snickers® bar in front of each of them. I told them that I wanted them to pay attention to this presentation...not lunch!!

I worked my way down to the last board member when I said, "Oh and here is a small one for your baby." That comment got everyone on both sides of the room laughing, because she was pregnant but not yet showing. It was very obvious through sight, sound, smell, taste, touch and feeling of empathy, that Mustang was going to be focused on Metro and their needs.

We drew them into a great conversation about their concerns. We talked about how Mustang would help solve those concerns, if Metro would help us minimize the bureaucracy and paperwork. Before the "presentation" was over, we were all working together to figure out how to take care of each other in a fully win-win fashion.

The most important thing that resulted from winning Metro was that 80% of our drafting room worked down at Metro from December through February, preventing a layoff. This saved our reputation with our people...and perhaps saved Mustang.

SNICKERS' STORY

This is why we serve small Snickers® bars at all functions. We want to continually remind people to be other-oriented in our ongoing effort to build trust. Being other-oriented in all of our actions is a very positive differentiator that many find hard to believe at first. Will *MUSTANG* really continue to create win-win scenarios, or become defensive and protective? We felt that as the right people were touched repeatedly, they would get past these concerns and become part of the ever expand-ing Mustang family of clients, vendors and new Mustangers.

Front and back of the original Metro presentation boards.

"Effective and continuous sales are the lifeline in a small business."
Bill Higgs, Salesman

15: ATLANTIC RICHFIELD COMPANY

Divakar Pathak was our first direct hire Mustanger and worked as a piping designer. He was part of a new group of young people we learned about while moving furniture from an engineering firm that was closing. Out of work and needing to support his family, Divakar had been selling cars at a dealership. He had been the top salesman for the previous three months but was happy to be back in a technical job. I told him that I had primary responsibility for sales but did not have much experience and wondered if he had any words of wisdom from selling cars. He said to just make an impression so you are remembered. In his experience, it did not seem to matter if the impression was good or bad...just that they remembered you.

A LITTLE HELP FROM SAM

The biggest surprise when I started calling clients in the second week was discovering that Sam Carruba, as president of CBS, had been very busy the week before calling everyone in the industry. He wanted to address the loss of three key engineers to preempt the inevitable chatter in the industry as the word spread. He told people we left our projects in good shape and we were not planning on pulling a lot of people from CBS. These calls were good for CBS's client relations and an absolute windfall for us.

Every client I called had already heard about us from Sam or a vendor and wanted to hear our story. They all knew of engineering firms that had closed or were closing and wondered why we had decided to start a new engineering company at such a poor time. These clients needed viable engineering firms to compete for their work and wanted to hear about

Mustang's potential. The energy that came over the phone to them and the earnestness with which I told our story was the first brick I laid in each new Mustang relationship.

Due to the targeted list I was calling from, I had a 100% hit rate on setting up a visit to the client office. Paul and I went on the first few sales calls together. We figured we could tag team and one of us could observe how the message was coming across. This worked until about the fifth call when we were visiting a very good friend of Sam's.

TIME TO SPLIT UP

Sam's friend sat there for fifteen minutes and said nothing while I worked through the Mustang story and brought Paul into the talk by asking him questions that the client should have been asking. It was a very tough fifteen minutes as I was carrying the entire load in what should have been a reasonable give and take sales call. Finally the client spoke and said Sam had told him we were out "fooling around," which I'm sure were his words and not Sam's. Now, I can always tell when Paul gets hot because the veins on either side of his neck bulge out and start pulsing, sort of like he is ready to tackle someone in football. The veins came out but he didn't say anything. He let me gracefully work us out of the meeting with a promise to return in six weeks to give this man an update.

Paul was incredulous as we talked out in the parking lot. How could I plan to go see that guy again? The fact was the client had work that would come out in a few months and we had time to soften him up. Paul took the "fooling around" comment personally, because he knew that we were already totally busting our butts to do great work. We decided that Paul would be better off chasing a specific project where I had already laid some ground work.

This would also help us split up, since we had been doing virtually everything together for the first three weeks. We were in the same office, sitting next to each other, hearing phone conversations and project discussions. We had the revelation that we essentially thought and acted the same in situations, so we decided to stop talking all the time to each other and invest our time in talking to vendors, clients, and Mustangers. This was a big step for us to learn early.

By the way, we ended up working for that client on a big job a few years and about twenty sales calls later. The "softening up" took longer than I expected!

RELATIONSHIPS BUILT ACROSS TIME

Chris Blair, with Atlantic Richfield Company (Arco), called me into his office...he was now district manager over half the Gulf. He had two new project engineers, one from the reservoir group in Houston and one from the operations group in Corpus Christi, Texas. He said tongue-in-cheek that he needed me to train them to be effective project engineers like I had trained him some years back. The engineer from Corpus had a compressor project coming up and he gave me his name.

He said he wanted all of his projects done by Mustang, because he knew he would receive tremendous value for the money spent. I told him we could take care of the compressor addition, but that I did not think it would be a good idea for all of his work to come to us for a few reasons. First, there would be times where we would not be able to staff a job and he needed to have good relationships, I suggested, with at least two other firms to insure he could take care of his work. Second, I pointed out that even though he would receive great value from us, big companies like Arco want that "feeling of value" proved by bidding regularly and there was no sense getting second-guessed by his own people. I used this "pass the work around" speech thousands of times to help build credibility and trust. I truly wanted our clients to be successful long term and coached them whenever I had the opportunity. Clients did not hear this kind of advice from our competitors who tried to limit the playing field, not expand it.

Never bashful when it came to getting work, I called the new engineer, Kurt, from Corpus from an empty office at Arco after leaving Chris. Kurt was in a temporary office a few halls over. He said to come on over and I surprised him a few minutes later.

Kurt had drawings out on his desk and after introductions said that they had a pump that was cavitating on an offshore platform. Cavitating meant that the fluid in the pump was essentially boiling, which would cause destructive vibrations. Operations wanted him to figure out the problem with the pump. Looking at the drawings upside down, I showed him that if the drawings were correct, the vessel had been hooked up incorrectly to the pump, thus causing the problem. He immediately called offshore and had them verify the drawing...turned out it was an easy fix. Needless to say, we won his reciprocating compressor addition without bid and took good care of him.

ENGINEER-DOWN-THE-HALL

Back in those days I was able to set up an appointment with one person at Arco and then just roam the halls to say hello to other engineers and see what was coming up. I'd go over every week or ten days and pick up small tasks that did not have to be bid since we had very quickly set up an "evergreen" reimbursable contract. The Arco contract person lived in my neighborhood and knew the head guys wanted to be able to work with us, so he expedited the contract.

Some Arco engineers started calling me "Mr. Mustang" as I'd come down the hall and I always worked to brighten their day with a smile or some antic like getting a vendor's donuts from the coffee area and handing them out.

Working with Arco's head of electrical engineering, Felix and I set up for him to electronically transfer data back and forth to our office to get the drafting support he needed. Most times he just worked directly with LD Cunningham in drafting and did not get charged for any engineering time from Felix. This worked so well that I started telling the other engineers that we were Arco's "engineer down the hall". We had a contract and the trust of their bosses, so use us to get your work done. We were able to leverage their small staff and accomplish a lot of work.

A LITTLE EXCITEMENT

The tough thing about this Arco relationship was that work of any decent size was bid and for the first few months it was awarded to our competitors while we were proving our sustainability. Then we bid a nice compressor addition for Helene Harding, who had come in from the reservoir (rock jock) group due to the workload Arco had in supporting operations upgrades. I was roaming the hall one day when her boss, Phil Inman called me in for a chat. Phil had come in from Lafayette, Louisiana to replace Chris Blair, who had gone overseas. Part way through our conversation he told me that we had won Helene's compressor addition...I jumped up unexpectedly and gave him high fives, drawing him up and out of his chair. His heart was pumping and he said that if he knew I would be this excited, he would have told me sooner. It was a moment he would not soon forget.

Phil should have seen the high fives and fun we had back at the office. This was a great project for us because it would use all the engineering and purchasing talent we had cobbled together and allow us to start an inspection group to check things in the field. Inspection would make us a "full service" engineering firm...a longer range goal.

Helene Harding was a "straight A" Chemical Engineer from Texas A&M, whose best friend in college was a runner-up for Miss Texas...I think it would have been hard to tell which of them was the beauty queen. This compressor we had to relocate from another platform was a six-story tall Ruston Turbine which would be good for Mustang's resume due to the complexity of the hookups.

Helene went offshore with me a number of times which was very good for morale and good for her learning curve. She is the only person I had ever seen in the Army or offshore that would put her weight on the helicopter flight manifest to the half-pound. Helene was super quick in learning facilities and we had a great project from concept through startup.

As Helene's project was starting, Jim Linder of Transco Exploration called to say he had been laid off, and he wondered if I knew where he might find work. Paul, Felix and I were known to be well wired in the industry and had helped many clients find jobs after layoffs. Generally these people were pretty shattered and also needed a pat on the back. I told him it was great to hear he was looking for work. He said, "what?" I told him that we needed a construction guy to head up our inspection group...please come in and interview.

If nothing else, I would get him out of the house and networking. In this case, we hired him.

16: CONQUEST EXPLORATION

My modus operandi was to build trust in me and Mustang with the client. Then I would work to transfer that trust to the even smarter folks back in the office. I discovered the engineer-down-the-hall moniker helped people understand Mustang as we progressed. For example, would you put unlimited liability on your own engineer down the hall? Of course not, so why try to put that risk on Mustang and have to pay for it? Felix loved this affirmative action from sales to help him get good contracts. Of course, at the time, Mustang was so hard to manage that if someone wanted to sue us we joked we would just hand them the keys and wish them good luck.

FIRST RIGHT

In general, I joked with clients that we wanted first right of refusal on their work. If it did not match us, or we were too full, we would help them place the work at the right company and even suggest the team they should use. We were building trust based on an all-encompassing performance in the client's eyes.

STRIKE WHILE THE IRON OF COURAGE IS HOT

Vendor lead

A vendor called after leaving Tom Raabe's office at Conquest Exploration, a small independent oil company. He said that Tom wanted to add some facilities to two thirty year old Shell platforms they had purchased and he was not sure if the structures could support the additional weight. The vendor said he had put us in the "same sentence" with possible engineering firms that could help him. After thanking the vendor,

I wondered if I should wait a day, since it was 4:00 p.m. Thursday afternoon, or go ahead and call Tom, whom I'd never met. It was the first week of December 1987, which traditionally was a tough time to find work and we really needed something for our structural guys. I figured that I'd call right away and maybe catch Tom still thinking about the project. Turned out the timing was good and Tom was very personable. We set up a meeting for the next day to discuss his needs.

Blow Him Away

Instead of going over to Conquest to have a discussion about his platforms, we decided to create a fait accompli for getting the work. We worked into the wee hours to set up a computer demonstration of exactly how we would analyze the platforms...essentially doing 10% of the project.

Tom was pleasantly surprised when we showed up with a computer on a Friday afternoon in downtown Houston. He knew we were very serious about his project as the meeting would put us into the impossible Friday afternoon rush hour traffic...essentially gridlock. He was amazed that we had a demo specific to his project and dug in to ask a lot of questions. We easily handled these questions and answered some by using the computer programs in real time. Our "just-do-it" work from the night before really set us apart in Tom's eyes.

> "Our 'just do it' work set us apart..."

Tom awarded us the structural analysis before we left... have to love the simple decision making process in independent oil companies. Tom later awarded us the facilities work once we had proven that the structures would hold up the new equipment. This work along with Oxy, Metro and Arco, helped us survive the winter of 1987.

WHAT GOES AROUND, COMES AROUND

We had each been in the industry long enough to know that as a startup company we could not accept all of the work that could potentially get earmarked for us. We used this knowledge to solidify the client's trust by encouraging them to use other companies. These discussions with clients allowed us to emphasize that we were thinking of the industry as a team to be used as effectively as possible to deliver the best project. By giving clients the names of people they should use at other companies, we showed good industry knowledge, showed a focus on the client and showed we were realistic about our own capabilities.

A clear and clean philosophy came across in everything we did. We were working to position clients, vendors and Mustangers into win-win scenarios...even if it meant Mustang taking a controlled hit to prove the point.

KEEP MARKET FORCES IN PLAY

Our strategy has always been to win work without bidding. We felt that we could have finished 20% of the project by the time the bid was awarded. However, bidding does keep market forces in play to help hone efficiency. We were never scared of bidding, because if we were not competitive, then we should not be doing the work. Many times we wanted to bid because we could capture a little more margin than our evergreen contracts allowed. Bidding also forced us to do a good execution plan and think harder about how to be innovative.

We worked hard to solidify our relationships such that we could get an audience with the client to explain our bid and win the work even if we were a little bit high. This was critical when we really needed a particular project.

CAN'T CHASE 'EM ALL

A retired Air Force officer called to say he could help us win a plant upgrade bid. The work would be in California and all the people were currently working on-site. Engineering firms in Houston had the lowest overhead markups anywhere in the country, he said. He felt the low overhead would create the value proposition he needed to win the contract.

I gave him the names of firms that did onshore plant work and wished him the best. My neighbor cobbled a bid together for his firm and put 30 people to work in California for three years at an above average profit.

> "Our job was resource allocation to create a profit."

Well, that would have been a nice shot in the arm, but our job was resource allocation to create a profit. We had to evaluate opportunities, make decisions and move on to the next hot topic. There was just too much going on for us to worry about lost opportunities like this one.

KEEP BEATING THE DRUM

We pieced together the message and beat the drum with a constant beat. We took care of our people first to develop loyalty and an esprit de corps. We wanted clients and vendors to hear this message, see that we were doing it, and feel the difference. Then our philosophy was to go beat the drum some more, emphasizing the successes, and just move past the people who could not hear the beat for awhile. We had worked for 18 different clients by the end of 1987. Many of our competitors just milked work from 5-7 clients they had good relationships with. We wanted to work for them all!

*"I'd rather expect the best from people and some-times be disappointed , than..." **Bits and Pieces***

17: PEOPLE

I called Roger Canale on a Friday afternoon. He was a new designer who was going to start on Monday. I needed a designer to go offshore with me Saturday on a hot job we had just won and Roger was the only one without a current commitment. I asked if he would start early and meet me Saturday morning.

Roger said yes and we took off for the job in my 12 year old Peugeot diesel automobile. My car overheated and died on the other side of Houston, so we were towed back to Mustang. Then we jumped into his 8 year old pickup truck...obviously times were tough in Houston! This just might have been the weirdest job start he had ever been a part of. We got to know each other pretty well that day, found out we have the same birthday, and have taken care of each other ever since.

MUSTANGERS at first anniversary.

MUSTANGERS

The moniker of Mustanger was natural and just rolled off the tongue early at Mustang. The impact of referring to ourselves as Mustangers was huge beyond all imagination. It felt like we were members of a club that others should want to be a part of. The owners stayed very close to the folks and invested themselves emotionally into relationships, figuring that every new Mustanger would be with the company forever. This club feeling made it logical that the only way to get in was through a referral from a current Mustanger.

Through our efforts, we established Mustang as a lean, hardworking place, where the focus was on people and projects. We had no titles on business cards. The owners were spread out and in offices just like everyone else, with total access from anyone. We didn't even lock our individual office doors at night. Everyone worked harder than they ever had before, because they could see what Paul, Felix and I were doing and knew that we just about lived at the office trying to make Mustang viable.

Word spread through the offshore industry that something different was being created at Mustang. Through the grapevine we heard that other small to medium size engineering firms were not concerned…"just wait, they'll become more like a business and less people focused before 12 months have passed." Top people at CBS, who knew us well, felt that Paul and I could not survive together because our styles were different and would grate on each other.

Most of the industry took a wait and see attitude. They thought it would be great if a company could be fun to work at, make a profit, take care of clients and survive long term… but they had not seen it previously in the cyclical offshore oil industry.

Mustangers, however, seemed to easily put their egos aside when they came through the door and figured out how to pull as a team. They saw how well Paul, Felix and I pulled almost as one strong person in wrenching Mustang toward reality. They saw us put time into fun company functions in September, October, November and December, despite the tremendous workload. They watched our example and from those observations determined our priorities.

The priorities Mustangers saw were very different from what they had seen in various companies throughout their careers. They liked what they felt in this very empowering environment and wanted to invest of themselves to make it work as a business environment. A natural outcome from this "want to" attitude was a significant amount of self-discipline generated by each person as they tried to do their part. Self-discipline from individuals meant the owners' time was freed up to commit to clients, knowing that the team would perform above standard.

> "Exciting culture of self disciplined, productive empowerment."

The Mustang name had generated the term Mustangers, which was in turn creating a different and exciting culture of self-disciplined, productive empowerment. We nurtured and fed this "Mustanger" feeling. This feeling was a "grass roots" development, coming up from the people as they helped create something they wanted to be part of.

I NEED AN ENGINEER!!

In early September, Carol Oberhouse asked Felix to purchase a "Quiet Writer" for her to use. Carol did everything from office management, to project secretary, to HR, to proposals for Felix, Paul and me. She had been using Paul's dot matrix printer, which he had brought in from home. A dot matrix printer is pretty loud and with the increased volume of printing, it was driving her crazy. Felix pulled us together for our first "Board" decision to purchase a Quiet Writer for $1300.00. Since we had each put in $5,000.00 to start the company, this would be a major purchase, considering that the dot matrix printer worked (engineers just think efficiently by nature!). We decided to buy the machine instead of ear plugs, and Carol and everyone within earshot of her desk was elated.

You can imagine how hard it was for Paul to pull us together a week later to say that he desperately wanted to hire Don Leinweber as a direct employee and our first engineer. Don had called Paul from CBS and wanted to come right after closing on a new house in late September.

This would be a significant commitment because we would have to pay Don whether there was work or not. But Paul was drowning, neighbors were asking Kay if she was single, and he could not fully count on Felix and me because of our workload. He needed a pressure relief valve in the form of an engineer he trusted, who worked directly for him. We all agreed that we would extend the six months we planned to go without pay, if we had to, in order to make sure we could pay Don.

This was a tough personal decision for me because our family finances were in a shambles. I felt our current mortgage payment was too high and asked Ann to look for a rental house in the neighborhood so we could sell our house and lighten the monthly financial burden.

Ann worked full time as a recovery room nurse and was not seeing very much of me. I came home to find her crying after looking at five rental properties. She didn't like any of them and wanted to work more hours to enable us to keep our house. She applied and was hired on an "as needed" basis by two other hospitals and eventually would be in that status at five hospitals. I really wanted to help her slow down to enjoy the kids, but this decision to hire Don pushed that back a few months. We knew the November to February time frame would be tough for Mustang due to the normal industry cycle of getting budgets approved. Ann and I decided to just "gut it out," like we had done a couple of other times when financial hardship had hit.

Don came in and was a Mustanger from day one; looking back we'd have to say he had Mustang DNA, he bled BLUE. Because we continued to get work, Don was quickly absorbed and we could not imagine surviving October without him.

Don Leinweber, our first engineer, with his wife on his shoulders is taking down decorations at a Mustang party. Paul is the stabilizing force...as always.

WE NEVER CLOSE

Paul worked extremely late to catch up when no one was around. I lived five miles from work and many times would come in at 2 or 3 in the morning. A friend of ours had started a competing engineering firm and would see our lights on when he went home. He started calling a couple of times a night and just hanging up when Paul or I answered the phone. We found out a few years later that we were driving him crazy because someone was always there. We didn't really notice what was happening as we were just doing whatever it took to get the job done. Twice a month I was there until midnight entering payroll...it was pretty crazy.

A FOURTH PARTNER

Jim Boarman was a neighbor of mine and came over in October of 1987 to say that he was interested in coming to Mustang. This was a big surprise because CBS had worked hard to blast him out of a large E&C company named McDermott. Sam Carruba had made him head of structural engineering... Sam's right hand man. Jim had wanted to be an equity partner in CBS, however, and that was not available. I had not really worked with him much at CBS but liked him as a guy and neighbor. He started on the varsity team as a freshman basketball player for Purdue and was super smart. I had been an intercollegiate wrestler, Judo combatant and soccer player. The drive it takes to compete at that level was always a good indicator of competence to me.

The next day I caught up with Paul and Felix at the same time and passed on Jim's interest in coming to Mustang. Paul's reaction surprised me when he said that Jim was one of the few people in the industry that he felt he could truly trust technically to run the structural engineering group. He also felt having that slot filled would help him from a time standpoint. He could put his engineering attention on facilities design and let Jim develop the structural design group.

We decided that we could give Jim a percentage of the company if he would go on our "no pay" plan until we started to pay ourselves. This would minimize his impact to our overhead and provide the "sweat equity" required to be an owner. His risk seemed less than ours because we had grown to 25 people and had 12 clients, but there was still a significant amount of risk. Felix and Paul wanted me to visit with Jim and his wife Kathy about what they would be getting into. We wanted to make sure Kathy understood the stresses and strains Mustang's startup was putting on our families.

I spent some hours in Jim's living room on a couple of nights discussing everything either of us could think of about running an engineering firm. Kathy joined us some of the time and I tried to lay things out for both of them. Despite my stating all of the realities, they decided this was the best move for them. At Mustang, with some ownership, Jim felt that he could commit himself and pull on all of his resources to create the best structural engineering group in Houston.

Jim came in for interviews with Paul and Felix. We wanted Jim to be equal to the founders in terms of making things happen. We were clear that the general direction was to follow Paul's lead and support him as he developed the Mustang organization. We reviewed the buy/sell agreement in detail, made some revisions and cut Jim in as a 10% partner in October. All partners would be paid exactly the same once we felt comfortable in the cash flow. Paying us the same would remove money from getting between us. This all took some time to make sure we were aligned and then...boom...we had a top-tier structural manager to pull a chunk of the load off of Paul.

You have to enjoy the ride.

18: TEAM BUILDING IN EVERYTHING

I heard a loud crash from the office next door and jumped into the hall to see what was going on. There was Don Leinweber standing like he was about to put a heavy engineering manual on the top shelf of one of our $5 particle board bookcases. All the shelves had collapsed down and he was covered up to the knees with books. Literally, that book had been the straw that broke the camel's back!!

MAKING BOOKSHELVES

We both started laughing at his predicament and I had to bring other people over to see the exquisite mess. That weekend I built a bookshelf unit that could hold a large number of engineering manuals. We decided that we needed 10 of them in order to eliminate our safety hazard. I pre-cut all the pieces for 10 units and a number of folks came over to assemble and stain them. My neighbors met Felix and Paul in their scruffy T-shirts and shorts and said they thought they were down to earth people.

Mustangers had never done anything like this in conjunction with work. Instead of just buying more bookshelves that would warp over time, we built them. It felt good and we were getting to know each other better. I heard comments like "we do this type of thing for the rodeo to save money...or for church camp...or for the Boy Scouts...etc." Bookshelf building was providing free space for people to interact. This mingling was breaking communication barriers down. From those conversations, we would talk about church or their family or other interests and learn things we could ask people about in the hallway or at the coffee bar.

I love to make sawdust and I love getting people together to do a project, so it didn't get any better than this. My kids also helped and saw Ann and I interact with quality adults out in the garage and in the driveway. A lot of learning went on in that bookshelf building environment.

Felix and Paul taking care of business.

Stephanie, (Bill's daughter) supervises the bookshelf building.

SAVING SNEED... THE BACKBONE

David Sneed had been a lead piping designer at S.H.Landis Engineering, Inc. a well-respected medium size firm. The company was closing down and David came into Mustang as a contract employee. We could tell immediately that he was a top talent who could be relied on in the hectic pace of Mustang... sort of our "controlled chaos" mode.

When Tom Raabe asked us to take on the facilities work on his old Shell platforms, he had a very tight budget which meant that we would have to get creative. Paul accepted the challenge and in a short amount of time had all of the engineering and purchasing lined out. In order to streamline manhours, he sketched out all of the piping and put it into drafting with directions to "not change anything, just draft it."

> "Engineering's reputation results from how good the drawings are for construction."

Although done with the best of intentions to take care of the client, these instructions really rankled David. If this was the way projects were going to be done at Mustang, then we did not need someone of his talent. He did not want to be spoon-fed piping design solutions by an engineer.

As I've noted earlier, drafting is the backbone of an engineering office. They are critical to creating your consistency and reputation. Engineers get a lot of their real world training from designers and then start to move toward coordination and management.

In the final analysis, an engineering firm's reputation results from how easy it is to build from the drawings that go out the door. A large part of that reputation is created by the drafting room.

Paul came to me and explained how he had set the project up for success but had hacked Sneed off to the point where he was going to leave. We both felt David could become the head of design when the group grew a little larger. Paul felt that someone else needed to sit and have a good discussion about how flexible we needed to be in order to make all of our projects profitable.

David and I had an honest talk about how Mustang was set up and the vision for the future. We discussed the specifics of the project and how Paul's heart was in the right place, trying to please everyone but having to work within constraints. A critical part of our vision was to raise drafting up to a more respected and professional level. We wanted to hold on to good designers with the same level of intensity that we wanted to hold on to good engineers. Our vision was that clients would pick Mustang as much for the drafting room as for the engineering capability and David would eventually become the lead designer in developing that vision.

Hearing the same things, worded a little differently from a second owner made the challenge of developing the strongest design room in Houston very real to David. The consistency of the message convinced him to stay and work to create something special. He quickly became our rock to build around. David Sneed and Paul Redmon are the true "Mr. Mustangs."

Paul and Kay Redmon

Dave and Donna Sneed

STRETCH LIMO RIDE

I answered the door of our home and there was a limo driver standing on the porch. He said that he was there to pick me up. I told him that I thought he had the wrong house and asked what address he had been given. It was our address. Then Ann came up behind me and said to go outside. As I did, the back window rolled down and Felix said hi!

I had never been in a limo and was excited by just how long it was, parked in front of the house!! I had a grin from ear to ear as I walked around it a few times and asked what was going on.

Felix had told Joyce that we pulled in $100,000 of revenue in September 1987 and she had called Ann and Kay to arrange a surprise celebration. Ann and I jumped in and off we went to surprise Paul. What a thrill to be unexpectedly whisked off in a limo to celebrate a milestone.

Paul was just as surprised as Felix and I had been and we had a good time driving around Houston, stopping at some sights and talking. We reminisced about how blessed we had been so far in the startup. We talked about the people and clients we had the privilege to work with. Our wives could tell that this had been an excellent decision to start Mustang, even though it was very tough on everyone. We were all in the soup together, so we could talk about and laugh at the same problems we all were having in balancing family, church, work, exercise (we were all losing weight without it!), friends and finances. There were some significant short term...we hoped!... hardships in some of these areas that we all felt were investments toward building a company where we really wanted to work. But mostly we just joked and had fun going for fast food and enjoying some Asti Spumante in the limo.

CAN YOU DANCE?

Although everyone was working very hard, we knew balance could be gained by also playing hard. We created our own special music and everyone participated and played their part to the best of their ability.

In September all the families drove to Lake Somerville for a picnic. We played horseshoes, volleyball and went boating. Everyone brought food for a pot-luck lunch and kids brought their Hot-Wheels® or trikes to ride on. We had a good amount of time and free space with families to get to know one another better.

MUSTANG picnic.   **Felix**

October was Felix's 40th birthday party at his home, where we learned the Mustang dance and song.

November was Thanksgiving lunch in the office with prayer and fellowship at a long table we set up.

Thanksgiving lunch at the office.

December brought hand addressing (Joyce's idea) Christmas cards to clients with me writing a note in each of about 500 to add to the personal touch. We were so thankful for the support we had received. The year was culminated with a "dress-up" Christmas party at my house...Mustangers can certainly look good when they want to! The guys resisted, but the women liked dressing up for a party during the Christmas season. Just before the party we handed out $50 bills to each person, which was something we had learned and liked at CBS.

We took the time to say thanks to the person and talk about some things we wanted them to work on going forward. Additionally, most folks also received a bonus check to emphasize our intention to share Mustang's success with them. We told them that they should spend the $50 cash on themselves. I remember spending my first one at CBS on some new Lionel® train track for the train I had received at Christmas when I was nine.

People could not believe that we also gave cash and bonuses to contract employees. Contract employees were normally treated differently at Houston companies despite working just as hard as direct employees. We were breaking down walls and stereotypes just by using common sense and wanting to be good caretakers of Mustang's team spirit.

Toward the end of the Christmas party, we gave each Mustanger a wrapped box and a small wrapped present to their spouse. Joyce, Kay and Ann had done the wrapping. A blue Mustang shirt with the Mustang logo in gold and a Christmas tree ornament of a toy soldier in Dress Gray turned out to be a great group thank you and had everyone looking forward to 1988.

"Things will be great in '88."
Divakar Pathak, Designer

SWOT Analysis, end of 1987...
Startup Phase of *MUSTANG*

A SWOT analysis is an objective look at the company internally for strengths and weaknesses and externally for opportunities and threats. The analysis helps everyone to see where action is needed in order to have a strong, vibrant company.

Strengths:
- Owners are compatible.
- Super low overhead.
- Could sell work at a profit.
- 28 people have been pulled together as a team.
- Technically we are very good at delivering projects.
- Relationships with vendors and 18 clients.
- All reimbursable contracts.
- Paul and Felix had run small businesses.
- Diversified from oil and gas.

Weaknesses:
- Learning the business side.
- Funding and cash flow.
- No technical depth...bench strength.
- All projects are of short duration.
- Owners are carrying too much load.
- Limited expansion space is available in the building.
- CAD development and training.

Opportunities:
- Top people are available.
- Could differentiate brand due to no history.
- Lower overhead than our competitors.

Opportunities (continued):
- Clients are not happy with competitor's performance.
- We have a head start using CAD.
- Grow the inspection group.
- Client personnel we know have gone overseas.
- Clients are decimating their in-house engineering capability through layoffs.

Threats:
- Big boys could "buy" the work.
- Differentiation of Mustang is not clear.
- No Mustang project history.
- Generally no new work from November thru February.
- Mess up and we could have a lawsuit.
- Cash flow from clients could affect payroll and loyalty.
- Current clients could run out of work.
- Competitors could steal our people.
- Value proposition is not "tangible" to clients.

Whys...Ands: Understand the "whys" behind actions...what was our "come from" place...in order to keep them going. Understand the "ands" that were learned to maintain balance.

"Why's" that were learned:
- Focus on your people first
- Balance work and play
- Treat everyone with respect
- Be humble
- Don't grab for every manhour
- Be caretakers of Mustang

"Ands" that were learned:
- Execute flawlessly and sell more work
- Innovate and be profitable
- Plan and act
- Timely projects and timely invoices
- Train and be billable
- Take care of people and projects

Wants:

- Reimbursable contracts
- Trusting relationships
- Repeat work
- To take money out of the equation
- Win-win behaviors
- To build technical competence on billable work
- To create efficiencies to reduce manhours
- To follow work through start-up in the field
- To diversify to different types of projects

Mustang-isms:

- Mustangers
- Upside-down pyramid
- Job on the corner of the desk
- Same sentence sales
- Mustang DNA, bleed blue
- Designers are the backbone
- Engineer-down-the-hall
- Mustang Motion

Sayings:

- Strong to the hoop
- "Free space" to connect
- Strike while the iron of courage is hot!
- We will satisfy you, Snickers®

Fast Facts:

- Opened the door Monday July 20, 1987
- $15,000 capitalization
- Ten drafting tables
- First CAD drawing August 1987
- $100,000 billed in September 1987
- Billed work to 18 clients
- Have 28 people
- Have 2,100 sq ft of office space
- Deepest project is in 140ft of water

Camaraderie:

- "Shingle" on door
- "Twice as good as Omega"
- Coffee bar breakthrough
- Mustang Song to Locomotion
- Hand...hoof...sign
- Bookshelf building
- Parties, lunches, picnics
- Collar shirts with logo

MUSTANG

End of 1985–1987
End of the Beginning

"You can't coast uphill."

Felix Covington,
V.P. Mustang

PART 2: MUSTANG 1988-1991
NEW GROUND
Differentiation of Mustang becomes a habit.
The future is unique from here on.

Initial startup had been much harder than we ever could have expected. The highs and lows whipsawed our emotions to the point where it would have been easy to become numb and just go home. The costs, problems, and challenges that came out of the blue from every direction were daunting, even though we had tremendous experience in our field. Our effort to create a company that was like a big project team also received push back from all directions because the approach had not been seen before in this industry. Our people, vendors and clients liked what they saw and felt, but were having trouble believing the concept was viable long term. They saw the toll it took on the owners' energy and time and they felt empathy for our predicament but did not see a solution. They thought that we would have to revert to normal business practices that were essentially win-lose propositions.

We still believed we could elicit the help of our people (Mustangers), treat vendors and clients differently to get some of their help. Then we could create a sustainable "Mustang Motion" to develop win-win relationships throughout the industry. Of course, my favorite musical at the time was Don Quixote.

Don Quixote fighting windmills (righting habitual wrongs).

"Butcha gotta have faith, faith, faith..."
George Michael, Singer-songwriter

19: UPRC AND MARK PRODUCING

January 1, 1988. I'm up early and while the family is sleeping I start to think about Mustang. As I reflect on where Mustang stands as a company, it seems that we have a lot going for us. We have all the pieces of a real engineering firm, but it feels very fragile. Figuring we have 28 people, billable 90% of their time plus some overtime, means that we will need 65,000 manhours of work this year to keep them employed. This was the limit of our strategic planning for the first five years! Considering that our average project has been 1,200 manhours, we will need about 55 projects...or effectively, one a week. The disturbing component of this train of thought was that I had no real idea where the next project would come from.

THEY CAME

Over the next few months, some key people came to Mustang. Beth Hebert, who would become the heart and soul of our Needy Family drives, and Merri Ziemak started in structural design. Chuck Cook, Henry Gomez, who would head up our Private Sector Initiative re-building homes, and Son Nguyen, all started in piping design and were solid players. Dave Rucker merged his engineering firm into Mustang as a no-cost acquisition, giving us some good technical computer programs and raising our profile with important people in the industry. Bob Floyd came in as a strong process and mechanical engineer.

We now had all the pieces to go after some bigger projects, even if we did not have a company history of doing them. We made sure that the resumes we crafted for proposals highlighted the companies where people had worked, in an effort to give the client a comfortable feeling. When clients saw names like Brown & Root, Bechtel, McDermott, and Flour in the resumes, we received a credibility boost. There definitely was some "smoke and mirrors" in the proposals, but we knew that no matter what, the four owners would work the hours required to deliver on the promises we made.

UNION PACIFIC RESOURCES CORPORATION

All of this work and preparation had a potential payoff in February when Jim Grinnan of Union Pacific Resources Company (UPRC), in Fort Worth, came to the office to discuss a bid. Paul and I walked him through our execution plan for a complete platform in the Gulf in 83 feet of water. It would include the jacket, deck, facilities for 20mmscfd natural gas production and a small quarters building. Then, he wanted to tour the office.

We had brought all of our people back from working at Metro, and they were pretty excited about the possibility of this work to "bring them home." Jim could tell there was a lot of camaraderie and mutual respect as we visited with each person in drafting and then started down the hall. We stopped at the coffee bar and I told him about our short term company goal of busting through the wall to get to the sink...and we all had a good laugh. As we walked further, we showed him the open offices and where he could set up when he was in town checking on the project.

He invited us into "his" office and closed the door for a discussion. We felt like he was going to spend some time telling us that he liked what he saw, but we needed to be more established, with more backup, before he could award a significant project like this one to Mustang. Plus, we knew our competitors were going all out and promising the world for the first nice project to come along in two years.

All of these thoughts went through Paul's and my heads as we sat down and then Jim quietly said "the project is yours." Not believing our ears, we asked him to repeat what he said and then jumped up to do "high fives" and got Jim to do the same. This was unbelievable, to win a highly sought project that was right in the sweet spot of what we had designed the company to do. We celebrated by going to the coffee bar, getting a cup and then asking Jim how he came to the decision of...Mustang. He noted the following:

- If he could believe our manhour estimate, we were the low "believable" bid with a very competitive manhour rate in case the scope of work expanded.
- We were very organized in how we broke the project down, scheduled the pieces, and had intermediate milestones to insure progress he could measure.
- He was getting a core team from CBS in that we would all be on the project. He knew project internal communication would be good.
- Our brains were turned on as we showed re-use of prior work and innovative thoughts on how to reduce the engineering scope. He wanted to move into construction with the right amount of schedule left to meet his weather window before hurricane season.
- This project was as important to Mustang's future as it was to his future. With such tight alignment, he knew he had our full attention.

From walking through the office he knew the energy was high with a "can-do" spirit and that the leadership was fully engaged with the people...Mustangers...he liked that term. Jim inherently knew something I had learned in the Army, that energy and enthusiasm is a force multiplier. It creates connection and fosters team dynamics that produce at a high level.

CELEBRATE!

After Jim left, everyone gathered around the coffee bar for some gung-ho banter and talk about how we had made it through the typical winter slowdown and were now poised for spring. Paul and I had everyone back up so he and I could get into a three point football stance in the hallway, take off and run at each other for a huge chest bump in final celebration. This would be the first complete production platform done by Mustang and installed in the Gulf.

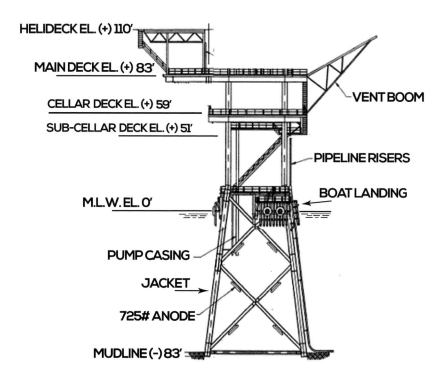

UPRC 4-Pile 20mmscfd Gas Platform done for Jim Grinnan.

CHOPPED TRIPOD

Minimal platforms had started to be stretched into deeper waters, up to 250 feet. We wanted to come up with something

that did not have the problems we were seeing in the current concepts as they were being stretched out of their comfort zone. Even the MOSS concept Paul and I had helped develop at CBS had been stretched beyond its sweet spot. We developed the "Chopped Tripod" and sold the first one to Mark Producing for a small reservoir in 180 feet of water.

Chopped Tripod minimal structure designed for Mark Producing.

David Davis, of *Offshore Magazine*, called me to say he was going to do a feature article on minimal structures. He wanted some technical background. I gave him input on the pros and cons of the various concepts to make his article very meaty for the industry. Then I asked if we could put the chopped tripod on the cover of the magazine. He said yes, if we could get a good picture.

This blew the industry away. Here was upstart Mustang on the cover of the magazine, essentially as the featured minimal platform. Over 30 concepts were described in the article, but we had the cover.

SPRING CRAZINESS

This new work from UPRC and Mark Producing, plus ongoing work from Oxy, Arco and others caused us to hire a number of new people. We expanded into a space on the second floor. We hired and assimilated people, while some good folks were enticed away for project specific bonuses. We were buying furniture and computers out of the cash flow as we still could not qualify for a loan.

To the people, Mustang was looking great as the changes all seemed to be making the company more "real." To us, everything seemed fragile as we worked tirelessly to fill the backlog while juggling to complete the work and keep up with the administrative tasks. It is hard to describe how exhilarating and horrible life was at the same time.

Our wives were shielded from a lot of the ups and downs but had to endure "absentee fathers" due to the time commitment. This flared up in various ways and caused stress and strain in our families.

That spring and summer got tougher and tougher as we worked to gut-it-through what we hoped was just a phase in company growth. We were hoping that at the end of a year, we would stabilize.

20: FOREST OIL

Things went well enough that we decided to start paying our-selves a salary in March. It was going to be about half of what we used to make, but would definitely be appreciated on the home front. Since I was inputting everything for payroll, I noticed we would be the 22nd, 23rd and 24th direct hire employees. My jer-sey number as sweeper (the last person before the goalie) on the West Point soccer team was 24, so I thought it would be fun to take that number! Paul and Felix had jersey numbers in football in the sixties. I figured it would be a few years before we had that many direct folks, so I just gave them the available numbers that put me on 24.

OWNER'S BONDS

Jim Boarman wanted to wait to get paid until he had the same amount of time at the company. He was an equal part-ner and wanted to be that in every sense of the term. Discus-sions around this and his feelings actually made it feel like he could never really be "equal." He had not been involved in the preparation for starting the company. He did not quit a job and have nothing on the horizon. He did not go through the first months of unbelievable anxiety and stress of trying to get someone to buy what we were selling. We found that the bond Paul, Felix and I had formed from this background was so strong that people could realistically only attach to it. They could not become integral within our bond.

WHO MOVED MY OFFICE?

We jammed people into all the open spaces of the building and decided we needed to find another home. Things came together very quickly for us to make the move to 4,000 square feet of space. In order to save cost, we decided to have a moving party and let everyone bring their families and pickup trucks to make the two mile move.

Layout of offices in the half round building.

We also moved furniture from two more engineering firms that were going out of business. At the same time, we had eight new people starting and twelve people returning from the Metro work. Over a weekend we went from a 28 person office split onto two floors to a 48 person office.

Gary Gonzalez was offshore and when he came in to work, he found the lights off and the signs down. He called Mustang to find out where we were and felt like he was starting at a new company. We walked him around and introduced him to 20 people he had not met before.

For years it would seem like we were a new company every three months, but this was the most vivid example of change as we grew in lock-step with what the industry needed us to be.

CHASING HARD

From May to August, I made a number of trips to Lafayette, Louisiana in order to chase a three platform natural gas complex with Forest Oil. Forest was a small independent oil company with little offshore experience. Bud Knell was the client project manager. He appreciated our help in showing him how to create a bid document that would get him good pricing and good control over his project. We spent nights doing part of the project front end conceptual work and giving it to Bud to help him make the bid document airtight. This project would fit us exactly: reimbursable engineering, structures, facilities, inspection, and a great relationship with the client.

All bidders were shocked when the package came out as a lump sum bid instead of reimbursable due to upper management over-ruling Bud in the eleventh hour. Forest Oil's electing to require fixed price bidding hurt our chances to win. We could not take the risk of the scope changing and the oil company deciding to play hard-ball over increases in cost. Forest Oil was a small independent without any track record offshore. If surprised negatively by cost, they could put us out of business or severely hurt us as we would do whatever it took to complete the project for them.

The bids came in very competitive and below the estimates we had provided to Bud, due to the lack of work in the industry. We probably could have won the contract but put some contingency money in our pricing due to our fear about the lump sum contract. Bud knew he would not be able to award us the gas platforms. He did however arrange for us to brief his management team on our proposal and capabilities. He gave us a lot of credit in the presentation for setting up his bid package.

DESPERATE TIMES

July and August were terrible as we worked feverishly to complete projects on time, while trying to find the next one. I was out every day in the Houston heat and humidity trying to find work, but there was none to be found. Paul likened me to Earl Campbell, the driving force behind the "Luv Ya Blue" Houston Oilers. He said that I just kept running full speed into the Pittsburg Steel Curtain Defense and getting thrown back on my butt, only to get up and do it again. He was amazed at my durability in the face of a dead industry.

We made what was probably a dumb business decision. The structural group was out of things to do since we had missed Forest Oil. We put ten people on overhead to design an efficient deck to use in the future. We were "putting our money where our mouth was" to keep people. Things were as bleak as the old "stay alive 'til '85" times.

SAY WHAT?

In mid-September, Bud called me to say that Forest Oil had made a significant oil discovery of 15,000 barrels per day in 220 feet of water in the Gulf and needed to get the project going right away. Oil projects were much bigger engineering projects because it was harder to clean both the oil to pipeline quality specifications and the water for disposal overboard. There were pumps and gas fired heaters, a 30-man quarters building and utilities like sewage treatment and power generation. In essence a big job on a much bigger platform than the three small gas platforms we had lost in August.

Bud ended the call by saying that he was sending a team over to scope the project with us and negotiate a reimbursable contract to do the entire project through startup.

WOW!!!

I don't think my feet touched the floor as I went to Paul's office to relate the news. One of the cool things about having our offices spread out in the company was that everyone was able to see our energy daily, but this was off the charts as we had it announced over the intercom system.

We had a guaranteed profit-making project that would go through the November to February time frame when projects were even harder to find. We could not plan this. All we could do was work hard, take care of our people, our clients, our vendors and trust that we would find a way. Briefly, we had broken through the steel curtain and were running down field. Now we needed more people with different skills to do a large oil platform. Thus the daily pressure cooker of Mustang continued at a brisk pace.

Forest Oil platform done for Bud Knell.

"Celebrate what you want to see more of."
Tom Peters, In Search of Excellence

21: PILING SAND?

Building up esprit de corps has always felt like piling sand...the effect does not last long. The second law of thermodynamics is in play...everything tends toward the lowest energy state. But I knew from Boy Scouts, West Point and the Army that creating esprit and a sense of team had always made my units a little bit better than they would have been. In our effort to rebuild trust and loyalty in the industry, it seemed like we needed to invest the time in building team spirit.

EVERY JUNKY OSTRICH TURNS YELLOW

As a second class scout, I was made patrol leader of six other boys. We came up with a patrol name and flag, while preparing for the troop's first ever Camporee where our skills would be tested in competition.

During the competition we came to a station where we needed to send a message using semaphore. I was the ranking scout and had not learned semaphore yet. I asked if we could use our own flag language and the grader said that would be fine.

Off we went to develop a flag language in fifteen minutes. We talked about using the flags in the shape of the letters or waving the flags to "make" the letters, etc. One boy asked if we could just wave a flag six times for an "F" and eleven times for a "K." Another boy brought up that we could use one flag for every fifth letter and the other flag for the letters in between. This sounded good so we wrote the letters down...E, J, O, T, and Y. Someone came up with the pneumonic of Every Junky Ostrich Turns Yellow for us to use and we scored well.

EJOTY at MUSTANG

We had the blue horse that we put everywhere to get a sense of pride in identifying with the organization. This sense of pride was solidified when we had a banner made for our first anniversary dinner and dance aboard the Colonel Paddle-wheel boat down by Galveston. The banner had the big blue horse, Mustang Engineering and Est.1987 on it. We took group pictures with the banner and carried it in front of us as we

Mustangers on the Colonel paddle-wheel boat at the first anniversary.

walked to the boat. Everyone took pride in the 1987 because now it was 1988 and we were still around! Mustangers took the banner to softball games, parties, shrimp boils, team building events, etc. for many years.

We had our Mustang motto of "Mustang will satisfy you" and our Mustang Motion song and dance. Sort of like semaphore versus EJOTY, we might not be able to work and communicate with everyone, but we were unbeatable once the client could understand us. We used the "Keep It Simple Stupid (KISS)" principle to the nth degree.

CO-OPERATE AND GRADUATE

The West Point experience began when we walked through a road barrier and left the "real world" behind. The first day we did more, learned more, and worked harder than we had in the last two years of our lives combined. Within one hour of this "Beast Barracks" training everyone became convinced that they could not do anything right...not even tie their own shoes unless a classmate was helping.

Every talent we possessed was used to help our classmates get through the next moment, trusting that we would be dragged along by them if needed. We learned to "Co-operate and Graduate," and it permeated everything we did.

CO-OPERATION AT MUSTANG

Mustangers had watched hundreds of companies fail, the foreclosures on every street, the savings & loan closures and various crises all over Houston. Our people knew that their well-being was in lockstep with the success of Mustang. Everyone was putting in extra hours that they did not get paid for in order to insure things were double checked to minimize errors. Mechanical, structural, electrical engineers, and designers all sat together to foster a sense of team and insure there were no communication gaps across interface lines. We knew that we could not take risks other companies did, because there was no buffer of cash if we failed. We had to get different types of contracts, work in different, more efficient ways and win work in a super competitive environment. Our intense work ethic and attention to detail permeated the entire organization to the point where people felt responsible to get the whole project out in good order...not just their part.

NEWSY NEWSLETTER

Everyone had ways to check and convince themselves that they were part of a different and better breed of engineering firm. This helped each person believe more in the things we were doing and put more energy into the difference. Drafters would call their buddies at other companies who couldn't believe Mustang funded parties for everyone including contract employees. They were also bummed Mustang had just won the latest project and attributed it in part to the gung-ho nature of the company.

We loved this feedback and I wanted to reinforce it by starting the *Mustang Newsy Newsletter* in the fall of 1988. I collected stories and pictures and tried to make it fun to read. We mailed it home to insure it got there. Spouses read it closely and showed pictures to the kids.

CREATING THE DIFFERENCE

We worked hard to develop a sense of team and accomplishment like the Scouts did. We pushed teaming and cooperaiton like the Cadets learned. And we reinforced the Mustang difference with the newsletter.

Despite how good we thought we were at hiring, setting up teams and developing efficient tools, our staff of people matched the typical bell-shaped curve of probability and statistics. We had some great performers, some poor performers and a whole bunch somewhere in the middle. In order to grow and achieve like we envisioned, we needed to shift the bell shaped curve to the right.

We were able to create the Delta (Δ) in performance from the standard workforce by putting continuous effort into creating a sense of difference and a pride in that difference. From being Mustangers, to mottos, myths, songs, banners, real mixing at after-hour events and treatment of others, we created an environment of difference. This difference was evident in our ability to put out better than average work at below average costs.

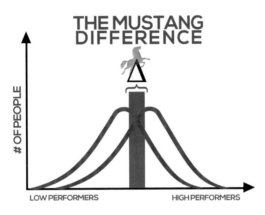

Best of all was that people other than the owners were putting real effort into the "piling sand" requirement of building a different culture. From the bottom-up this difference would permeate through all actions at Mustang.

Piling sand...a continuous effort .

"That which does not kill me, makes me stronger."
Neitzsche, Philosopher

22: LOUISIANA LAND AND EXPLORATION

The highs are high and the lows are low when going through the startup of a company. Sometimes the ups and downs happen in the same hour. You have to know that your heart is in the right place and that no one believes more or could work harder than you to keep everything moving in the same general direction.

At the Philmont Scout Ranch high adventure hiking camp in New Mexico, they do "Roses and Thorns" every morning. Everyone stood in a circle and each person had to say a rose and a thorn from the previous day...something good and something bad. By the fourth day, when some tempers were flaring, this really helped get things out in the open to be worked on as good crew dynamics were built. Sometimes it felt like we should do this at Mustang...

OVER THE TOP WITH ACTIVITIES

Our first Shrimp Boil was in April 1988...Tax Day...come celebrate. The invitation was a CAD drawing that went to 200 clients... showing we could do CAD. About 60 clients came. A number of vendors came to this "target rich environment" as they could chat up the clients. All Mustangers came...unusual in an industry that just took care of clients.

We had bowling leagues, softball teams, plus client and Mustanger golf tournaments. We developed "Club Mustang" days from thinking about Club-Med™ after the air conditioning went out for two days and everyone wore shorts to work. Electrical design set up a tent and fire ring in their area and started answering the phone "Mustang Engineering...we never close." Support for this positive Mustang Motion came from all levels at Mustang, from clients, and from vendors.

IT'S THE WAY WE ARE

In 1989 when we had the second Anniversary Party at the Adam's Mark Hotel, about a third of our people did not come, figuring it was "just another hotel party." It was a '50s themed party and seven groups put together lip synch programs. The Mamas & the Papas had an encore, Gladys Knight & the Pips (four women with great dance steps) and the owners doing "Leader of the Pack" on Hot Wheels® while their wives danced in poodle skirts finally moved everyone into the action. It was one of the best parties anyone had ever been to and caused quite a buzz in the office for weeks.

People were reticent about letting their hair down and opening themselves up, but we had shown that with persistence and involvement by the owners, we could get there. We knew that we could create memories, touch people, perhaps change them...but at a minimum get a smile.

We had people come up to their boss, e.g. Sneed, and say they would rather have extra money in their paycheck than have it spent on parties, picnics, and team building. Sneed told them that this is the way things were going to be at Mustang. The owners wanted Mustangers and their families to get involved with each other and build camaraderie unheard of in the oil patch. He and others enjoyed the difference being a Mustanger was making in their work environment. Sneed and Redmon got the point across and turnout was 100% at my house for the Christmas party.

People could not believe that they were going to an owner or lead designer's house for a party that included everyone. Organizational lines were blurred and a team personality focused on doing good work to take care of each other materialized. We provided "free space" for people to interact and relationships and trust were developing.

DEEPWATER TRIPODS

Lift vs. Launch

McDermott was winning deepwater tripod work because they had the only lift barge big enough to install them. We convinced four oil companies to fund a study to design a deepwater tripod that could be launched off of a barge like we did for some four-legged structures. Once launched, about 5 lift barges were capable of moving it into position.

For Louisiana Land and Exploration (LL&E) we bid installation of their 467 foot tripod from design sketches to pick lift or launch. We locked in the price for installation and then proceeded with detailed design. This was truly market and business driven engineering.

McDermott DB-50 lifting deepwater tripod jacket.

Skirt Piles

The big cans at the bottom of the legs on the LL&E tripod are sleeves through which "skirt piles" are driven to anchor the platform. There was big savings to be gained by not putting the piles all the way through the legs.

LL&E jacket ready to be upended.

Marry Deepwater with Shallow

Our deepwater structural experience helped us develop a new tripod design for Walter Oil & Gas in 223 feet of water. It married deepwater and shallow water design methods. In deepwater we used skirt piles at the mud line instead of having the pile go up through the jacket leg to support the deck. This eliminated 500 feet of piling at each of the three legs for LL&E...a lot of steel!

Tripods worked well in shallow water due to fewer wells and generally smaller decks and eliminated a lot of steel by having one less leg. It turned out that a skirt piled tripod in 223 feet of water had some major hidden savings not seen in deepwater. The cross bracing was smaller and could be made out of standard tubular shapes instead of fabricated tubular pieces. It was light, easy to weld and easy to install offshore.

Our design was in a yard being built right next to an Exxon tripod for 224 feet of water that was designed conventionally. The difference was astonishing!! We took a number of clients to see them both and talk to the fabricator about cost, weight and schedule.

THE "O" BEAMS

Our focus was on being the absolute best at facility design and using structural to support that effort. We used to jokingly say that the entire structure was just a big pipe support...the money comes from the "O" beams (pipes), not the "I" beams (structural shapes). As facilities became larger, we found that their weight and space requirements began to drive the structural design.

ARCO INDONESIA

Chris Blair had a huge project that was going out for lump sum bidding in a few months and the project was in a shambles. He trusted Mustang and wanted us to clean up all of the conflicts in the bid document. This would get better bids and give him control. Arco would have to pay for this work directly, since they were not using an Indonesian approved contractor, but Chris felt this was well worth it on a $700,000,000 project called Pangarungan. In two weeks we staffed up with secretaries and nine very strong engineers of various disciplines to help us do the work.

To this point, Paul would not let me chase Conoco and other "Big Boys" because he did not feel we could stand toe-to-toe with their technical people and we had no "bench strength." He started to soften his stance after the influx of new talent. I brought in Amoco, Conoco, Marathon and BP for briefings on Mustang's capabilities. Although we were small, they saw that we had cranked out many tough projects. A big plus was having done medium size oil platforms. They saw low turnover and could feel the esprit in the office. We ended 1989 in a strong technical position.

23: FORD BACON & DAVIS

In November 1990, Felix got a call from David Edgar, Senior Vice President of Engineering at Ford Bacon & Davis, a 100 year old pipeline company in Monroe, Louisiana where he used to work. In order to grow his operation, David felt that he needed an office in Houston where many projects originated. He and Felix set up a meeting to review his needs and our capabilities. Part way through the meeting he had seen enough to know that he wanted to buy all or part of Mustang.

STRATEGY TO MERGE

We worked with David to develop an integration and synergy plan that he could present to his Board of Directors.

I talked to his CEO in the beginning of December and found that he was starting three weeks of performance reviews, strategic planning and presentations to the Board. He could hear the poorly disguised mirth in my voice while I was talking to him. His response was that he knew what I was thinking. While he was in meetings, I would be out calling on clients and booking the first quarter's work. I said, "exactly and that is why we may not fit into a larger organization. We just want to get work and do work; not talk about it." I thought...strategic planning, bah humbug!!...we've got work to do in order to keep everyone busy.

The Board thought that we were too expensive at $2,000,000, which was three times our net profit extrapolated from our fourth quarter since we were growing so fast. It was interesting though, to try and put a value on Mustang.

CONSOLIDATED CONTRACTORS COMPANY (CCC)

Then CCC out of Athens, Greece came to buy us and said they would stack money until we said yes. They were a big international player with fabrication yards and the financial strength to go after large lump sum projects worldwide both offshore and onshore. They wanted a Houston presence.

Felix, Paul and all three wives jumped on a plane and left me with two kids and that screaming baby...Mustang! They were wined and dined on a superb yacht in the Aegean Sea, ran on the original Olympic track, and met with our possible future bosses. They came back with a $2,200,000 offer and a reasonable structure for how things could work. This was very tempting considering the stress we were under.

We realized however, that the stress would not diminish as CCC would expect us to grow and give them a good return on their investment. We worked the numbers and felt that we would grow enough to put the same amount of money in our pockets in two years without selling. Plus, we all agreed that we were babes in the woods when it came to working internationally with a company like CCC.

We decided to not let Mustang become a chip in the game of another company's growth plan. We felt that we were the only ones who knew how fragile the loyalty and trust was that we were building. We needed the freedom to be the best caretakers of Mustang growth.

David Edgar of FB&D came back a year later, at the end of 1991, to talk about buying us again. We showed him that we had doubled in size. He decided to quit FB&D, come to Houston and build the pipeline group we had planned...from scratch. What a great reverse-acquisition strategy we had developed...for the price of hiring one person!

THE BOARMAN QUANDRY

Our fourth partner became a tough challenge for us. We had worked to make sure we all knew what we were getting into, but little things seemed to put wedges between us.

Fortune Magazine interviewed us for a new entrepreneurial section they were going to put inside the back cover. They interviewed five companies in each of twenty major cities. Jim was out the day they came to interview Mustang and take a picture of the owners. Ours was the most compelling story and Mustang had the first article...including a picture of Paul, Felix and me. Jim was not in what he called the "family picture" and it made him feel slighted.

The biggest rub between us was that Felix and I put Paul first in everything. We did whatever it took to ease his load. Jim would stand toe-to-toe with Paul and not back down. The friction was palpable and really bothered me. I would come to work and when I pushed the fifth floor button on the elevator my stomach would tighten up as I was not looking forward to watching Jim interact with others.

Jim came into my office one night around 11 p.m. to discuss a project. I moved the conversation to his relationship with Felix, Paul and myself. Finally, I said that Paul, Felix, and my relationship was not going to change, and that I felt it was probably time for him to leave Mustang.

The four of us worked hard to figure out how to split the sheets. We were astounded when Jim's lawyer found holes large enough to drive a truck through in our buy/sell agreement. We finally agreed on a dollar figure and Jim was off to his own pursuits. There was no doubt that all four of us were happier immediately, and I didn't mind pushing the fifth floor button!

PEOPLE

Innovate Houston Award

In 1989 the Greater Houston Chamber of Commerce originated the "Innovate Houston" awards. The idea was to gain notoriety nationwide by showing that Houston was coming back from the oil price collapse. We submitted in the "People" category. Our people wrote an application lauding company get-togethers, helping needy families, children's parties and the computer loan program to teach people the new skill of CAD.

A team of people came to interview Mustang. Our designers discussed how putting computers on their desks through a cooperative effort and providing free training had changed their careers. The team declared Mustang the most people oriented company in Houston...an award that will be cherished forever. On the announcement in the Newsy Newsletter I hand wrote "Mustang Motion is alive and well...People taking care of People!"

401K

We started a 401K plan in August of 1988. We announced in early 1989 that we had put 5% of everyone's 1988 earnings into the plan as a thank you from Mustang. We did not require any matching funds and made vesting three years. One of our goals was to give back and money talks.

Slow down!

The May 1989 newsletter read; "Whenever you hit a slow spell, don't be concerned...take some regular hours and get home to do everything listed on the refrigerator door. We need to enjoy 1989-it is already May! Call Carol if you need to get your home address."

24: BRITISH PETROLEUM

A vendor salesman called me in the fall of 1989 and said he had just left Randy Peters' office at BP. He said that I should call and meet him as he had a big project coming up. I called and got Randy on the line. I told him who I was and asked if we could get together for lunch in the next week or so. He knew that we had an evergreen contract with BP and that we had done a few small jobs, but other than that, he really did not know much about Mustang since he had come from BP Alaska. We set up lunch for the next Tuesday and I promised to catch him up on our capability.

The next Tuesday morning was absolutely crazy but for some reason around 11:50 it popped into my head that I was supposed to have lunch with Randy at 11:30. I'd learned to not hide when I mess up, so I called him to apologize. Randy answered the phone and was obviously eating in his office...but he was ok about setting another date...for a meeting...no lunch! Well at least I had made an impression for the sales call.

FIXING A DARK HORSE

Randy's project was in Mississippi Canyon Block 109 and was named Amberjack. Amberjack was significant in that it would be the third-deepest structure in the Gulf at 1,030 feet, with an overall height of 1,250 feet, same as the Empire State Building. The production rate would be 20,000 barrels of oil per day and it would have a 50 person living quarters. This was a huge, world class project... a little daunting to our 43 man company. We decided that the best approach might be to team up and work a deal where the project would be negotiated instead of bid.

MCDERMOTT

We now had the core facilities team from BP's last two major projects done at CBS and Omega. McDermott had close ties with BP top to bottom and would be preferred for the structural design. They had state-of-the-art computer programs and had done BP's EB-165 Snapper platform in 863 feet of water. While doing a modification on Snapper we heard operations complain about McDermott's facilities design for layout and maintenance.

We set up a meeting with top McDermott people to discuss the two of us going together and offering to just negotiate the project with BP. Management listened, but felt that they could win the entire project due to their structural design capability in this water depth. They were thinking the old way...that the facilities were a small portion of the project and their facilities engineering would be fine.

BID ALONE

Strategy

We had taken BP's previous large project up through award of equipment and 70% of engineering at CBS. We knew everything that could be re-used on this project and how to schedule for BP's input. We decided to bid alone for the structural deck and production facilities design.

BP was stretched thin on technical talent so Randy hired two contract engineers, John Echols and Chuck Stephens who had worked for me at CBS on the previous BP project. They would know what we planned to re-use. Randy's boss, Judy Wagner liked our Tom White for project manager. Randy liked our Dave Rucker for Project Engineer, putting us in position to have me and Paul not involved day-to-day on the project.

Past Work

We were short listed for the bid and invited to present our proposal to the BP team. We had heard that there was some "hallway talk" at BP about Mustang making a mistake on a pipe spool. The spool did not fit a piece of equipment on a modification we had done for BP a month earlier. The holes on the piece of equipment's flange were rotated 12.5 degrees clockwise from the industry standard and we missed it. They cut the pipe spool and re-welded it offshore to make it fit. This was one of 50 tie-ins to an operating platform.

We pulled the drawing we had issued for fabrication and it clearly showed the 12.5 degree rotation and recommended that the weld be done in the field (called a field-weld). When we talked to the fabricator, he said that the BP project engineer took all of the field-welds out of the design and had them weld them in the shop prior to going offshore...essentially taking quite a risk on Mustang's accuracy. The fabricator was impressed that everything fit except the one flange that had to be rotated...somehow they missed this during fabrication.

Presentation

As anticipated, toward the end of our presentation, when it would do the most harm, we were asked about our error on the previous project. Instead of dumb stares and confusion, we put up a slide showing the drawing that was issued with the 12.5 degrees of rotation and field-weld clearly noted. We spun it that the BP project engineer had taken a good, calculated risk in having the field-welds removed, but that he needed an inspector in the yard to insure the pipe spools were built to the drawings. We wanted to sell our inspection services if we lost the design of this project. Knowing the hallway talk had set us up to be well prepared for the critical question.

AWARD

The next day I was back in structural drafting with Diane Daniels when I was paged for a phone call. It was Judy Wagner's boss, Scott Preston (rarified air at BP!!) calling to award us the deck and facilities design. After the call I let out a breath. This was an unbelievable award for Mustang, but BP would test us like no other company could. When we got through this project we would be much stronger but it would be tough. The daunting challenge I knew was in front of us took some steam out of celebrating this win. We had been the dark horse and had won a project that would require us to hire fifty more people in the next three months.

Merri Ziemak makes the drafting room "kinder and gentler".

Mustang won the deck structural design, production facilities design, all steel purchasing, including the 1,030 foot jacket and project management assistance to Randy. Brown & Root won the deck and facilities fabrication at their Houston yard. McDermott won the jacket design and offshore installation of all components or about 15% of the project. We thought McDermott could have won the entire project through negotiation, but BP developed a super project with awards of pieces to different companies.

BP DOMINATES US

After four weeks, BP ran off Tom White and Dave Rucker to have them replaced by Paul as Project Manager and me as Project Engineer. BP was not re-using anything from the CBS designed platform. Everything was being created from scratch. For three months Paul and I lived at Mustang working to yank this project out of the depths of despair. We worked seven days a week, sleeping on cots and eating out of our filing cabinets, which were stocked by our wives.

BP never let up red-lining and "wordsmithing" every document numerous times. At our indoor putt-putt tournament the BP designed hole had a ramp up to three holes. One hole dumped the ball into a sea of red pens, another returned the ball to the starting point and the third one just ate the ball! They knew what they were doing to us.

We decided to "prime the pump" by working a simple bid from specification through purchase order. This set the baseline for the documents and procedures. Then we streamlined bidding by having the vendors fill their information out on our customized bid evaluation forms. One of our secretaries could do the bid spreadsheet and save engineering time.

Since BP pushed so hard, we became very good at what we did. I'll never forget Paul taking on the re-work of a study that would not die. I was in his office when he came back from a meeting on the study where it was torn apart. He came in, threw the study across his desk and said he was done. I was now Project Manager.

This was a good thing, because Amberjack was a black hole that just absorbed great talent. Due to our spreading reputation, there was a lot going on all over Mustang and Paul needed to put his fingerprints on the organization as it grew.

Amberjack top "drilling" deck being floated over the main deck.

Amberjack 3,600 ton deck being installed in 1,030 feet of water.

Amberjack with drilling rig, cranes, life rafts, vent
boom and quarters installed.

UNOBTANIUM

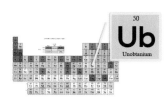

Over-engineering due to studies and wordsmithing created equipment specifications our purchasing people called "Unobtanium." They could not easily source the valve or pump because it was not standard. This drove up cost and schedule through startup.

Trust people to communicate and deliver.

25: MATRIX ORGANIZATION

We went to organizational management seminars because we were in peril of breaking through the "glass ceiling" of 120 people. We had seen six other companies like ours get to that level, fall back to 80 and then fluctuate between those numbers long term. If we were going to break that mold, we thought we might get some value from management training. We were all aware of the glass ceiling and were blown away when we blinked in the spring of 1991 and were closing in on 200 people with impetus to go to 250.

SILO MODEL

The silo was the standard model in business and in engineering firms. Each group within a company was responsible for delivering a bottom line and developed its own structure to do that. Each one of these silos could handily report out at the top to the organization, which could then roll everything together for projections and results. The reporting and organizational lines were very clear as well as career paths and job descriptions. Everything was set up well to be "managed to metrics" that had been proven to deliver a healthy bottom line.

SEEKING HELP

When we would go to management seminars for training, the participants as well as the instructors were incredulous when we described the matrix organization we used. To them it sounded like complete chaos with no way to know real time how the organization was performing. This type of organization had to be home grown and even could be sort of typical for a startup where everyone had to wear multiple hats.

The experts felt that once you reached 15-20 people the organization needed to gravitate into silos in order to manage growth and profit in each of the company's main areas. After two such seminars we decided that management gurus really could not help our situation. We were on our own for organizational development designed to match our strategy.

MATRIX MODEL

In the matrix organization everyone has two bosses.

One boss is their department manager (electrical, mechanical, etc.). The department manager is responsible for keeping their people billable, for hiring, firing, raises and bonuses. They staff projects with the right technical and personality mix to support the project manager. The department manager is also responsible for developing more efficient ways of getting the job done and transferring that information to other projects.

The department manager had to understand project work flow and load and unload people to insure that they had productive work to do on projects.

The project manager is the other boss. Their job is the day to day direction of the people accomplishing project tasks to insure they "move, shoot, communicate (Army phrase)" in concert with the rest of the team. They are responsible for taking care of the client and delivering value to the project.

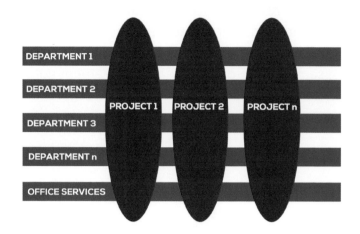

MUSTANG **Matrix Organization.**

PROFIT

The most unusual aspect of our matrix organization was the project manager not being responsible for delivering a "bottom line" profit to Mustang. This totally messed with project managers' minds who came from other companies where the bottom line was their primary responsibility and where they earned their bonus.

We did not want Mustang's invoices to be a source of conflict between our project manager and the client. Our project manager was free to sit on the same side of the table with the client and figure out the absolute best way to deliver the project in the current industry reality. Sometimes this meant that we gave some of our scope to vendors or competitors that had a very efficient solution. At other times it meant we put an engineer or designer into a vendor shop to help them get their product done on time. The client was involved in these decisions as we worked a "best player plays" mentality along with an open minded project execution philosophy.

This put the client's prime point of contact, our project manager, squarely on the client's side. He could shed people back to the department managers and it was their responsibility to get them billable on another project. Mustang's attention was on delivering quality projects in the best possible manner for the client, and we took care of Mustang's business internally with a constant juggling act.

We had a method to the madness of the matrix organization. Profitability was set by Felix, Paul, and me when we set the schedule of rates for the reimbursable contracts. We held the department managers responsible for maintaining a high percent billable for their staff, moving people to the projects at the right time, and insuring they worked well within the project team. We kept the overhead low by performing many administrative tasks ourselves with minimal help. We did not have a human resources group, just a super clerk in Tina Kutach to help department managers and folks.

All recruitment interviewing and hiring was done by the department managers. They were accountable and had the autonomy to take care of business.

Perhaps the toughest part was that project managers generally are control freaks and think they are the be-all, end-all to project execution. The matrix organization stroked those egos and at times project managers would come down hard on a department manager who was juggling many conflicting inputs.

Paul was the master of identifying good discipline leads in the early years and then developing them into department managers. He was able to coach them to keep their egos in check and work toward solutions for the project managers. Because Paul had the respect of the project managers he could also knock them down a notch when needed to smooth some feathers.

PERFORMANCE

The matrix organization greatly reduced our overhead as the department managers were fully billable for the first eight years, had no staff, and did all of their development and staffing as part of the projects they were on. We had a few very knowledgeable and industrious clerks like Sandie Bamber to help Felix with hiring paperwork and insurance questions. Project managers worked out the contracts for projects, obviating the need for a lawyer. Our efficiencies in loading and unloading people to match the project workflow; re-use of prior work, and use of new efficiencies we created, allowed us to benchmark well. Our engineering cost that was half to two thirds of the industry standard, while generating four times the profit per revenue dollar.

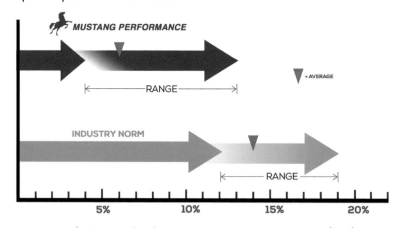

Engineering as % of total installed cost (TIC).

The net/net result was that Mustang was able to put out about 30% more projects per capita than the competition, allowing us to get involved with many clients on a huge number of projects in a short period of years.

Being a sub-contractor mitigates risk.

26: OCEANEERING AND DRESSER

Work came to us in many ways--vendors, clients that had moved overseas, partners of clients we had worked for and fabricators speaking highly of our drawings being accurate.

Dave Rucker helped bring in Craig Devenney's gas platform for Union Texas Petroleum in early 1990 and then the Gulf went totally dead for about 18 months. But we could chase projects elsewhere.

FLOATING PRODUCTION STORAGE & OFFLOADING

Oceaneering

Paul chased and won the oil facilities on a floating production, storage and offloading (FPSO) tanker based facility, a new idea in the oil patch. FPSOs directly offloaded to a tanker on a regular schedule. Once a field was depleted the FPSO could be moved under its own power to a new location. A marine based contractor named Oceaneering was taking the risk of building an FPSO named the Ocean Producer for lease to an oil com-

pany for use offshore Gabon, Africa. Paul became the driving force for Oceaneering on the project as it was done in the cheapest manner possible due to a projected three year life span. Additional years would require reinforcing the hull steel. Only Paul could have pulled off the impossible schedule and cost Oceaneering had agreed to in their contract.

Equipment on tanker.

Paul walked me through the tanker and production facility when it was near completion. I was amazed at all Paul had to learn about marine and ship regulations in order to design the 15,000bopd production facility with 500,000 barrels of storage available in the tanker's hull. The production facility actually used some of the tanker's onboard utility systems in order to reduce equipment costs.

Modularization

Paul's team modularized the production equipment and the pipe racks in an effort to minimize construction work on the tanker. Many pieces of equipment required special internals to handle the tanker's motions and deck flexing.

Paul liked the work and felt there might be more projects as the concept was good for marginal fields like the one in Africa, where the three year life could not justify running expensive pipelines to shore.

Ocean Producer FPSO en route to location.

This project put Mustang on the cutting edge of floating production systems for any water depth.

BIG TURBINES

PDVSA

We had hired Ralph Kinley from a vendor that did production modules for Solar Turbines. Solar liked Ralph and asked us to bid the engineering for a full production facility in Lake Maracaibo, Venezuela for Maraven, a subsidiary of the state owned oil company Petroleos de Venezuela, S.A. (PDVSA). Because the turbine compressor was the longest lead item and most expensive part of the project, Maraven was making the turbine compressor vendor take responsibility for the entire project. The scope included everything from production equipment to living quarters and utilities. The skids and modules would be installed on concrete piers in the lake.

At the same time, we were courting Dresser Rand to support them on their turbine compressor projects for PDVSA. A competitor of ours, Paragon, was doing a lot of work for Dresser, but some of Paragon's people had come to Mustang, facilitating introductions.

Dresser Maraven

Don Anderson of Dresser called me in one day and said they were awarding us three concrete platform complexes consisting of about 80 modules for Maraven. We had been talking to Don and his team about getting something small to start a relationship and here he was handing us 80,000 manhours of reimbursable work. This was much bigger than what we had been talking about. He agreed, but his team felt Paragon was stretched and Mustang had floated to the top in their evaluation of all other engineering houses in Houston! We hired Dick Westbrook from Metro to run the Dresser work.

We built a new team, from engineers to secretaries, around Dick and let him sort it out. We hired our first document control person on Dick's job as the project secretary could not keep up with the workload. Dick created our "large project" document control system as the project progressed.

Solar Maraven

When Solar heard we had the Dresser work, they did not want to give us their project, thinking Dresser may learn some of their competitive advantages. We ended up putting the projects on different floors in the building.

Dresser Lagoven

A few weeks later Dresser came back and gave us the procurement and construction management on the Lagoven (another PDVSA subsidiary) project that was designed by Paragon. Dresser liked what they had seen of our purchasing and scheduling capability. We had just hired Craig Devenney, our client at Union Texas Petroleum, because he was available--not knowing what we would use him for. Craig had a lot of field construction experience from having worked for Brown & Root, so he was perfect to take on the Lagoven work, but we were out of space in the building. We rented a floor in an adjacent building to house his project team, which was pulled together from everywhere.

Construction started on Craig's project without final vendor data, so we put a design team in the Houston Brown & Root yard to incorporate the data and stay ahead of fabrication. Our inspectors counted people and progress, allowing our newly created Project Controls Group under Randy Alton to accurately calculate productivity. By using an "Earned Value System" we calculated the productivity at 62% while the yard was claiming 92%. Productivity in construction of the four six story modules was so far behind that we were able to talk the client into letting us bring an offshore hook up crew into the yard to start the final module (super innovative thinking). This innovation allowed the final module to catch up seven weeks in three weeks of effort and spurred the normal yard workers to better productivity.

A lot of people rolled off of the BP MC-109 Amberjack project onto these compressor projects and we grew about 40% in the spring of 1991 as we looked like a compressor company. We were definitely being whatever the industry needed us to be.

ADDING INFRASTRUCTURE

The Venezuelan State Oil Companies wanted the 100 or so modules we were in charge of to be built in Venezuela. We went and looked at the fabrication yards available and they were full with other PDVSA projects. Our evaluation presented that the Gulf oil patch had fallen into another slump, leaving the fabrication capabilities stagnant. We showed the cost difference between shipping completed modules to Venezuela versus shipping most of the pieces and trusting local supply for the rest. Due to the importance of getting all of this compression on line, we won the day and spread the modules from Corpus Christi, Texas to Gulf Port, Mississippi. For 80% of the shops this was the bulk of their work in the fall of 1991. We never received acknowledgement for helping to bring this work to the Gulf. We did however, develop very strong relationships with the fabrication yards as they worked off of our drawings and relied on our purchasing to make their schedules.

Dick Westbrook, Craig Devenney, Ralph Kinley and Dave Rucker were all new project managers to Mustang and ran the bulk of the company day-to-day in our matrix organization. Mike Hunt and Richard Shirley (former clients with Union Texas Petroleum and Oxy respectively) came in to grow our construction and inspection capability for these modules. Ted "I'm not an engineer" Kelly had come in from Paragon to set up our in-house purchasing and expediting spreadsheets for BP Amberjack. He used them to the max on the Venezuelan modules. Mary "think I'll have a vendor for breakfast if I don't get their vendor data" Budrunas helped Ted set up our expediting systems. Randy Alton came on board and helped set up our scheduling and cost control systems for large projects. Our systems were developed on projects, moved to new projects and improved as they were used. The systems were developed with no extra "bells and whistles" as there was no time for frou-frou.

We didn't get a pat on the back from fabricators, but we received everything we needed: reimbursable work, domestic and international that stretched everything we had to the next level.

This picture shows half of one of the compression modules for Lagoven in the Brown & Root yard. The full project had four full compression modules along with fifteen other production modules.

FOLLOW THE WORK

One of our reasons for looking so hard at being acquired by CCC was the oil companies starting to move work overseas to find bigger reservoirs--"elephants" in their terminology. We did not know that there would be another big downturn in 1990 and 1991 but could feel things moving in that direction. We called this having our "antenna up" due to our network. We were concerned because the international work went lump sum, and we could not afford the risk required to participate.

Being open minded and opportunistic, we landed major international projects in Venezuela and Africa by using our expertise to help vendors and contractors feel confident to take on the risk. They knew that we could deliver the engineering, purchasing, and project management assistance they needed in order to sell their equipment or services in a lump sum manner. They were taking on more risk than we would have been comfortable doing in their shoes...because their bottom line was tied to our performance.

> **"Our focus on completing projects instead of selling manhours made an impression."**

We had found a win-win way to move into international work and were learning where we fit into projects. Our unwavering focus on completing projects instead of selling manhours was making an impression.

27: GO-BYS, SKIDS & SCHEDULES

Vendor Data...Vendor Data...Vendor Data!!!! To our way of thinking, that was the key to a good offshore platform project. There were no books on how to design an offshore platform. We learned as we went, kept the things that worked and adjusted the things that didn't work. We had learned that if we designed with good vendor data, we controlled our engineering costs and lowered the project total installed cost, by giving the construction contractor better drawings. Without vendor data, we called our efforts "cartoons" because they might as well have been building from concept sketches.

GO-BYS

When I left the Army in 1979 and started at Petro Marine, I found it crazy that there was no book to read on engineering for offshore platforms. When I learned from someone, I asked how they knew that information and they said, "from experience."

In offshore engineering at that time, the calculating part of the engineering was pretty straight forward. We had a flow stream from a wellhead that had to be separated into natural gas, water and condensate by using gravity in pressure vessels at about twelve hundred pounds of pressure. We kept the pressure high so that the gas could be dried a little with glycol contact, metered and put in a pipeline to shore. Generally the water was cleaned with more settling time to meet the Federal Government's Minerals Management Service requirements and put overboard. The small amount of condensate produced was cleaned through settling and pumped back into the gas pipeline. The real work was in specifying the equipment, purchasing it, getting it delivered, figuring out how to support it on the deck, and hooking it all up into a processing system.

Every processing system was different due to reservoir characteristics, drilling requirements for the deck and operator preferences. Many companies had tried to standardize process systems like was done onshore, but the cost of equipment was so high that it was always worth some engineering to optimize the design.

During the downturn in the '80s though, we had to figure out how to design these platforms with as few engineering hours as possible. We figured out how to re-use parts and pieces of past platforms in the new design. We never wanted to start from scratch on a project. We wanted to buy some pieces using old data, while putting our effort into the pieces that were specific for the new platform. Using "go-bys" from past projects was critical to winning work. Paul and I became masters of this method while at CBS.

FELL INTO SKID DESIGN

Flowrates per well offshore were 100 to 1000 times higher than onshore. The wells were clustered to a platform, raising the flowrates for processing much higher than the design rates for onshore equipment. We also had a salt-laden marine environment to deal with, making paint selection and corrosion avoidance a small project in itself.

Most of the platforms Paul and I managed at CBS were designed to support a platform drilling rig. The rig was installed on the bare top deck of the platform and drilled all of the wells. Part way through drilling, flowrates were picked for design of the production facilities based on well tests to that date.

We designed skid packages for all of the production and utility equipment to be installed offshore when the drilling rig was removed. These skid packages would then be hooked up offshore to create a producing platform. Each skid had hundreds to thousands of component pieces that had to hold up in a rugged offshore environment, requiring close specification. Additionally, we needed to keep the number of different types of components limited as much as possible due to the *long logistics tail* from offshore to onshore to the suppliers all over the world. The "devil was in the details" of skid design as small errors would cause large re-work costs offshore.

Typical separator skid with piping, valves and instrumentation.

It was very lucky that Paul and I developed our modus operandi around skid designs that essentially modularized a production facility. We unconsciously created a company that had the close communications required to do detailed skid design. With structural, mechanical, electrical, instrument, procurement and logistics requirements closely interrelated, trade-offs had to be handled continuously in real time. It felt right to us and would position us to improve industry benchmarks.

PROCUREMENT DRIVEN SCHEDULE

Because we did back-to-back projects for clients who had their own operating personnel, Paul and I learned what equipment they liked. We could lay out what we termed a "procurement driven schedule." For each piece of equipment or skid we would figure out the time to specify, bid, award, approve vendor data, fabricate, inspect and take delivery. Then we would look at the need date in the yard for a new deck or offshore if replacing drilling equipment. The need dates would take into account our first thoughts on the construction sequence timing. We would leave a couple of weeks for schedule slippage (lagniappe in Louisiana lingo) and fix the end date, letting the schedule float to the front end.

We would then set up our engineering to match the purchasing needs at the front end of the schedule. This would not be an optimal method to schedule engineering because in many cases we would be doing things in the wrong order. However, due to experience, re-use of known equipment and occasionally heroic efforts, we pulled it off with significant manhour, cost and schedule savings for the client.

From our experience in back-to-back projects, we had developed a scheduling method we then used successfully even with new clients.

"Custom design with a manufacturing mentality."
Bill Higgs, Mustang project engineer

28: ENGINEERING OFF THE CRITICAL PATH

Our competitors would engineer, then procure and then construct due to the complexities of an offshore platform and the fact that each one was essentially a prototype. Due to optimization to match the reservoir, each platform was designed singularly, purchased and put together in its own unique fashion. Attempts at standardization generally fell apart in the second week of design.

LIMIT ENGINEERING

A major problem with prototype design was that engineering could go on forever as more possibilities to optimize were seen as the design would unfold. We called this phenomenon "filling the void." Engineering expanded to fill the time available. If we wanted to control engineering costs, then we needed to limit the schedule and force engineering to finish.

"Engineering will expand to fill the time available."

I used what I termed the 80% solution, while Paul would use 95%. Get the engineering 80% complete prior to bidding, do an 80% vendor data review while evaluating bids; do an 80% quality job reviewing of the real vendor data after award, do an 80% quality of inspection in the field and an 80% quality inspection prior to startup. Different things will be caught at each of these stages of the project, resulting in a 100% quality project. If we waited for engineering to get everything perfect before bidding, we doubled the engineering time and then often had to change the design anyway to match what we decided to buy. This extra engineering time negatively impacted vendor and contractor schedules for fabrication.

CRITICAL PATH

We used the procurement driven schedule to take engineering off of the critical path for the project. We made the critical path, which were the back-to-back events that forced the length of the schedule, go through equipment procurement, delivery and field hookup. Once we had this schedule laid out, engineering was no longer on the critical path, like it was in the rest of the industry. Thus, we had adequate time for engineering to develop quality drawings, while at the same time squeezing it into the time slots allowed in the schedule.

> **"Engineering is a necessary evil to get into procurement and construction."**

Perhaps one of the craziest phrases I used in sales was my belief that engineering was a necessary evil to get into procurement and construction. I used this phrase to help the clients understand what we were trying to do...our "come from" place. I was a professional engineer and part-owner of a quality engineering firm saying that engineering is a necessary evil.

Clients would be surprised when I would say this but would then listen closer to my presentation of our project execution methodology. We needed their close attention because what they were going to hear had subtle nuances that would result in extraordinary projects for them. The client had to become comfortable with a little controlled chaos  in that we blurred the lines between engineering, procurement, and construction as we busted silos.

PROJECT INFLUENCE CURVE

Arco project engineers were very open minded and liked our procurement driven schedule with its non-intuitive benefit of getting engineering off of the project critical path. One day I was sitting in an Arco engineer's office when he became tied up on a long phone call. He handed me a notebook he had received in an internal Arco project management course to flip through while I waited. Here it was 1991, and I'd been in offshore engineering for twelve years when I saw a diagram that gave me an epiphany on what we had been doing. It was the Project Influence Curve as depicted below.

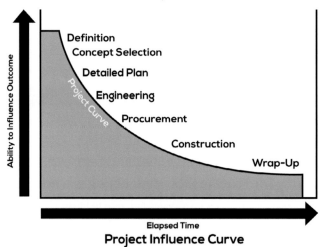

Project Influence Curve

This curve shows that you have the greatest potential to influence the outcomes of a project for cost, schedule, quality, and safety in the earlier stages of the project. As the project moves from concept to engineering to procurement to construction, the scope of work becomes more and more fixed, making the ability to change outcomes very hard. Wow!! This curve put into a picture what Paul and I had been building our company's project execution strategy around for years.

FRONT END WORK

We always put a lot of emphasis and innovative thought into the very earliest stages of a project to set it up for success. We had questionnaires to pull out of the client organization all of their preferences for equipment, flexibility and operations. We pulled go-bys from past projects that would be applicable to this client and project. We figured out how to optimally lay out the project for bid packages, for construction and for operations down the road. With this information we developed our procurement driven schedule and set up our engineering deliverables to match the project execution strategy. We worked the hardest at the front end of the project, where the influence curve was showing that we had the most capability to affect cost, schedule, quality and safety. Because our engineering was squeezed, we allowed more time for the vendors and fabricators to do their job, increasing quality and safety, while lowering their cost.

PROJECT COST CURVE

While working with the Project Influence Curve over the next few months, another thought came to us. We added a Project Cost Curve to the same graph and things became clearer. As the project progressed, each phase became much more expensive. The concept selection and front end work were cheap because we were just doing sketches, pulling go-bys and doing planning. When we started detailed engineering, procurement and then fabrication, the dollar expenditures went up exponentially.

When changes were made in these successive steps, it would cause us to get off of the planned cost curve, always jumping the curve upward as shown on the next page.

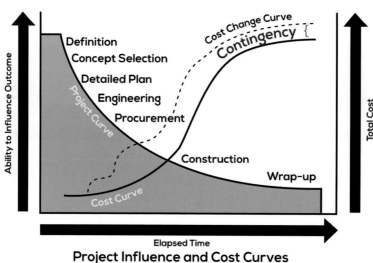

Project Influence and Cost Curves

PROJECT MANAGEMENT

Project management evolved for us as we moved from small gas platforms to much larger complexes like BP Amberjack, Maraven and Lagoven. These were "world class" oil and gas projects. It boiled down to figuring out the pieces and scheduling them to control where the big dollars would be spent--in construction. By developing an engineering and procurement system that took engineering off of the critical path and delivered vendor data early, we were able to put out the best quality drawings in the industry. This was being proven on project after project as our people continued to innovate better ways to implement our execution strategy.

Paul was focused on building strong teams that could deliver. Felix was working to insure distractions to project work were minimized. I was working to find a way to explain the Mustang difference to clients. The Project Influence and Cost Curves gave me a visual tool to help my efforts by crystallizing in a client's mind where the Mustang difference originated.

"Time sheets provide transparency into operations."
Stephanie Higgs, CEO Cielo

29: MORPHING THE ORGANIZATION

We had built the "Upside-down Pyramid" organizational structure gurus talk about. The owners were on the bottom, supporting the engineers and administrative staff with tools, people, work and encouragement. Engineers and administrative staff in turn supported the drafting and secretarial folks, giving them everything they needed to be successful. Drafting and secretarial put out the final product that supported the industry needs. Add the fact that there were no titles on business cards and we were breaking all of the old mores.

KING OF THE MORPH

Paul didn't like all the second guessing he heard after announcing an organizational change he felt was pretty minor but logically needed. He always wanted to work well with people and this felt like he had thrown a monkey wrench into the works. People focused on what this change meant to them personally and what this change potentially put in motion for the future.

Paul went around talking to people, "smoothing their ruffled feathers," saying he did not know the future and explained why he had made the moves to match the current and foreseeable future's needs. Everything was driven by the projects we won. In reality, people loved Paul and would follow him anywhere but couldn't help questioning what they read in a memo. Paul wanted another way to effect organizational change because it seemed, and actually was, constant. He felt there was a lot of wasted time and effort generated from simple memos that said only what they meant to say. Paul's solution was to start morphing the organization in baby steps.

Paul did not call it morphing. The rest of the organization came up with that term in order to explain to new people what was happening. New people were always trying to figure out the organization top to bottom. Just when they thought they had it, they saw me go be a project engineer under a project manager, or a designer seem to be the lead but working for others on a project. People were put in positions on jobs to "earn their stripes" with the people we wanted them to lead. As it became obvious to everyone that this person was the right person to lead, they just sort of assumed that role. Paul nudged the process from behind and worked to see how key folks felt about how things were working.

Morphing was the art of continual change in the organization that allowed our matrix to be whatever the industry needed of us. We could look like a 15 person company fixing little things, or a world class organization that could stand toe-to-toe with the big boys technically, while executing in a much leaner fashion. Mustang's structure was more determined by the mix of project organizations than anything else. These project teams were industry facing, allowing their capability to be the look clients had of the Mustang organization.

This sounded and seemed very confusing both internally and externally. Imagine trying to explain a morphing organization to a new hire or while qualifying for a project with a client. We tried to get people to see that the company was essentially a large project team with a number of tasks to get accomplished. The organization of that project team seamlessly molded itself to match those tasks in the most efficient manner we could devise. The molding happened as everyone moved to be on the tasks that needed their expertise and were ready to be done. Highly efficient productivity emerged from this continual shifting of resources.

POLITICS

The only detailed organization charts produced were the ones for project teams. The organization chart for the company just illustrated groups of people to show a client the capability we had, e.g. drafting, inspection, etc.

A side benefit of Paul's efforts in morphing was a reduction of politics, as it seemed everyone had "situational power" to take care of business. If they needed power or stroke to solve a task, it was given by those around them. Our feeling was politics and turf building inevitably added overhead and slowed things down. We had the pulse and knew who caused friction, allowing us to move them out of the way either in the company or push them out of Mustang through coaching.

> **"Politics and turf building inevitably added overhead and slowed things down."**

Probably the most significant benefit of morphing was that if a change did not work, it could be quietly morphed back without losing good people. Good people, who were moved to a place where they no longer fit, could move back and stay long term...pretty cool.

GENETIC TESTING

Getting comfortable with a morphing organization was part of what we called "genetic testing" of new hires. If they had Mustang DNA, then they would feel right in a totally project and client focused organization. Their office size, who they reported to, what their title was, etc. did not matter to Mustangers. What mattered was ability to get the job done in a team environment and bring in repeat work from the client for job security.

HIGH GRADING

Although Mustang seemed soft and cuddly with the people taking care of people mantra being implemented, it was a tough as nails business just under the surface. Part of morphing was a continuous high-grading of personnel by moving non-productive talent out and bringing in new talent. We were surprised that some people who were lifesavers in the first few years did not survive through the morphing. We couldn't identify a reason or theme that resulted in these people not making it while others grew with the organization and thrived. We were not prepared to move people who had become friends out of the organization and this was one of the toughest things during this phase. We thought we'd all "hold hands and grow old together," but it just wasn't meant to be.

> "Although Mustang could seem soft and cuddly... it was tough as nails..."

Most of the high grading happened through a natural selection process of people who wanted to surround themselves with people who could produce at a high level on a myriad of tasks and stay upbeat day after day. As we found them, they became Mustangers and helped us find more.

THE 1991 DOWNTURN IN GULF WORK

The 1991 downturn resulted in no work in the fabrication yards and none of our normal offshore Gulf work. We went to New Iberia, Louisiana to tour the fabrication yards in anticipation of awarding the 80 Maraven modules. It felt like a ghost town. Parking lots were empty, no cranes were moving and the management teams had no work to bid on.

We were able to talk a small Independent oil company into starting a job they had shelved due to the recent drop in oil and gas prices. We showed them that if they would kick us off to design and then build "out of cycle" with everyone else, they would get top teams and significant price reductions. Since they had the money, they earned a 40% reduction in cost and schedule. Meanwhile, we had a project to do.

By booking work going into and during the downturn, we were able to bring in some top people and increase our capability as layoffs again shook the industry.

PULLING THE LOAD

Normally 20% of the people in a company pull the bulk of the load. We worked to develop a company where 80% of the people pulled the load. We did this through small things like letting secretaries and drafters hand out their business cards to clients and show how they helped the project. We disseminated information broadly to "make all eyes informed eyes." By having informed eyes and people's brains turned on in an encouraging environment, we caught problems and conflicts while they were still small. As we needed additional folks, we asked our people, vendors and clients if they knew people who would thrive in an environment like ours--an open, transparent, fun environment that also required a lot of personal accountability. Our weekly timesheet gave everyone immediate feedback on how they were doing on their projects. The payoff for joining and performing would be continuous work in a company that would not disappear out from under them, as happened all too frequently from '83-'89 and again in 1991. They focused on the work while we continued to work hard on their behalf to create a strong, stable company.

OPERATION HORSETHIEF

Good people know good people. That is about all we could believe in for hiring. We started calling our hiring process Operation Horsethief...identify the horses in other companies and go get them. By having a fun name for identifying top performers we kept it at the front of people's minds, resulting in a very successful hiring practice. We brought people in, had them drop all of their bureaucratic training and asked them to just take care of projects and people. They found this simple philosophy invigorating.

Sometimes we brought in people for interviews, liked them, but the timing was not right for either them or us. We may not have had enough work to add them, or they may have wanted to complete a job in order to not burn any bridges with their old company or a client. We often agreed to keep talking and they were put on a department manager's "want to hire" list. In many cases we worked out compensation and just put it in a folder. We wanted to be continuously interviewing in upturns and downturns--looking for good people that matched our criteria.

"Hurry up to the next disaster."
Greg Higgs, Offroader

30: NO GROWTH MOTIVE

We needed a method of paying a bonus to our department managers and project managers to thank them for taking care of business. As we discussed how to do bonuses, our thoughts kept coming back to transparency, simplicity and adequacy in aligning goals. We sort of liked the bonus method described in the book Up the Organization. *The method distributed profits to everyone based on their relative value to the company as inferred by their compensation. We felt, however, that this was handled with our 5% 401K contribution that had no matching requirement. We needed to take care of the leaders and producers in addition to the 401K.*

DEFINED NET BONUS METHOD

Manhours

Since we sold manhours instead of lump sum projects, the bonus needed to be based on manhours. We wanted project managers to take care of the client but absorb some inefficient manhours at times to help the department managers meet their goals. We wanted department managers to keep their people billable on projects. The department managers picked their people's classification in the billing rate schedule to insure the billing rate produced a profit.

We set a "Defined Net" that the bonus would be based upon. We would take a person's pay, multiply by 1.25 and subtract that from the billing rate to arrive at the defined net. Overhead hours were just put in at the 1.25 multiplier and subtracted, making their impact very noticeable. We made the multiplier of 1.25 artificially low in order to prevent any grousing. The bonus was then set at a percentage of the calculated defined net.

Calculation

Managers knew that overheads and some other costs had to come out of the defined net, keeping it gray enough to minimize any second guessing of the percentage provided to the manager. In this manner, the bonus moved with the various schedules of rates used for different projects and clients. Similarly, it helped align department managers and project managers to maintain billability. Department managers became used to trying to create a differential between the billing rate and a person's cost when they hired someone and gave them a job classification. Project managers challenged the department managers if they classified someone too high, giving the system some self-correction.

REWARD VS. GREED

Our defined net system was based on "reward" versus the normal standard of "greed." It was a thank you for taking care of business in our reimbursable manhour environment.

Project managers in a lump sum environment with a bonus based on the bottom line could get greedy and destroy the future relationship with the client. This difference seemed huge to us in creating a project-client-people focused environment and culture.

SPREADSHEET

The defined net bonus system lent itself to spreadsheet calculations for simple implementation of a quarterly bonus to our key players. These numbers also told us how healthy Mustang was and we pulled another percentage amount to use for individual bonuses. In the spring of 1990 we gave nice bonuses to a number of lead designers and engineers.

Mini-Review

Each department manager kept a spreadsheet showing when and how much of a bonus was given to each person. In general terms, we knew about how much we wanted to give a person each year, outside of the 401K's 5%. This allowed us to sporadically give a bonus to someone that had worked exhaustively for three weeks or came up with a new idea, while still staying in control of the overall bonuses.

These timely bonuses as a thank you were well received by direct as well as contract people. Some contract people told us that it was the first bonus they had received in 20 years of working. They could not believe how well contract people were accepted and relied on as part of the team at Mustang. Each manager handed out bonus checks confidentially and used this opportunity to tell the person what they were doing well and point out areas for improvement.

This "mini-review" happened without the person knowing it was coming and was shown in the manager's spreadsheet. We liked this method better than formal reviews on anniversary dates or the end of a year. Reviewing in this manner took stress out of the situation and kept more energy directed toward projects.

Another benefit of working the bonus spreadsheets was a better "gut feel" for what was needed to maintain a strong bottom line. By constantly working with the numbers, we developed the knowledge that let us estimate better. This was true both in projects and in the business. We were forever estimating and then crunching numbers to get comfortable.

> "We were forever estimating and then crunching numbers to get comfortable."

RUN THE NUMBERS

We occupied one-plus floors in 1990. The building owner demanded that we sign a "real" five year lease which would leave us without the ability to unload space as needed. We ran the numbers and checked cost per square foot to buy buildings in Park Ten. For a couple hundred thousand dollars over the five-year lease agreement, we could buy the entire six story building.

We talked with the owner and they wanted our lease signed in order to use it in selling the building. We then negotiated a price to purchase the building at a very low point in the Houston commercial real estate market. In order to keep Mustang debt free (either the lease or the purchase amount would have to appear in our bids to clients) and thus looking financially strong, we bought the building in our names under a separate company. By owning the building separately, there was no "funny" pressure put on Mustang to grow. Mustang just paid the going rate for the space it occupied.

NO GROWTH MOTIVE

We had no growth motive, which actually enabled growth very profitably. We just wanted to keep the people we had and take good care of projects. Growth meant more people, which meant more headaches in the very fluid matrix organization. Why should we take on more work and lower our overall profit margin? Thus we did not decrease rates for bigger projects or cumulative manhours per year. Clients pushed us to provide discounts, and our response was that if we did not sell the manhours to them, we would sell them to someone else. We were a small fish in a big pond. It was a weird philosophy, but the clients could not refute it and knew we were always busy.

HOUSTON 100

An indicator of how busy we had been came from our application to the Houston 100, recognizing the 100 fastest growing companies over the previous three years. We were recognized in the award's first year, 1990, for our growth from '87-'89 and came in fourth!! Then in 1991 we again made it for the '88-'90 time frame. Only about twenty companies were able to sustain enough growth, without being purchased or disintegrating, to be in the top 100 two years in a row, telling us that we were doing something special. It was also interesting to note that only about 15% of the companies were in the oil and gas business as Houston worked hard to diversify.

OVERHEAD LAGS

One of the neatest things that happened during growth spurts was that our overhead lagged the growth curve. Felix set up our support staffs to help instead of hinder growth and productivity. By using clerical people in human resources, finance, legal, office moves and setups, we were very responsive to needs while no territory was being built in these staffs. The clerks were stretched at times, but they did not have a boss drinking coffee in the corner office...they were both doer and boss.

New people were amazed that they would come in on a Monday morning, were signed in, briefed, put in an office with a working computer, all the supplies they needed and a bag of Mustang goodies, and were billable by 10 a.m.!! They had never seen anything like it. Everyone they met was pleasant, said hello and was obviously industrious. The experiences in those first hours made them want to jump in and get after the work.

Understaffing in overhead positions made us gravitate to the "real stuff." This meant we had fewer balls to keep in the air, allowing us to run leaner. We didn't have a controller managing our budgets and saying we needed to let an engineer go because he was on overhead. We had engineers and project people making the right decisions.

RECEPTIONIST SETS THE TONE

Charmaine Sakos was our receptionist and sometimes we felt everyone worked for her. She had an energetic personality and a sixth sense for where everyone was at any given time. Just the sound of her voice could whip the organization into shape. She took it as a personal challenge to make sure that when a client called in, she could get them hooked up to the person they asked for. I'd be in someone's office or in drafting and the phone would ring (only land lines then). Someone would pick up and darn if it wasn't Charmaine patching a client through to me. How did she know where I was? If she paged you and you did not call her right away, a very stern voice would come over the PA system and you knew you'd better call her. Clients loved her and everyone in the office admired her ability to keep everything moving smoothly.

> "Suck a vacuum on the industry and pull it toward a win-win environment."

It was evident from the receptionist, through the energy in the hallways, to the quality drawings going out the door that Mustang was setting a new standard that others would have trouble following. We did not spend much time worrying about our competition. Our philosophy was to build a different type of organization that would suck a vacuum on the industry and pull it along toward a win-win environment.

A.

B.

C.

D.

A. Tracey "Mrs. Mustang" Bayles. Set up new offices and got people billable.
B. Felix "The Man behind the Curtain" as they say in Oz, with Joyce.
C. Purchasing Manager Ted Kelly rides the Big Wave on "Club Mustang" Day.
D. Bill with Charmaine Sakos, Best Dressed Winners - "Go Texan" Day.

"Turning sand into concrete."
Greg Higgs, CEO FabFours

31: BECOMING SOLID

We created our project systems as needed on projects. Our scheduling, specifications, bidding, expediting and other procedures were generated to provide the information needed to match the size and complexity of each project. Since the projects ranged from small three or four person jobs to 100 person large international jobs, we needed a lot of flexibility. We wanted these systems to support the people and not get in the way of their productivity.

PROJECT SYSTEMS

We knew the bigger engineering firms used their systems to insure projects were accomplished even if the people were not top-notch. They would generally get good projects but not industry changing performance. Their systems relied on a few good people filling the gaps and leading, while the systems generated the daily tasks and checking protocols.

We brought in a great project controls person named Randy Alton to start our project controls group when the Dresser projects became so large. He knew state of the art software for scheduling tasks and knew how to manpower load engineering as well as field construction onto the schedules. At the same time, he understood Mustang's need to match the systems to the project. Randy brought in some top people he had worked with and jumped us four years into the future in about six months. One of the best things they did was set up our first computer network and loaded tools that Paul said were our latest and greatest from projects. Now updates were controlled, and enhancements easily pushed to all projects.

PACESETTER AND PDMS

Randy merged the tools we had created to develop our Pacesetter™ and PDMS™ suites of programs.

PDMS™ was our Project Document Management System. This system controlled all of the paper on a project, including specifications, drawings, correspondence and vendor data. At times we felt it took a ton of paper per ton of steel to create a project. Knowing who had what and what revision required a strong system.

Pacesetter™ put all of the tools Paul and I had created into a logical project execution methodology. We had pieced together a method of streamlining the front end of a project in order to get into purchasing and construction earlier and in better shape. The name and brochure helped me explain to clients how our methodology should earn us an "efficiency factor" in bid evaluations. This effort helped us "win the ties" in bids and book the work.

Pacesetter™ picture we used in brochure ads.

USER FRIENDLY

Clients also gave us plus points (Ranger School term) because our systems were easily transported into their companies for use and were not proprietary. This was a discussion point between Paul and me as he was pretty proud of the systems that had been put together. He felt we should control them and hold them close. My contention was that everyone had some method of tracking things. After all, we're just counting drawings and keeping track of where they are. Keeping things simple and open to use would make us more user friendly to clients and vendors, which should improve communications and work flow.

Our systems naturally gravitated to moving with the project to clients and vendors because it made sense to everyone, but the discussion was interesting.

EARNED VALUE

Randy Alton brought a new term with him that helped us control projects. The term was "Earned Value." For every deliverable on the project we set up three to five milestones and assigned a percent complete to that milestone. This took the subjectivity out of reporting. The user could not claim an earned value milestone's percent complete until it was reached. This prevented a project getting to 80% complete and then sitting on that percentage for a long time. We had our fingers on the pulse and could put more resources on lagging areas. Earned value reporting was a significant development.

> "Earned Value took the subjectivity out of reporting."

CROSS-FERTILIZE

The Project Controls group also helped us cross-fertilize good ideas between projects. The project controls folks were another set of eyes and ears out on the floor looking at the status of deliverables and talking to everyone to insure the reporting was accurate. As they learned of neat things a project was doing, they brought them up on other projects where they were applicable. We had department managers, project controls and the owners all working to identify best practices and moving them across the company. I was tightly in this loop as the best practices were also great things for me to show clients while chasing new work.

SALES AND MARKETING

Our first ad was done by the people at *Offshore Magazine* from pictures and notes we gave them. We put pictures in the ad that would allow clients to mentally "check-off" our experience. The editor introduced me to Bob Mahlstedt, who owned Ram Mark services and could be paid as needed to create ads.

We spent some hours in three or four sessions with Bob, working to get him "read in" on Mustang's capabilities and how we were trying to differentiate ourselves. The first ad Bob created used a picture of the Ford Mustang with a young Lee Iacocca standing next to it. The second ad he did was on Pacesetter™ and the third on offshore platforms. When I saw the proof of the third ad, it dawned on me that all three ads had a similar layout, and I said as much to Bob. He smiled and said "That is why you hire a professional." It was pretty neat that we received so much experience wrapped up into his fee.

GIVE AWAYS

Another part of external marketing we pushed was to have something with a blue horse on it, on a client's desk five times a year. We hoped it would stay there awhile and remind them of us. This could be a "trinket" or our client newsletter that was quick and easy to read. Our Christmas card was always innovative and tied in with the blue horse. We would stuff a Mustang magnet, or date wheel calculator into the card--something that would last forever and help the client. One of our Christmas cards, with three mustangs pulling Santa's sleigh, won an award for design.

A lot of thought and action went into promoting Mustang internally. We gave Mustang goodies to people on their first day, at parties, to their kids, or just out of the blue something would be on their desk. We wanted to always be saying thank you for your efforts and earn their hearts and minds through our actions. We wanted to demonstrate giving and being other-oriented so they would do the same.

BUSINESS REPORTING

Our banker and CPA did audits and said that we were running a very tight ship financially with very simple reports. We never borrowed any money which made it easy for the banker; he just cashed checks and watched our checking account grow.

One of our challenges was internal. People got so used to "Mother Mustang" taking care of all their needs, that they would take advantage of her. Felix and Paul had to be very vigilant in looking at expense reports and internal spending to nip unwarranted expenses from going onto our overhead. We gave a lot of mini-talks about Mother Mustang and how to keep her healthy.

STRATEGIC PLANNING

Our plan was to improve in every area of the company while continuing to put out quality work. Each department had a list of things they wanted to improve, and Paul had a list of project management things he wanted to improve. On each project we looked for opportunities to do one or two things off of the lists during the course of the work.

We got into a yearly rhythm of clearing the decks for action in the first quarter, growing and busting in the second and third quarters, then pushing for work to last the winter during the fourth quarter. We would high grade our people in late October so people were settled for the holidays. This gave us our number of people in December as the number we wanted to hold onto as a minimum the following year.

COMPETITION

All of our clients had other qualified options for engineering services besides Mustang. There were over 100 petroleum related engineering firms in Houston, Dallas or New Orleans. Clients liked the service and experience of working with Mustang but could not keep us from going out of business. With some of the tough bidding practices we faced, at times it felt like no one cared if we survived. This understanding helped us hold the line in bids to make sure we would be profitable.

We knew that if we kept our project teams together and improved their ability during downturns, we would be a better company long term. Our industry was like arriving at the elevator...you were either going up or down. We worked hard to only get on the elevator when it was going up!

REAL WORLD MBA

We felt like we were getting a real world MBA as we worked through hundreds of questions, problems, and decisions monthly. If someone had the time and inclination, they could have done a business school case study on us every quarter. Many times it felt like we should have had more training or experience for the decisions we faced. However, by working to keep things simple and in front of us, we were able to work through them. We were also very open about asking for other opinions as we had three previous owners of engineering firms and six prior clients working for us.

"Exposure means casualties" was a catch phrase in the Army. We worked to limit our exposure to things that could hurt Mustang. We stayed away from real tough clients, onerous contracts, taking out any business loans, and taking on projects that seemed set up for failure. This meant we had to work harder to find clients and projects right for us, but we did not get our management team tied up in unproductive shenanigans.

Sitting around jaw-jacking at the end of 1991, it seemed like a company run by technical people was working. We had 220 people with a good backlog during a big downturn in the oil patch. We knew all of our people and knew our strengths and weaknesses. We had designed Mustang to run differently in order to continuously differentiate. It felt right.

Demonstrate giving and being other oriented.

32: DESIGNING MUSTANG

At the 1991 Christmas Party, two different people come up to us and make sure we were listening closely when they made their point that their spouse had changed since coming to Mustang. Their spouses put more energy into being with the kids, were generally happier and woke up ready to go to work. The people talking to us wanted to make sure we knew that we were making a difference in people's lives and they wanted us to keep doing it. These conversations sent tingles up and down our spines as that was the ultimate purpose of the company as envisioned in the planning stages from 1985 to 1987. We reveled together in the fact that by "staying the course" over these first four years, we had created a difference people could see and feel. We could not have anticipated all of the twists and turns we had experienced, but we could enjoy the results of our efforts in staying true to our core beliefs for four years.

MUSTANG MOTION

Like Brownian movement in cells, we worked to make Mustang Motion perpetual by keeping it in the front of people's minds. We had Mustang Motion sports teams and the Mustang Motion Newsy Newsletter. We had the Mustang Motion song and dance routine. We had the slanted and bold blue letters of **MUSTANG ENGINEERING** and the rearing blue horse on one hoof...either going up or down, but not keeping still.

We kept everyone moving offices, including ourselves in order to get project teams co-located. We changed the pictures and announcements every few weeks at the coffee bars to generate enthusiasm and visually change the environment.

CHANGE

All of this effort was directed at getting people used to change to the point where it was embraced and laughed about, as in morphing the organization. People moved quickly from one project to another or from one task to another because that's just the way it was at Mustang. Move offices, change desks, bring in a new person, no problem, all done without interrupting the flow of work.

Our thoughts, actions and the habits we created were all centered on being comfortable with change. Our hopes were that this environment would move us toward a destiny of unbeatable responsiveness to the changing world of upstream offshore projects. We knew everything was changing as oil companies went into deeper waters or harsher environments trying to find bigger reservoirs. They were moving into international markets and stretching their capabilities in an effort to survive. We needed to be able to change and mold and adjust our people, systems, and execution methodologies to match the oil company needs on a continuous basis.

PROJECTS

"Our feeling was that there was no reason for Mustang to exist other than doing projects for clients."

Track Record

We let projects drive everything: hiring, organization, profit, technical development, insurance, contracting, etc. Our feeling was that there was no reason for Mustang to exist other than doing projects for clients. Anything that did not contribute to this goal was seriously questioned.

We established a track record of successes in projects that were unusual, high visibility to the owner and aggressive in terms of cost and schedule. These types of projects were getting bigger, which helped our "going out of business" curve stretch way out to a year. These projects let us develop close relationships with clients and gave them plenty of time in our offices to understand the difference we were bringing. Examples of the "Mustang difference" abounded and documenting them set up future sales.

Project Changes

On BP MC-109 Amberjack, the big stone rolled and crushed our plan. They tested a new well when we were 70% done with design and on very tight schedules delivering drawings to the Brown & Root fabrication yard. The new well showed we needed to add quite a bit of heat to the process due to the cooling effect of going through 1000 feet of water to get to the deck. Generally a significant design change like this would take four weeks to evaluate and eight weeks to implement into the design...after negotiating an engineering change order.

Being reimbursable and used to change, we did the engineering in three days, located space for the equipment in the very tight design and negotiated additional equipment with vendors who were already supplying similar equipment. We got vendor data in two days, changed the design over a weekend and did not slip our issue of drawings to the fabricator. BP knew they had the right company after we took care of what could have been a major problem in less than seven days!

Similarly, on the Dresser Maraven project it became clear after a few weeks that the three "identical" complexes had very different design parameters. We minimized the effects of these differences in many ways and kept the same schedules despite ending up with three "one-of-a-kind" projects.

Despite changes, we always told our people to "stay the course" and do it right while we ran interference. Getting the drawings right and checked was always of utmost importance as it saved the client major money in fabrication. Overcoming these problems helped create very strong teams. When people saw Mustang's owners intimately involved and working with clients to put good work out the door, they knew that the company had its priorities right.

"Projects and engineering activities were king at Mustang."

Projects and engineering activities were king at Mustang and everything supported that fact.

FIT-FOR-PURPOSE

We understaffed projects a little in order to give people a few more hours and a bigger paycheck. This also meant there were fewer people on each project, providing shorter and better lines of communication. Fewer people meant we did not do "nice to have" things on projects. We came up with the term "fit-for-purpose" engineering. Generally, this also meant we reduced our deliverables to just what was needed for construction. The process of understaffing and creating a fit-for-purpose engineering design philosophy kept our costs unnaturally low, despite being on a reimbursable contract.

Our people saw we were able to win almost any project we focused on getting, due to our ability to execute. They started to believe in the company and invest themselves to make it better.

A culture built on loyalty needs trust, transparency, confidence and history. After four years we had built the bridges with our people, clients and vendors to earn that trust.

GIVING BACK

Two designers, Beth Hebert and Henry Gomez, visited with us about supporting a few needy families for Christmas. They would take responsibility for running the effort on their own time.

The outpouring of gifts from Mustangers was tremendous and required many more hands for wrapping and putting things together.

The best part of this effort was that we were allowed to deliver the gifts to the families in person. Ann and I took our children, Greg and Stephanie, who were 12 and 6 years old respectively to Mustang to load the cars and pickup trucks with everything for delivery.

A.

B.   **C.**

A. Needy Family presents wrapped and ready.
B. Diane Daniels with a lot of wrapping to do!
C. Henry Gomez at work.

PRIVATE SECTOR INITIATIVE

Henry Gomez was also instrumental in getting Mustang involved with the Private Sector Initiative (PSI). For PSI we took on the job of fixing someone's home that needed help...many times an older person or a person with disabilities. Materials had been donated by companies around Houston, and we supplied the know-how and labor. In some cases there would be a few weekends of preparation at the house and then a *long* Saturday with 20-30 Mustangers doing projects inside and outside of the home. Again Mustangers brought their kids to help and learn. Sitting under a tree eating lunch with a multi-generational group felt like we were at an old-style barn-raising as we shared stories and built great camaraderie.

Henry, Felix and James at PSI.

SWOT Analysis, end of 1991...
MUSTANG has legs*!*

Strengths:
- Owners leadership...worked through fourth owner and possible sale of the company.
- Every job is profitable due to being reimbursable.
- Contractors and vendors are pulling us into international work.
- Mustang Motion (Spirit) remains high.
- Conceptual and front end design strength is setting us apart.
- Multiple clients...over 40.
- Working for a few major oil companies on large projects.
- Auditable invoices, financial report and contracts are in the drawer each month.
- Strong cash flow.
- Project and department managers are taking more of the load off of the owners.
- We easily mold to what the industry needs from us.

Weaknesses:
- CAD development.
- Training in all areas.
- Project controls are weak for major projects.
- We can only handle two of the bigger projects at one time.
- Only doing the front end on international jobs limits feedback from construction for improvement.
- Culture has holes due to the influx of new people that all went on the same projects.
- Offshore industry is in another major downturn.
- We are not covering the bases in sales with our clients.

Opportunities:
- Companies are still cutting top people that we can hire.
- We have leaner more efficient teams than competitors.
- Clients are not happy with competitor's performance.
- Use CAD for structural and piping design.
- Client personnel we know have gone overseas on projects.
- Reputation for saving contractor's money could help us work internationally.
- We have kept strong teams together through the downturn and are ready for an upturn.

Threats:
- Big boys could "buy" the work.
- Big boys have hired people away with project bonuses.
- Differentiation is not clear to clients we are pursuing.
- Industry downturn may continue past our current backlog.
- If we mess up, we could have a lawsuit.
- Mustang could crumble under industry pressures.
- Our value proposition is still not "tangible" to clients.

Mustang-isms:
- Steady Work...for Steady People
- Engineering off the critical path
- Procurement driven schedule
- Morphing the organization
- Mustang DNA
- Operation Horsethief
- All eyes informed eyes
- Defined Net bonus method
- Fit for Purpose Engineering
- Mother Mustang

Camaraderie:
- Mustang Micro-wave at softball games
- Mustang Motion
- Needy Family drives
- Club Mustang days
- Private Sector Initiative
- "Horse-Thing"
- Shrimp Boil
- In-house putt-putt
- River rafting with families

Sayings:
- Energy and enthusiasm is a force multiplier
- Piling sand
- Target rich environment
- Chip in the game
- Prime the pump
- Best player plays
- Antenna up
- Yearly rhythm
- Exposure means casualties

MUSTANG Double helix DNA
People and Projects

"Why's" that were learned:

- Energy begets action
- Help others be heroes in their jobs
- Families are important
- Demonstrate trustworthiness
- Esprit takes energy
- Reduced scope is a win-win
- Skids control construction scope

Wants:

- Better project management for large projects
- The ability to get international work
- Better CAD capability to do detailed design
- People's brains turned on
- To do part of the real project in the bid
- To apply the KISS principle everywhere

"Ands" that were learned:

- Pray and work hard
- Ups and downs are constant
- We can do tight and achievable estimates
- Do current work and invest for the future
- Exhilarating and horrible
- Work hard and play hard
- We must do big and small projects

Fast Facts:

- $3,200,000 billed in September 1991
- Billed work to forty clients in 1991
- Have 220 people
- 55,000sq.ft office
- Deepest project 1,030 feet of water (jacket by McDermott)
- Top flowrate 20,000 bpd, oil 100mmscfd gas

MUSTANG

End of 1998-1991
The future is unique from here on...

"Little pigs get fat, big hogs get slaughtered."

**Paul Redmon,
President of Mustang**

PART

PART 3: BUILDING MOMENTUM

MUSTANG **1992-1995**

Repeated success fuels the engine.

Unstoppable... Unique... and Fragile

We thought that by the end of the fourth full year we would have a company that we knew how to run and that would have enough "flywheel effect" to keep going over the rough spots. By then our philosophies on people, projects, business and organization should have been tested and adjusted to create our ongoing formula for staying in business. The lack of structural work from July through September of 1988 and the total shutdown of Gulf work in 1991 made us think harder about trying to keep enough reimbursable work coming in to feed 220 people.

By being willing to chase international work as a subcontractor to vendors or contractors that would sign the risky contracts, we avoided a large layoff in 1991. We also saw that our expertise in figuring out the front end of a project to set it up for success in purchasing and construction was valuable to owners who had to bid their international projects lump sum. A solid front-end design minimized changes and helped the owner control their costs and schedules...generating an earlier revenue stream.

Going forward we needed to expand the number of ways work could find its way to Mustang. Our filters of good clients, good reimbursable contracts and projects that were technically within our capabilities were getting established across a broader range of opportunities. We wanted to find a way to change some of the possible good work to match our filters by getting close to clients and showing them how reimbursable engineering could create a win-win scenario for their project. We needed to get some clients to take a risk on EPCM and then make them HEROES.

33: TEXACO & HYUNDAI

All of the Houston engineering houses were abuzz. Texaco was moving from New Orleans to Houston and we would finally get a chance at their work. We used to say that we had the wrong area code for doing New Orleans work as we lost bid after bid in that city. Proximity, for ease of coordination, was worth a lot in engineering bid evaluations.

Texaco had put a project offshore Angola out for bid and we wanted to get their first job. We knew that they had tight relationships with firms in New Orleans and that if they did not like the Houston market, they could still use those firms. The "Company Plane" called Southwest Airlines made that very possible. Alas, Aker-Omega won the project.

AKER

I called Aker's salesman Greg Rhodes to congratulate him on bringing Texaco to Houston. He wasn't real excited about the win and said that sales had nothing to do with it. Since Aker (a Norwegian firm) had bought Omega (a company like Mustang), they had been unable to win any projects. Clients were not sure if the cultures would work and did not want to risk their projects in an unknown environment. He said that Aker had decided to "buy" a project to get things going. Due to the low manhour rates quoted, they were going to have to hire most of the team "off the streets" and cobble it together.

Wow, this shocked me. I told Greg that we needed to impress Texaco in order to keep their work in Houston. He agreed and was afraid that they were going to let the Houston engineering community down. I asked him to keep his finger on the pulse and let me know if things started to go poorly.

YOU JUST NEVER KNOW

Greg called me in January of 1992 to say that his management team and Texaco were at each other's throats. The Angola project was not progressing, the contract rates were a problem and neither side would back down. He felt that his management might entertain Mustang putting a few good people into the project to help clean up the flow sheets, which were the basis of the design. I told him I thought we could free up Dave Rucker to come over and size things up. Greg knew Dave was a "water walker" for this type of effort and said he would go talk to both parties.

Greg was able to get approval for Mustang to supply some people to come in and "sweep" the design to clean it up. It was a compromise both parties could agree to doing. Dave went over and after two days requested that we give him Keith Mitchell and two others to help. Now we had two top project managers plus two other engineers plugged into the Aker-Omega 50 person team. We sent them in with instructions to support Aker-Omega, get things cleaned up and back on track. Act like you are Aker-Omega employees and come back in six weeks.

After two and a half weeks the four people had turned everything around and essentially were de-facto in charge of the project, even though they did not have those positions. They just had all the answers so everything started to move through them. Upper management at Aker-Omega saw what was happening and breathed a collective sigh of relief.

Aker had bought Omega in order to get into the Houston market because that is where key decisions were being made for worldwide projects. Aker wanted to get in on the front end of floating production systems so they could supply the hull that was required. Facilities design of production equipment to produce the oil and gas were more of a nuisance in their strategy. The Texaco project was tying up their management team that needed to be chasing hulls to supply their fabrication yard in Norway.

Instead of being hacked off at Mustang, Aker was pleased that we had now provided them a way out of their predicament. The Texaco and Aker-Omega management people would at this point not even want to be in the same room due to their conflicts. Dave and Greg worked as intermediaries to get a break point agreed to, and the project was moved to Mustang. We used an Evergreen Contract we had set up with Texaco when they first moved to Houston. We had a reimbursable contract we liked and now we could insure Texaco was well taken care of on their Angolan work...in HOUSTON!

THERE IS ONLY ONE GOOD PROJECT MANAGER

Part way through the project, Texaco needed to start another project and they wanted Dave to run it. We told them that we wanted to put Ralph Kinley on it for better control. They were very happy with Dave and felt another project manager would be a step down. We asked them to trust us and if they were not satisfied in three weeks we would roll the job under Dave. Both projects grew significantly and each of the Texaco project managers felt they had the best project manager at Mustang.

Trust in our staffing ability was crucial as Texaco then became very busy. Keith Mitchell was next to pick up a project and then Dick Westbrook. Each time we had to convince them we were putting the right team together for that specific project. Redmon was the master at staffing and finally they would just ask Paul to pick the team. All projects were very successful and the business relationship was close to nirvana.

CONTRACT CONCERNS

We liked the large international projects Texaco gave us, but contracting became an issue. Each time they awarded us a project they squeezed a different piece of our rate schedule with the understanding that they were not bidding on the open market. We had not felt this squeezing on projects. They bid and put quality equipment and materials into their projects and paid our invoices on time. This squeezing of rates for each project, however, was to the point where we would rather bid and get a higher rate!!

I went to the Texaco manager of projects, and explained how our numbers had been squeezed across time. Then I showed him where the numbers were on projects we had just won for other clients through competitive bids.

He told me that he looked at this contract as being sort of like buying a used car. You keep pushing on the price until the screams get too loud and then you figure that you have the best price you can get. Since he was planning to award us a major project without bid and I was in there pushing back so hard, he felt that he must have reached the right price point.

> **"Relationships stay strongest if market forces are kept in play."**

That was a good business lesson for us on how relationships stay strongest if market forces are kept in play. Both sides would know that they are getting value out of the relationship. We saw that we had to manage the client's perception of value in order to hold our rates.

Our relationship stood the test of time and we worked for Texaco offshore Myanmar and Indonesia all from the Houston office.

HYUNDAI HEAVY INDUSTRIES MEETS MUSTANG

Technical Test

Solar Turbines had won the job of providing a large turbine compression module for India's Neelam field through Hyundai and hired us to do the engineering and procurement for them. Although Solar had a lump sum contract, they contracted with us on a reimbursable basis. Hyundai had a huge ship building and fabrication yard in Korea and took on lump sum turnkey projects around the world to feed the yard. They put people in our offices and brought in technical experts for a design review. Our process, mechanical, instrument and electrical work was praised, but they wanted another meeting on structural. They had not anticipated the module weighing so much when they had bid the platform and wanted a closer look.

We worked for an hour going over equipment weights and structural calculations in detail. At times the Koreans would huddle to discuss things in Korean and it did not seem like we were satisfying them. We decided to try moving forward and flipped to the next drawing which showed a side elevation view of the module. One of the Korean experts said "Oh, it is two levels! The weight is fine." This exercise boosted our engineering capability in Hyundai's eyes.

Build the relationship

Hyundai came to us two months later with a large offshore platform they had won. They wanted us to do the detailed design and assist with project management like we were doing on Neelam. As we were working through the drawings and specifications in my office, everything was looking good until Paul dug into the instrumentation and controls system.

This platform was highly specified for a complete offshore automation system that would allow the platform to be operated and monitored from an onshore base. Paul did a quick estimate and felt we would need eight instrument and six controls systems engineers at the peak, which would be about four months from now. These were the hardest people to find in Houston and Paul knew that he would not be able to staff that portion of the work. We could do everything but this instrument and control system portion in the time frame they wanted.

We had a long discussion with the Hyundai team about who we would recommend they use in Houston in order to not get into trouble with the design. We made some good friends through this meeting, especially with their USA sales representative. Hyundai appreciated our being honest with them. We were also able to talk with them about our need for reimbursable contracts and that Solar had worked with us that way on the Neelam project.

Neelam platform.

> **"Build a better mousetrap."**
> **Ralph Waldo Emerson, Essayist**

34: AIR PRODUCTS, WEPCO & ADCO

Air Products spent three days touring three fabrication yards in Louisiana and Texas discussing their need to modularize a helium plant for Algeria. Each yard told them that they should talk to Mustang Engineering about modularization, due to what they had seen from our Maraven work. Air Products called me from Corpus Christi and said they had a four hour layover in Houston on their way back to Pennsylvania...could they talk to us about modularization? Modules are essentially very large skids that are multiple stories tall...right in our sweet spot.

MODULES 'R US

Ralph Kinley and I met with them to discuss modularization. Air Products had what we called a "stick built" design group. This meant that their designs were built piece at a time in the field. We had seen stick built firms try to modularize refineries with very costly mistakes requiring things to be taken apart and rebuilt in the field. Ralph was a master at both types of design and could ask them questions that made it obvious they would have troubles with this project.

They left feeling that they had found a flaw in their execution strategy in that they were not module experts and their people did not communicate well enough to design modules without errors. They were thinking that they should have us do the design for them.

It turned out that their engineering group was slow and needed work. We sent a team into their office to line out the modules and help them with coordination. Our head of construction, Mike Hunt, helped them immeasurably with logistics planning and field coordination of the module fabrication.

OUR NICHE

Our skid expertise on small offshore projects developed as a way to control costs offshore. We had become experts at skids and developed an organization that lived with them every day. We had grown from single level skids in the 5-30 ton range to six story modules as big as buildings that weighed 100-400 tons. We were finding that this modularization concept generated cost, schedule and safety savings while delivering a superior facility both offshore and onshore in remote areas. What seemed like business as usual to us was an expertise niche with application worldwide.

WEPCO

We had a good relationship with Allen Tank, an equipment manufacturer owned by Vince Cueves, Gil Weisberger and Walt Hampton. They introduced us to their agent in Egypt, named Tarek Marei, with whom they had worked for a long time. We had met a number of agents over the years and pretty much steered away because they wanted retainers. It was hard to keep track of what they would be doing for your investment.

Tarek was different in that he would go to work and get paid based on finding the right types of projects and winning them. The fact that each of us had a healthy relationship with Allen Tank created a good trust foundation.

Tarek found an opportunity for us to bid engineering of a 15,000 barrel per day oil facility in the Western Desert of Egypt. Our oil experience and modular skidding capability moved us to the short list for WEPCO...Phillips Oil Company in Egypt. After interviews we ended up winning this project over a team from Fluor. Fluor was a huge international player, so we were getting some people's attention on the world market.

Modularized facility in the Western Desert of Egypt for WEPCO.

The WEPCO project allowed us to develop onshore specifications on a project. We also were involved in international bidding and award of the equipment. The bidding effort introduced us to many more equipment and construction companies, which could see our capabilities... more potential clients! The project went well and helped load our spring of 1992.

ADCO

Things were looking slow in the summer of 1992 as we looked toward fall...gotta love that roller coaster ride! A fabricator named Baker Mo approached us with a bid possibility in Abu Dhabi for the National Oil Company, ADCO. They had done work for ADCO before and felt they had a good chance at a lump sum turnkey project that would involve building skids for a remote facility. We felt it was somewhat of a long shot but had nothing else concrete that we were chasing.

The bid package was very incomplete and would require a lot of engineering to enable Baker Mo to price everything from materials to logistics. In order to minimize our investment, Paul took this bid effort on himself, with a small team.

Instead of doing expensive drawings, Paul's team did sketches of everything to enough detail for Baker Mo to do material takeoffs. The more detail we could produce, the lower the contingency Baker Mo would have to put into their bid and thus the more competitive they would be.

Bidders would have to do about 30% of the engineering in order to put in a tight bid. From talking to Baker Mo, it sounded as if bidders would only do about 6% of the engineering and then use factors and contingency to get to their bid price. They would only invest more engineering dollars to answer bid clarifications if it looked like their bid was in contention.

We learned more about lump sum bidding over the next six months as Baker Mo received clarification after clarification request. Since Baker Mo had heard they were in contention, they wanted to work the clarifications in detail. It turned out that every clarification started with more work by the engineer. Once we were in this game, we could not back out as Baker Mo was totally dependent on our helping them clarify each issue.

Baker Mo project in Abu Dhabi for ADCO.

ADCO awarded the project in early 1993 and we took it all the way through startup. In order to meet an aggressive schedule and earn Baker Mo some bonus dollars, we flew some of the equipment to Egypt on a Russian Antanov-124 super cargo plane.

On the ADCO project we learned how different construction methods were used in countries where labor was cheap and equipment not readily available. We knew that going forward we needed to get better local knowledge if our front end estimates and design decisions were going to be accurate internationally.

DIFFERENTIATE

We wanted the diversity of chasing and getting international work in order to give our workforce more stability. At the same time, we wanted to create a value proposition in this type of work that would set us apart.

> **"Engineering could help a contractor execute profitably."**

As owners our brains were turned on to find a way to differentiate and create an international market for our services. Engineering was a small part of a lump sum bid, but engineering could help a contractor execute profitably. We knew that our good front end engineering design methods could create repeatable quality projects for clients whether they were contractors or oil companies. Repeatable success was a better mousetrap to these clients that typically saw every third or fifth project have horrible benchmarks.

A better mousetrap.

Complexity provides opportunity through simplification.

35: MOBIL PRODUCING NIGERIA

We had our first Offshore Technology Conference (OTC) booth in May of 1992 and met a number of international players. Dennis LeFleur was the salesman for Unifab, a fabricator in Louisiana that we worked with on Maraven. He introduced us to Toyin Akomolafe at the show. Toyin owned a company called Index Brook that did small engineering projects in Nigeria. He had helped Unifab bid and win work for the Nigerian National Petroleum Corporation (NNPC).

Toyin took Paul and me over to the Nigeria booth at the show and introduced us to a number of key players in NNPC and Mobil Producing Nigeria (MPN). It was obvious to us that he had a long term relationship with everyone we met and knew how their bid and award systems worked.

NNPC

First bid to MPN

Five months after the OTC, Toyin picked up a bid package from MPN to do the front end design on the Edop compression platform for offshore Nigeria. For years NNPC had been producing large quantities of oil and flaring (burning) the natural gas as a by-product they could not use. NNPC had been coming under international pressure to stop flaring the natural gas and save it for the future when it might be pipelined to shore. NNPC had passed this international mandate on to MPN, requiring them to start extinguishing their flares. This project would extinguish the 100 million standard cubic feet per day flare at Edop.

We toed the line on this bid and gave them pretty much everything they wanted. We added about 30% to our budgets because we had not worked with Mobil or MPN before.

We did one innovative thing in our bid to hopefully differentiate us. We included a proposed table of contents for the lump sum bid package that would result from our work along with examples of the final product we would create for each section. We felt it was important to show the level of detail we thought was necessary in each type of document, as this clarified what our manhour budgets were based upon.

Who is Mustang?

Our sample products prevented MPN from throwing our bid out for being too low and therefore not understanding the requirements. MPN sent a team over to interview this "Mustang" they had not heard of, to see if we could really do the work required. We were awarded the project with the level of detail we had proposed. We had been bidding against Fluor. They had done the last three projects at four times our estimated bid cost, which was why MPN checked us out so thoroughly.

Contract

Felix had a tough time re-working the MPN contract as it was written for a construction contractor. In the past, all front end work had been done by construction contractors (e.g. Fluor, Bechtel, Brown & Root, etc.) who would then bid for the full lump sum EPCI project. If they won, then the contract was good for the full scope. The "teeth" in the contract, however, were horrible for a reimbursable engineering contractor. MPN and NNPC finally decided to re-write the contract per samples we gave them...unheard of in the Nigerian market!

COST EFFECTIVENESS PROGRAM

We started our cost effectiveness program on Edop. Each week I would ask everyone on the project for ideas that could save cost or schedule. We had a very experienced team and generated quite a list. We were essentially cross-fertilizing ideas from other oil companies and engineering firms into this project by turning our people on to the possibility of showing our client a better way. The savings totaled to over half of our engineering fee. This demonstrated that we had our brains turned on for the client. It also created a nice "black & white" sales reason to choose Mustang.

MPN KNOWS NIGERIA

Nigeria would be my first trip outside of the United States other than across the borders into Canada or Mexico. Most of the people at Mustang at that time felt that Louisiana was a foreign country and had not ventured that far from home!

When we arrived in Lagos, I was following Jack Sirman of MPN down the escalator. Suddenly people in front of him started falling down and I yelled "look out" as I jumped over the side. Jack was knocked down, while others behind me turned and ran up the escalator. There was not enough room between the bottom of the escalator and passport control for all the passengers from a full Boeing 767 aircraft. Normally the escalator is turned off and is just used as a stair, but some-times it is mistakenly...perhaps mischievously...turned on. ☺

Our bus from the airport to the MPN compound had a se-curity escort front and rear. We were now in the MPN security system and were told to stay in it while in Nigeria.

36: BOUYGUES

We sent the detailed process flow sheets to Nigeria two weeks before we would arrive for a week long review with operations. They would have time for a detailed review before we came and we would get what they really needed out of their heads. The reception we received was phenomenal because in the past they would receive incomplete flow sheets when the engineering firm arrived and they could not review in detail during the meetings. They were very helpful in lining us out to give them a good compression platform.

NEW POSSIBILITIES

In these meetings we were also able to reduce scope, which always helps ensure project success in cost and schedule. We showed MPN ways we had of getting the information nailed down with fewer documents. This was critical in the front end work because things keep changing.

Due to the cooperation of the in-house MPN team, we were able to meet every milestone in the schedule with top quality products. We issued the 15 volume lump sum bid document on time and received permission to bid on the detailed design with any of the bidders that wanted to use us.

This was a huge development we had not considered...bid as a subcontractor to the construction bidders after doing the front end engineering design (FEED). Due to our knowledge from preparing the documents we could bring a lot of value to the bidders.

> Bid as a sub-contractor to the construction bidders after doing the FEED.

We negotiated with the bidders to supply our engineering bid for free, but to charge them at a reduced rate for their bid support requirements. This was a win-win-win for MPN, Mustang and the bidders that chose to work with us. The bids should be better because of the jump-start Mustang's detailed knowledge would give the bidders. The bidders had a more level playing field as none of the competitors had been involved in the front end work. Mustang would get the chance to follow the project through detailed design, construction and startup...great for feedback and learning.

ADDITIONAL WORK

Edop 250,000bopd platform with 100mmscfd flare.

We still had funds left in our budget. MPN decided to keep us working on an increased scope. We did the detailed design of the modifications required to the existing Edop platforms. This kept MPN and a smaller Mustang team working together and available to answer bidder questions.

We provided bid support to Bouygues out of Paris, France. Bouygues had done many projects for MPN and had all the capability required for this complex combination of new platforms and modifications to old platforms.

The five bids came in very close to each other, meaning that the bid document was very clear and did not require a lot of contingency. The bids were also lower than MPN had expected. These results were far better than their past construction bids and they gave a lot of credit to Mustang in talks with NNPC.

BID SUPPORT

By being the FEED engineer and having a separate team help Bouygues do their detailed bid, we learned about things we could do better.

Bidders did their own engineering verification of the design as part of the effort to develop their material estimates. It wasn't until this verification was complete that their purchasing people were given documents to get pricing for equipment. Two thirds of the bid time was used up in verification and the equipment pricing could not be worked very hard resulting in a large contingency.

Two bidders wanted to bid a "float- over" installation technique instead of using a lift barge that had to be relocated from the North Sea or the Gulf of Mexico. Float-over was a new technique that required different leg spacing in the deck than we had. The savings could be significant either by using the concept or the threat of it being available and forcing the lift barge people to reduce their cost. Since the deck had been through a complete hazards analysis during the FEED, we could not allow a float-over bid.

STAGED TRANSFER

Bouygues won Edop and gave us a reimbursable contract. We worked an execution plan where we completed the structural design in Houston ready for construction. Mechanical engineering went through equipment award in Houston and then to Paris for vendor data review and expediting. Primary piping, electrical and instrument design was completed in Houston and then transferred to Paris with some of our people for detailing. This staged transfer of design kept things from changing, which helped Bouygues make their budgets.

EKPE

New Team

A few months after the Edop construction award we were called by MPN to check our interest in doing their Ekpe gas compression platform. MPN had been admonished by NNPC because their cost for managing the Edop FEED work had been as much as Mustang's cost for doing the work. In an unheard of move, NNPC had agreed to MPN awarding Ekpe to Mustang without bid if MPN would reduce their costs. MPN sent a totally new team to our offices to develop the scope of work for Ekpe. This time however, they had a good feel for Mustang and reduced their staff from 23 to 4.

Incorporate Lessons Learned

For Ekpe we provided equipment bid packages in the bid document. The bidder's purchasing departments were able to start bidding equipment in the first week. This allowed the bidder to narrow the contingency in their bid.

We designed the deck with two possible leg locations...narrow for lifting into place and wide for a floatover installation. This helped "boil the fat" out of the lift bids for NNPC and the floatover installation method ended up winning the contract!

A float-over deck being installed.

Create short communication loops.

37: AGIP, CHEVRON, TEXACO

International bids could become very complex as bidders worked to differentiate themselves from their competitors. Sembawang was a large construction company in Singapore that was bidding lump sum on an offshore project in the South China Sea for the Chinese National Oil Company (CNOOC) and ACT. Agip (Italian Oil Company), Chevron and Texaco (ACT) were the partners that had issued the bid for two 50,000 barrels of oil per day platforms with quarters buildings and captive drilling rigs. This was a huge project that would tie in to four other platforms in the area.

SEMBAWANG

Teaming up

For added strength in their bid, Sembawang subcontracted the basic engineering and procurement to Kvaerner from Oslo, Norway. Knowing that the ACT players would be heavily involved in the basic engineering, Kvaerner subcontracted the project to Kvaerner Earl & Wright in Houston. Kvaerner had bought Earl & Wright a few years earlier in order to have a Houston presence. In looking at the scope of work, Kvaerner Earl & Wright decided to subcontract the deck and facilities design to Mustang due to our large oil platform and current Texaco international experience.

We had a full team engineering and bidding out all of the equipment components in a short time frame. We had to allow time for everything to come together at Sembawang's offices for final pricing and bid submittal. It took three months to prepare the bid and six months for clarifications. This was a long shot project, but we had been paid for our effort.

Move to Mustang

Sembawang won the project and moved a team to Houston. We had a weeklong set of kickoff meetings with top people from eight international companies. Part of the kickoff meeting agenda was to work communications.

It became obvious that the bulk of the decisions that would need input would be concerning the deck, facilities, quarters building and drilling rigs. Since this scope was with Mustang, the decision was made to house the ACT personnel and Sembawang purchasing team at Mustang.

After a few weeks of trying to work decisions through Kvaerner and Sembawang it was decided to let Mustang work directly with ACT to get the basic engineering and procurement completed. Here we were with a reimbursable contract under a lump sum contractor and de-facto in charge of setting up a billion dollar project for success...couldn't be better!!

ACT decks being transported from Sembawang's fabrication yard. Note that the quarters buildings and cranes are already installed to save offshore hookup time.

Staged Transfer

We developed soft break points to move the project in stages to Sembawang's fabrication yard. First we moved structural along with some of our people in order to keep the design progressing without major change. There was a lot of set up required to get detailed design rolling in Sembawang's offices, so the piping, electrical and instrument folks delayed a little longer before moving. Sort of like in a relay race, if the next person isn't jogging and ready for the handoff then time will be lost. The last piece we moved was all of the purchase orders for equipment.

> "Like a relay race, if the next person isn't jogging and ready for the handoff then time will be lost."

INTERNATIONAL STRATEGY

Our ability to work with U.S. based oil companies to get decisions and efficiently put those decisions into drawings and specifications for contractors to bid and build from, without major changes, was a differentiator.

FEEDs were a significant size project for us and we put our best people on them to nail the scope of work for the client. Construction bidders did FEED as a "loss leader" to get close to the client. Their best people were put on construction bids they had won, where their profit was at stake. We could differentiate ourselves.

We found that we did not have to take on additional risk if we found the right clients, projects and situations where our execution strategies could not be beat.

"Good things happen when you make sales calls."
Jim Vogt, Mustang Sales

38: BROOKLYN UNION & PETROBRAS

Taking a lead from a vendor, I cold called Ross Frazier with Brooklyn Union...a small Independent Oil Company...our perfect type of client. I told him that I wanted to meet him to discuss how Mustang might help him on some upcoming offshore projects. He then took over the conversation for a few minutes to tell me that he knew all about Mustang. He felt that we had been taking advantage of clients with our reimbursable engineering hype and lack of focus on delivering cost and schedule to clients. He did not feel that we had anything in common with the way Brooklyn Union planned to approach projects and he would appreciate it if we would not call him again. Wow, I was stunned by the turn this cold call had taken...to frigid... and went to see Paul.

Wonder Why?

I told Paul that I had just been totally blown off by the principal project guy at Brooklyn Union and wondered if he knew of any possible reason. I recapped the conversation and Paul was also astonished. Paul was super-wired into the industry and could not fathom why Brooklyn Union felt this way. I told Paul that this was not the end...that I was going to find a way to get in front of Ross eventually, even if we never worked for him.

The next week I was called by a fabricator in New Iberia, Louisiana and asked if I could come over for a meeting to discuss chasing an offshore platform. I said sure and the meeting was set for Saturday morning in their offices...obviously a hot prospect. I drove over Friday night in order to be fresh for the morning meeting.

We got down to business Saturday morning with the contractor starting to show me the probable size of the platform and flow rate when the client walked in. They introduced me to Ross Frazier of Brooklyn Union and I immediately wondered how this meeting is going to go. Ross never brought up the conversation from 10 days prior and I certainly never did!! We met for two hours and Ross awarded the project to the fabricator and Mustang right there on the spot.

Celebrate

Winning this small project in the Gulf seemed like the most exciting thing in sales since Jim Grinnan gave us that first full project in 1988. Monday morning after telling the news to Paul and Felix, I said we needed to celebrate. We went down to the front of the building where we had our picture taken jumping off a small wall in our "Oh what a feeling" moment!

Every phone call can change your world!
Paul, Felix and Bill

UNPREDICTABLE

Probably what I liked most about sales was what Paul liked least...the unpredictable nature of what might pop up, and figuring out how to respond. Paul liked best to work on things that were real, while I had no problem investing some energy trying to nurture something along until it became real or died. This gave us a great one-two punch when I found something worth progressing.

STEVE PYLES

Steve Pyles called one day and asked if we were part of the Mustang Engineering he had worked with in California. We were not, but I did not answer his question directly, wanting to find out more before answering. I asked if he needed help on a hydrocarbon related project, which was about as open ended a question as I could come up with on the spur of the moment. He was with Sun Exploration and they were opening an office in Houston to pursue offshore Gulf work. He had found our name in the Yellow Pages. I came clean and explained that we were not part of the California based Mustang Engineering, but that we were the perfect choice to help him with offshore production.

This started a relationship that is still going strong. We set Steve up with an office at Mustang, bought some golf pictures and some artificial plants to make it feel homey, since he would be in from out of town, and we started doing his work offshore and onshore. We followed him as his company changed names to Oryx and when it moved into deepwater... all from a phone call!

CON STEERS

Con Steers, of IMC, called me one day from Rio de Janeiro, Brazil to say that he had canvassed Houston looking for the right engineering firm for an offshore project to be done with IVI Shipyards in Brazil. He was a Canadian with a banking background and said he needed an American company to make a deepwater Floating, Production, Storage and Offloading, FPSO, project viable. The shipyard would supply the tanker, while Mustang would supply all of the topsides production equipment. The project would be for Petrobras, the large state owned oil company of Brazil, and just needed financing of the Mustang part. He assured me that we could qualify for Export-Import, EXIM, Bank financing from the U.S. Government to the tune of $80,000,000 for the project. If approved, it would be the largest amount outside of the aircraft industry ever done.

Typical large FPSO leaving a shipyard.
Production equipment is gray.

I listened to all of this and Con sounded like he knew what he was talking about. Our scope would be to design all of the equipment into skids, bid fabrication in the U.S., inspect and expedite the skids to an international packing and shipping terminal. This was all great and matched our capability perfectly. But then I told him this sounded a little far out...and that his first name being "Con" also raised questions...to which he laughed. He was coming to Houston the next week and we arranged to meet. Three months later we were doing the job and bringing some nice skid fabrication work to the Gulf fabrication yards. The EXIM Bank paperwork drove Felix crazy, but it was a profitable eight million dollar engineering and purchasing project for Mustang and used a lot of our capability.

COMPUTER IS A LEVELER

Con took me to a small engineering firm in Rio to see if we could work together and have more local content on future work for Petrobras. This was in 1995 and I saw something that was both scary and challenging. The designers were using the same computer programs we were using. The quality of their product would look exactly like the quality of ours. Programmers at the software companies were making it easier to "clash-check" piping interfering with steel supports and doing dimensional checks. Engineers were loading components of designs into the software and vendors were loading their designs to make it easier and more accurate for any designer to create a great final design.

Paul, Felix and I had heard about the large international engineering houses using low cost engineering centers, but this was the first time that I had been behind the door to see what could be produced...very interesting!

Having professionals can change the game.

39: ASHLAND OIL

Due to our bigger footprint in the industry and my being on projects, we were getting some weird pressure from our clients. They were pushing me to visit with them regularly. I had a habit of showing up when there was work, getting it, and then handing it off to operations. My network was good and I wasn't the kind of person to just go by for a visit...I always felt like I needed a reason to call on a client.

INFORMATION

Clients wanted to know what was going on at Mustang so they could continually access our capabilities. The visits were all about information flow as they knew we worked on a lot of projects for a wide range of clients. They knew that our view of the industry was different than our competitors and they wanted that input. They wanted my take on the pulse of the industry. They needed input on fabricator work load, where good people were moving to and what new things were being done technically. Felix, Paul and I agreed that I needed to hire a salesman to help cover the 50+ upstream clients.

JIM VOGT

Dick Westbrook asked me to interview his friend Jim Vogt. Jim had been let go from an engineering and construction company where he had been in charge of sales. I interviewed Jim and explained that I needed a good salesperson to touch base regularly with 50-70 clients.

MARY NEEDHAM

I wanted to make an offer to Jim but he had a contract with Reserve Technology Inc. owned by Mary Needham. I called Mary to negotiate her fee because Dick had actually found the job for Jim. Mary sounded very professional on the phone and requested a face-to-face meeting in order to learn more about Mustang.

Mary and I had a good meeting primarily to discuss Mustang's history, where we were at present and possible future steps. She couldn't believe that we were at 250 people with just me part time in sales... but could fully understand our maniacal focus on keeping overhead low in a capricious industry. She felt that our total focus on "quality out the door" would bring its own growth. She also felt that the right sales people could help us identify more projects to choose from, since we wanted reimbursable work from clients that valued engineering and paid their bills. She knew we were limiting our possible client slate but could understand why.

> "We wanted reimbursable work from clients that valued engineering and paid their bills."

When Mary asked about our strategic direction, I really had to think, since we never felt that we could push a direction, but rather would go where the industry pulled us. I told her that we had followed vendors, contractors and clients into international work...some of it for major oil companies. I told her that offshore projects in the Gulf were moving into deeper waters and we wanted to be part of that. I told her about my hiring a sales person for the downstream refinery and petrochemical market that did not work out, but that this seemed like work we should be able to do.

Mary then summed up our conversation with a strategic twist. She said that she felt Jim was the right person for Mustang at this stage of our growth. He had the experience and maturity to help position Mustang better in the industry. Having someone 100% focused on upstream sales would also help Paul and me to have more predictable sales...a term Paul and I had been discussing for some time. She felt that strategically it sounded like we wanted to work directly for the major oil companies in order to get more stability with larger projects and develop the stronger technical capability required on such projects. The next step strategically would be to move into downstream as a way to broaden our sales base while using the same technical people we already had in upstream.

THIS WAS AMAZING!! I thought I was going to have a discussion about what Mary wanted to charge me for representing Jim and here I was having the first real strategic discussion about Mustang since my first meetings with Paul and Felix from 1985 to 1987.

Mary amended her price on Jim since she did not find the Mustang job, recommended to him that he come to Mustang and asked to stay in touch.

MARY NEEDHAM...DENNIS FRAKES

About a year later I met with Mary to ask for a sales person to penetrate the major oil companies. We had worked for a few majors directly and for many as subcontractors to construction firms. She recommended and we hired, Dennis Frakes whom I had met about 10 months earlier while chasing a job with Parsons, a large international engineering and construction firm out of California.

RELATIONSHIP SALES

Jim and Dennis had engineering and project backgrounds but had moved out of doing any day-to-day engineering activities. They worked to develop a relationship with the client and from that relationship ensure we would be treated fairly in the bid and award of projects.

Things were getting tight in 1994 and there was a project coming up with Ashland Oil that Paul wanted. I tasked Dennis with making sure we won this job as it would help us keep some key people during this downturn. Paul pulled out all the technical wizardry he could muster to put us in position to win the job.

Part way through the bid evaluation Paul heard rumors that the project was going to Aker- Omega and he wanted to know why. We needed a meeting with Ashland's management to clarify our bid. I asked Dennis to try and set up the meeting although communication at this stage of a bid was very limited and controlled. Dennis was able to use his relationship with the project manager to get us an audience with the entire Ashland management team. Our better solution won the project and we did a number of projects in a row for Ashland.

I knew that I could not have invested the time Dennis had in developing the relationship required to set up that meeting. Dennis did not have to understand the project solution, did not have to schedule the project or work any of the details like I did. He developed relationships and put technical people in position to win. This was very different from what I had learned to do and was very effective.

We truly had professionals in Jim and Dennis. We needed to understand them and learn how to support them in order to take our story directly to the major oil companies.

"All problems are communication problems."
Dennis Frakes, Mustang Sales

40: COMMUNICATION IS CRUCIAL

When I was at CBS Engineering and working in sales for those six months, I just tried to develop clients and find work to chase. Once I found a possible job, I put on my "project hat" and tried to figure out the best way to do the work while pulling on CBS resources for ideas. It never occurred to me that there was a broader sales challenge that used the same skill sets.

ESTABLISHING THE BRAND

Internal sales

I felt that internal sales activities were a significant part of my job. I wanted to be continually selling Mustangers on the fact that they were in the best job and best company they would ever be in. Quality "people resources" were at a premium in Houston and this was a place where I could help operations by working to reduce turnover. Engineers and drafters could easily move between about 50 companies in Houston. Reducing turnover also helped sales as teams that worked together over multiple projects became more efficient and did a better job, which brought in repeat business.

As part of internal sales, we started having a regular activities meeting to set up budgets and schedules for outside activities like the Shrimp Boil, bowling leagues, roller skating parties, etc. At West Point we called our cheerleaders Rabble Rousers and I used this term with the group to incite them to action. They were going to help me invigorate people from apathy toward putting themselves into making Mustang different. New ideas were hashed out and volunteers took charge of each activity. We issued a 1994 Mustang events list so people could mark their calendars with things to look forward to.

I was still writing the Newsy Newsletter, but I was getting a good flow of material and slowly turning it over to the Rabble Rousers. We were still using the coffee bar to drum up interest, but with better material. People's brains were turned on to create a fun and productive culture. Activities provided free space for people at all levels to interact.

Blimp flies over the shrimp boil.   Mustangers with the Shrimp mascot.

"Young Gun" engineers as Smurfs.™   Mary Budrunas and Ron Smith.

Horse

Everyone thought they could improve on the horse logo and I had to be the enforcer. People would be amazed that I could see if the horse was rotated two degrees...but it was important to me and to Mustang as that logo meant a quality engineering product worldwide. We wanted people to see that blue horse or a construction drawing with a black and white horse on one hoof and immediately think of Mustang.

SUBTLE SALES

Our business cards had in small letters under Mustang Engineering the phrase "A Project Management Company" as a quick description of what we did. Wanting something different, I came up with the phrase "People Oriented...Project Driven™." This phrase would immediately move people into the space we were creating in the industry. It summed up what we were about in terms of trust and loyalty and allowed us to get into the right type of conversations early in meetings.

We sent out calendars toward the end of 1994. They were large 24"x 36" with a big blue Mustang horse lightly in the background and *MUSTANG* across the top. The calendars were laminated and came with a marker ready for project planning. We sent them everywhere, to clients and vendors and they showed up in conference rooms as well as personal offices. We also gave them to all of our people, which was unheard of in the industry. This resulted in there being blue Mustang horses everywhere throughout our offices and conference rooms. Greg Rhodes of Aker-Omega called to tell me it was a little intimidating talking to an Arco client in Dallas with the *BIG BLUE HORSE* staring down from the wall. ☺

For Christmas we gave clients and our people *Life's Little Instruction Book* embossed with the Mustang logo and the owner's signatures...showing our belief in what it was presenting. Sort of like "same sentence sales" early in Mustang's history, this was linking us by association with strong beliefs and moral codes. We also gave out a water timer with a wheel that would spin when turned over, hoping it would go home and take the Mustang horse to the toy box...working the hearts and minds of clients, receptionists, vendors and Mustangers in as many ways as possible.

ADVERTISING

Bob Mahlstedt still worked for us part time, consulting on marketing and advertising. He did our ads and we worked together to pick where we wanted to advertise. We put four small ads in three Pipeline magazines to give our pipeline group a boost. We advertised four times a year in the *The Oil & Gas Journal* (top industry magazine) for credibility and four times in *Offshore Magazine* to demonstrate technical ability in our main area of expertise. We picked specific months in magazines based on their featured topic and created what we called a "Media Calendar." Bob dug into Mustang and tried to understand how we were selling a culture of just-do-it! We were also selling the "experience" of an engineering effort fixated on setting up win-win contracting. Talking with Bob helped us understand better what we were trying to sell and develop ways to express it.

Early Ads

SALES ORGANIZATION

Proposals

We moved a secretary into sales. For the first time, I would not have to beg project secretaries to help me with a proposal! We started doing a sales hit list, so that with minimal effort, Paul and I could keep up with what we were chasing. We created single page project sheets with a picture and delineating our scope and experience on each as fodder for proposals. We started a "goodie file" of things we could re-use in proposals.

I was a perfectionist when it came to proposals because I was trying to move the bid evaluation to a discussion of ideas and execution strategies and away from price. I felt that as the proposal presented the story, the spell could be broken if the reader came upon a spelling error or a page out of place. Then they might start to wonder if our engineering was as sloppy as the proposal effort.

Earn it...don't accept it

Jim came to me with a contract he had developed with an oil company that would guarantee us 85,000 manhours of work a year if we would lower the rates we charged.

This contract scared me to death, because it could allow us to grow "fat" in the organization. A department manager could put someone on the project to "use" the hours without being as productive as we desired Mustang to be. If we let this start, it would end during the next industry downturn when we would find ourselves too fat and sloppy to compete.

I explained that bidding keeps us "lean and mean" and competitive. We liked Services Contracts where we had to scope each project and win based on our effort to define it well, and be innovative in the solution.

41: OPERATIONS STEPS UP BIG TIME

International projects were being done to a new standard called ISO 9000. This standard started in Europe and required a company to document all of its procedures and have them verified. The idea was that the client would be able to reduce their inspection requirements. Bids between certified vendors were also supposed to give the client a comfort factor along with a quality product.

ISO Certification
We did not want to go through the ISO certification process because once you were certified; ALL of your projects had to be documented per the ISO requirements. This documentation effort would render us uncompetitive on our small-to-mid-sized projects, which were critical to our maintaining a high billability rate.

Since Solar was ISO certified and was doing the Neelam project to ISO standards, we asked them to audit our procedures. The audit told us that we fully met the intent of ISO, but with significantly less paperwork and organization due to the quality of communication within the company. From this exercise, operations got a gold star and we decided to stay away from actual ISO certification for as long as possible.

"It bothered us when a client would say that they did not need to expedite or inspect a vendor because they were ISO Certified. In the real world, the squeaky wheel gets the grease."

ARROWS IN THE QUIVER

We worked to get operations to give us "arrows in the quiver" for sales. This was hard because operations people generally do not think about how to help sales until directly confronted with a bid. By having me on projects and some Management by Wandering Around (MBWA from Tom Peters book *In Search of Excellence*) we were able to get good material to use in meetings and presentations to clients. The more communication we had between sales and operations, the better we were at selling and conditioning a client to set the project up for success.

REFERENCE DIRECTORY

Paul set up a Reference Directory of technical talent available in Houston and had the department managers contribute to it as they found great resources. Every talent required for any project worldwide was available in Houston...you just had to be able to tap into them when needed instead of carrying them on your payroll. Paul's list grew to 28 categories of expertise. He had everything from compressor vibration to naval architecture available to draw upon. We did hire some experts direct as the volume of work in a particular area increased.

Unabashedly tapping into the Houston talent pool gave us confidence that we could produce technically sound designs for any upstream project worldwide.

YOU CAN'T EAT PRINCIPLES

We started to bid the White Tiger project in Vietnam with both Bouygues and Hyundai. Then we went exclusive with Hyundai when they offered to pay all of our costs.

The client was a Partnership between Vietnam and Russia. During the bid meeting in Vietnam, we sent the proposed deck design back to Mark Doing in Houston saying that it looked wrong. He sent a sketch of how we would design the deck and said that the deck we had sent to him looked like some railroad bridge trestles laid flat and welded together.

The Russians explained that the deck was made of bridge trestles because they could weld those in Russia and send them by railroad to Vietnam for assembly. Hyundai was then center stage to explain how they could provide supervision and build the deck correctly in Vietnam.

The bid came down to a tussle between Hyundai and Bouygues. Hyundai found out that Bouygues was showing Mustang as an alternate for their engineer. Bouygues people figured that if they won, then we would work for them.

Verbally and in writing, we restated our position as being exclusive with Hyundai to all parties.

After Bouygues was awarded the project, they called to ask us to take on the $5 million reimbursable contract.

We had done what we had set out to do. We had been the desired engineer in a reimbursable contracting mode under two of the strongest contractors in the world on a large international lump sum project. We had to stand on the principles, however, of being trustworthy in the international market. We decided to face letting people go instead of taking on the project.

CYCLICAL INDUSTRY

In 1993 we were going full out on projects with big international jobs as well as medium to small domestic work. We had added people and were at about 250, doing the work of about 350. Then in 1994 everything slowed down in the oil patch and we were scrambling for every little job we could find. Roger Canale had me come back into the drafting room to calm the troops as we hustled for work. We liked being at 250 people because of the mix of projects we could handle and worked like crazy to find work to keep our folks.

We were working hard to achieve "stability through diversity"...onshore, offshore, small, large, pipeline, subsea, Nabisco®, gas storage, specifications for Oxy Oman, Lyondell Chemical, carbon black for Sid Richardson, cold weather, rain forest, remote...

It got so bad toward the end of 1994 that most companies cut out their Christmas parties because they had just gone through a round of layoffs. We had a terrific Christmas party with a sit down meal, white and gold table and chair trimmings, a band and dancing. I remember looking out over the festivities and wondered if this was like Nero fiddling while Rome burned. We had scraped through the year without losing any talent and seemed to be ramping up work going into 1995.

Being a small player gave us the advantage of not needing a lot of work to keep us busy. With the new markets we had opened internationally, there were more opportunities for work even in a global downturn in the oil patch. Since we did not have construction capability, we could live off of pure front end engineering projects that did not proceed into purchasing or construction. Although the environment was bleak, we were actually pretty well positioned to find what we needed to survive. But it wasn't fun.

42: SANTA FE ENERGY

Santa Fe's Energy's Larry Leavell had a problem. His company planned to drill on its first offshore lease in the Gulf and they knew nothing about doing a project in that environment. They were spreading their wings a little, by moving from onshore work to the potentially more lucrative offshore oil fields where the reservoirs and production flowrates were orders of magnitude higher than what they were used to doing onshore. At the same time, Larry had heard the war stories and knew the risks had similar magnitudes. This first project would be a large investment and could materially damage Santa Fe if it went out of control.

LUNCH & LEARN

Many Choices

Larry asked us to organize a few "Lunch & Learns" in his conference room to bring his staff up to speed on doing their first offshore project. We quickly taught them the terminology with pictures and drawings. We reviewed estimating, contracting strategies, schedules and responsibilities of all parties for an offshore project.

Other engineering firms were meeting with Santa Fe in an effort to steer them toward using their proprietary structural concept for this 150 foot water depth project. These firms provided concept drawings and estimates to Larry's team for 20 minimal platform concepts. Larry's team was able to ask good questions due to our luncheons and became much better educated on their options and risks. At the same time, this knowledge created confusion and apprehension about which concept to pick and how to nail down a price.

Industry Game

John Ellis explained the "industry game" they were stepping into. Clients bid with very little data to allow the "market" to give them the right answer. In reality, the bid process turned into a "liar's game" where the bidders would choose their optimal off-the-shelf design to bid.

Clients then evaluated the bids based on the steel tonnage quoted. Since no real site-specific engineering had been done, the tonnages were essentially educated guesses squeezed by the pressures to win the project.

Surprises in weight growth and installation costs materialized after award and the "lump sum" award had to be increased. Lump sum was really only lump sum in the eyes of a neophyte if the project had not been completely engineered before bid. Lump sum was really just a semi-firm "starting price."

MUSTANG CHANGES THE GAME

We suggested and Santa Fe agreed to pay us to get a soil survey at the location and do a $6,000 study. The study would size the piling based on the soil strength, water depth, wave and weight criteria. Our structural engineers could then estimate tonnages, installed costs and risks for the various concepts. These estimates were all done using the same criteria, the same engineers and eliminated the "liar's game." Santa Fe picked a standard tripod. They felt that the 4% increase in steel cost was far outweighed by the minimal risk of cost overrun due to installation offshore.

After startup, they had a surprise when the wells produced 1,800 barrels of condensate per day. They were heroes for selecting a stable platform that could handle the additional equipment needed to process and sell the condensate!

Santa Fe Energy's first offshore deck loaded on the barge.

FIRST POSTER

We offered our expertise to *Offshore Magazine* for preparing a poster on minimal platforms. The sales manager sold ads around the border of the poster and put our blue horse and name on the outfacing fold. Companies in the industry bought the ads because the posters would be on walls everywhere and used in concept selection for shallow water.

This effort put us in the great position of the industry coming to us, reducing sales efforts and having us only talking about real projects to new and old clients. By being in early at the concept development stage we could steer the contracting strategy and bid process to set up a win-win project.

43: SIERRA CHATA

Like Paul Harvey would say...here is the rest of the story concerning Santa Fe Energy and Larry Leavell. He called on a Friday afternoon to say they had purchased their first international prospect and had a meeting scheduled with their partners the following Thursday to get project approval for development. Due to a natural gas sales contract they had signed to insure viability of the field, they had to be operational in 14 months or the contract would revert to an existing supplier. I asked if we could meet him for breakfast Saturday morning and collect all of the information they had. He was excited to hear this response and said he would bring a couple of people that could supply all the data they knew.

SCOPE

FEED

The Sierra Chata field was in a remote area with no infrastructure, two hours outside of Buenos Aires, Argentina. The facility they needed would include flowlines from three groups of wells to a central processing facility with its' own power generation and living facilities. The cleaned natural gas would then be metered for sale and put into an 80 mile pipeline that would run to a tie-in at a bigger pipeline. We needed to do the front end design for this project in less than a week for presentation to the Partners.

For the presentation, we went all out to make Larry a hero. We had a project description with first pass layouts and estimates through startup. We pulled this data together into a Level II schedule based on our execution plan of skids shipped from Houston.

Check the Price

Everything went well in the presentation except the estimated bottom line of $82,000,000 which included a 15% contingency. Contingency was for known unknowns and unknown unknowns. The partners were impressed with the level of detail in all of the deliverables and found no glaring errors. But, they had done a similar flowrate facility in the state of Wyoming, USA for $38,000,000. Larry asked us to verify that our four-day estimate was not 115% high!

We estimated the Wyoming facility in the same manner we had done Sierra Chata. The plusses and minuses resulted in a $52,000,000 estimated price tag for Sierra Chata done in Wyoming. Normalizing construction and logistics between rural Wyoming and a remote area of Argentina, resulted in a $78,000,000 estimated price tag. So the $82,000,000 we had estimated compared favorably.

LET'S DO IT!

Award

Larry went to the partners and asked to award the project to Mustang with a reimbursable contract for design through start-up. He felt that the schedule was too tight and could not afford a six week bid cycle.

Early on I asked the project manager, Rik Williams (an Eagle Scout), why he had helped push for Mustang. He said that in his career he had always tried to do "More than expected...Better than expected" and he had seen that we had a team that met this personal mantra of his. We liked this phrase and started using it at Mustang to help explain our culture.

> "His career mantra was 'More than expected... Better than expected'."

We had some surprises. The site had a 12 foot rock semi-cliff in the middle that would impact our equipment layout. The pipeline route was mainly rock which would be much harder to bury the pipeline in. We learned how difficult it would be to transport our skids and materials from Buenos Aires to the site. The well test showed some hydrogen sulfide, H_2S, requiring equipment and material upgrades. With this information we revised our estimates to use some of the contingency and started detailed design.

Results
The remote area, difficulty of the terrain, level of construction talent and equipment blew up some of our budget and schedule. Through super-human efforts we were able to get the plant started up three weeks before the contract deadline and at a cost of $78,000,000.

A few years later I was in Larry Leavell's office and saw an unbelievable picture of the Sierra Chata plant that was taken as the sun was going down. It looked like the "city of gold" was in the Sierra Chata.

Sierra Chata plant.

"Growth results from quality."
Bill Higgs, V.P. Mustang

44: "INC. 500"

Since we had been placing well in the Houston 100 for fast-est growing companies, based on three year periods of growth, I filled out the paperwork to see how we might fare in the American market. The Houston 100 recognition did not seem to do anything for our business, but it did give us another positive thing to talk about with our people. If we could place in the Inc. "500", which was based on five year growth, it would show we were experiencing something special. In addition to reflecting well on our people, I felt that I could also spin the award positively to clients.

REMARKABLE GROWTH

Too Fast?

Many clients were concerned that we were growing too fast and started looking for cracks in our project execution. Clients felt that they needed to coach us on the business to help make sure we stayed viable for their projects. They had seen very good companies build up and then disappear.

We worked to equate growth with quality throughout the Mustang experience to our clients.

Lists

We were on a number of lists. We made the Engineering News Record list of the top 500 Engineering firms as determined by revenue volume. We were in the top ten of the list for both Offshore Upstream and Pipeline. We liked seeing the names of the "company we were keeping" on these lists because they had been the "who's who" in these fields since we had started our careers.

HOUSTON'S GROWTH LEADERS

Eight of the 10 fastest growing private firms are service companies. To qualify for the list firms had to have 1987 sales between $75,000 and $25 million.

Company	Product or Service	% Increase from 1987 to '89
1. Veragon Corporation	Manufacture Drypers - disposable diapers	5,664%
2. Adminstaff Inc	Employee leasing	1,759
3. Space Industries International, Inc.	Space design engineering, manufacturing	1,702
4. Mustang Engineering, Inc	Engineering design for oil and gas industry	1,658
5. Robert Lamons & Associates	Commercial Advertising	1,456
6. Collections Unlimited, Inc	Accounts receivable management	1,538
7. Douglas Harding Group	Graphic design services	1,037
8. PKS Special Supplies	Aluminum construction elements	1,031
9. Business Systems Group	Network computing systems integration services	965
10. MEP Group	Design engineering & construction management	873

Source: University of Houston Small Business Development Center

Houston 100 fastest growing companies for four years straight.

The coolest list seemed to be making the Inc. 500 List of America's Fastest Growing Companies for the five year period of 1987-1991. We placed 42nd on the list and were the number one company for engineering. Software and computer companies were primarily the fastest growing companies at that time. Wall Street called us to see if the oil patch was rebounding!

We also made the Inc. 500 in 1993 which was more real because the partial first year of revenue had been dropped. We moved down into the 270 range on the list, but it was clear that we had experienced remarkable growth, far above the national average. In many ways the ride was killing us, but it was exhilarating at the same time.

MANAGE MUSTANG LIKE A PROJECT?

Staffing Schedules

In 1994 we developed and started using a simple Gantt bar chart method to track our people resources. Project managers were required to review schedules and notify the department managers if they were going to need more or less resources. Project staffing was always in a constant state of flux because we did not want to let resources "sit" on a project waiting on client decisions or vendor data.

> **"We did not want to let resources 'sit' on a project waiting on client decisions or vendor data."**

We envisioned the personnel schedules as a way to codify our intentions and provide a weekly method for re-aligning resources. The schedule did ease tension for the department managers by giving them an indication of whether they needed to be increasing or decreasing resources.

Rubber ball Management

It took four sweeps and startups over a one year period to get the discipline of updating schedules. We were learning how to move away from rubber ball management, where you give someone a task and it bounces right back to you. From this experience Paul and I felt that anything we wanted to have as a habit needed to be done weekly for six to eight weeks with one of us directly involved and a champion who had the task as a critical part of their job.

PERSONAL TIME MANAGEMENT

One day I received junk mail from Planner Pad, Inc™. I reviewed their system of having a full year in a spiral bound book ½" thick. Across the top were seven columns for weekly lists of activities by categories; perfect for someone wearing many hats. The middle section of the pages had the days of the week with dates and space to list daily things to do. The bottom section had time slots by day for appointments from 7am to 8pm. The far right column had space for notes and calls, expenses and small calendars showing the previous month, this month and the next month.

I bought one and started using it in 1991. From 1991 to 1993 my Planner Pads™ had many blank weeks, sometimes for a whole month as I worked to train myself into the habit of using it correctly. By 1994 and 1995 I was an expert and could manage a lot of tasks. Whenever I fell off in the upkeep of the Planner Pad™ I could feel my performance slipping. Things were so crazy in 1995 that the Planner Pad™ really got used and I became a big believer in Sunday evening planning for the week and daily revisions to the plan each morning.

Actual Planner Pad used by Bill Higgs circa 1997.

MUSTANG BECAME A BIG PROJECT TEAM

We were close to the top in our field for managing project teams to deliver benchmarked best-in-class projects by 1995. We knew how to build these teams with no "fat." They had great communication internally and externally, and were fluid enough to react to the continuous changes inherent in the offshore oil & gas development market. We took that capability and worked hard to build Mustang as a big project team using the winning formula we had been developing on projects.

TEAMBUILDING

We did a number of activities on project teams to weld them into a unit. We did everything from offsite games with planning sessions to in-house bridge building competitions to having clients like Tom Hall of Mobil wear crazy hats to monthly reporting meetings. Anything we could think of to get people comfortable with each other top to bottom and in a manner where if there was any problem, there would be no barriers to bringing the matter up. We provided free space to develop communication and relationships. This project teambuilding lined up well with the activities Mustang sponsored monthly in developing the same feeling company-wide.

"For every beginning there is an end."
Old Proverb

45: ANALYZING THE BUSINESS

We hired a consultant named Russell Beasley to help us develop a three year plan. He helped companies determine their goals in their main business areas and then evaluate options for achieving those goals. One of the components of his strategy was to interview a number of key players outside of top management to see how well their perception of the company and needs matched with what he heard from top management.

KEY PEOPLE (THE GROUP) INTERVIEW SUMMARY

Employee satisfaction

"The Company is a good place to work. They like the loosely structured organization, the belief that Management appreciates their contribution, that their compensation is competitive, and that Management works hard to maintain a business backlog to maintain the staff at its current number. The Group see themselves as long-term employees."

Current Business Strategy

"The Group understands the current business strategy of obtaining a blend of jobs with the goal of maintaining a steady flow of work supporting a steady workforce of 400 people and assuring a steady cash flow for the Company."

Growth

"There are conflicting opinions within the Group between realizing that most companies must continue to grow to survive, and recognizing that growth can create changes which may result in a working environment that is less pleasant."

Company Organization

"The Group feels that the current organization provides an unstructured environment in which employees can work with optimum freedom."

Company infrastructure

"The Group believe that offices project the right image to customers and provide a comfortable environment in which to work."

Future Involvement of Owners

"The Group believe that the continuing hard work by Management has been a key to the Company's success. They believe that if an Executive Manager leaves, care will be taken to locate a professional to replace the vacated job function, with no adverse impact. All believe Felix wants to retire."

SUMMARY OF OBJECTIVES

"The owners want personal satisfaction while associated with the business. They have an interest in the well-being of company employees. And they want the ability to achieve investment liquidity at some time in the future.

Key requirements were to reduce personal pressures to manage the business, thus reducing demand on personal time.

The key elements of the business that needed to be addressed were: finding work, keeping people and delegation of responsibilities."

From this analysis, we determined areas requiring action were marketing, organization and liquidity.

Market Analysis

We looked at markets both geographically and by industry where we could be viable. We defined our current market size, in order to determine possible revenue dollars Mustang could reasonably obtain.

We reviewed our deployment of sales personnel and our systems for proposals. We reviewed the current advertising and trade show activities. We identified that we were essentially growing our market by finding ways to obtain reimbursable work in areas that had traditionally been lump sum.

Organization

Our organization in operations under Paul was adequate for continued organic growth. We had department managers for facilities, structural and electrical/instrument engineering groups. We had a manager of construction, one for inspection and one for pipeline services. Paul headed up senior project management personnel directly as well as our quality assurance person.

The organization under me for business development was adequate for continued organic growth. I managed the upstream business development effort and monitored David Edgar's efforts in managing the pipeline services sales activities.

The organization in commercial services under Felix needed strengthening to manage the organic growth we anticipated. We wanted to get more free time away from Mustang for Felix in order to entice him to stay longer and help us achieve the liquidity all three of us wanted from the business. The commercial services structure was fine for organic growth, but needed some additional people.

The main driver for any additional organizational changes would be our decisions relating to growth and obtaining liquidity of our investment in Mustang.

Liquidity Strategies

We could continue "business as usual" and achieve *organic growth* by following the people and companies we knew. We had been growing at a 30-50% rate year-over-year and it seemed that we should be able to continue this for a few more years.

During the analysis we had identified geographical markets, different end-user industries and placement of technical services personnel as ways to create *layered growth* using our current organization and hiring a few people with the right skills.

We looked at financing alternatives to obtain *leveraged growth*. These included being purchased and merging with another company, doing an Initial Public Offering (IPO), doing a private placement of stock, or obtaining convertible debt.

The four possible plans we put numbers to were:

Plan 1- stay as we are. At the end of five years each of us would have $6MM in cash and $6.5MM of equity. An offshoot of Plan 1 would be to sell part of the company into an Employee Stock Ownership Plan (ESOP).

Plan 2- buy Felix out for one third of receivables plus some of the "goodwill" value or about $3MM. After five years Paul and I would have $6.25MM in cash and $10MM of equity.

Plan 3- sell 50% of the company into an IPO or Roll-up IPO (multiple companies do an IPO together). After five years each of us would have $0.5MM in cash and $9MM of equity.

Plan 4- we all sell with an earn-out. After five years we would each have $5MM in cash. This is the smallest total value after five years but the value is locked in up front.

So it seemed as it had in the past that we were better off just continuing to do what we were doing and take care of business.

"A rolling stone gathers no moss."
Old Proverb

46: CREATE A PROJECT

During the big slow-down mid-way through 1994, I had an idea of a way to create projects. We had close relationships with a number of vendors who did production skids for us. When I was in their shops pushing to get vendor data or their status in fabrication I met their engineering and drafting people. Most of their drafters were "contract hires" that allowed them to load and unload staff depending on the workload. I generally found my-self coaching them into giving me the quality of vendor data we needed in a timely manner. Due to the whipsaw ups and downs in the industry, many times we took their submittals and just had our drafters re-do their design and gave it back to them.

VENDOR DATA

David Sneed worked up what we would charge to do the vendor data package for the vendors I had visited. We were very comfortable that we could do the work for less than their budget. One of the first vendor packages we did was a com-plex production skid that would be submitted to Brown & Root (B&R) for a large international project. The B&R bid package did not give all of the information we felt was required to get the design right the first time so we gave a list of questions and information needed to the vendor. B&R supplied all of the answers and data and we did the vendor data package the way we wished they would come to us from vendors. The pack-age was approved on the first pass with laudatory comments from B&R to the vendor. The vendor was able to jump right into purchasing and fabrication, six weeks ahead of schedule and was rated highly by the B&R Purchasing Department for responsiveness.

DIVERSIFICATION

Pipeline

David Edgar set up our Pipeline sector including a small office in Monroe, Louisiana to tap into the pipeline talent he knew and trusted. We started switching contracts and hiring pipeline people based on David's reputation. The onshore pipeline industry in the United States is like one big family, where everyone knows each other, their spouses and kids. David's move to Mustang gave us instant credibility and the people he brought with him just solidified that Mustang would become a new epicenter for the industry.

Our first project came from United Gas and consisted of a 60 mile pipeline. We would do the pipeline design, purchase of the right-of-way, provide construction management and inspect the final installation. This project allowed David to bring in a few of all of the resources he would need to be a legitimate player. Within nine months he was able to start getting engineering for the things that are attached to pipelines at either end and along the line...gathering facilities, compression stations, pumping stations, tie-ins to refineries, etc. These "attachments" were the things we were hoping to get by being involved with pipelines.

Picture of a pipeline being installed.

DOWNSTREAM

Jim Vogt talked me into going to the Engineering and Construction Contractor (ECC) conference because the "who's who" in the downstream refinery, chemical and petrochemical industry would be there.

Jim was working to get me more comfortable that we could do downstream work. He felt that we could compete with our current resources plus some specific downstream talent. After meeting clients and attending seminars showing that they had the same concerns in project development that we had, I was sure he was correct. A few months later we were working for a company called Enterprise Products in Houston and the downstream work was well within our capability.

GIG'M ALLIANCE

We formed an alliance with Gulf Island Fabricators for construction, Gobal Contractors for installation, and ourselves, called GIG'M after the Texas A&M slogan Gig'em Aggies. This was sort of an experiment in a "Roll-Up IPO" to see if the market would jump on this combination of companies. Although all three companies were "A" players, we never achieved any traction in the industry.

We had seen companies spend a lot of money moving in a direction they thought was strategic, only to find out that no one was buying. It was great that we could check out this GIG'M grouping for the cost of a few meetings while we were getting together anyway on current projects. We all kept doing our own thing while we fished around to see if clients were interested and it fell pretty flat.

SID RICHARDSON

Sid Richardson had purchased the equipment needed for a major upgrade to their carbon black plant. They were dissatisfied with all of the engineering houses in their industry and wanted to find a new firm that "could just execute projects well." Richard Shirley took on the project and figured it would take ten years to get the black powder out of his system when he was done.

OFFSHORE PROJECTS INTERNATIONAL (OPI)

OPI won a loading terminal in Pakistan and gave us the contract for design through start up. The terminal consisted of onshore pipelines to large oil tanks like you would see located near ports anywhere in the world. Then there were pipelines from the storage tanks to a large pier with anchorage for tankers and loading booms to put the product into the tankers. OPI only wanted the pier installation but had to take on the entire scope of work.

Fauji oil terminal designed for OPI.

"Defense is a skill. Offense is a talent."
LTC Marty Walsh, Battalion Commander

47: DRESSER AND ARCO

Dresser Rand had stretched us significantly as the Maraven and Lagoven projects developed for Venezuela. Maraven was a cost-reimbursable project for Dresser and the management team they put into our offices started out pretty loose, thinking that they had a very big budget. We met with them a number of times early-on to caution them that project scopes of work and budgets generally only grow over time and that they needed to be frugal from the beginning.

SCOPE CHANGE

The three identical platform complexes for Maraven became three unique complexes due to different reservoir and infrastructure require-

ments. The schedule became tight due to contract requirements and we were in a design-build mode at about fifteen fabrication yards.

During the module concept work we found out that we could not get a large lift barge into Lake Maracaibo where these modules would be installed on concrete piers. The only "big lift" barge on the lake had a fixed double boom. This meant that the prime six-story compression modules would have to be split vertically for lift and then be put back together on-site. This increased every discipline's scope and took significant coordination.

COSTS

The Dresser and Mustang teams pulled everything off smoothly and Maraven felt they had the best operating platforms on the lake. Maraven did not, however, like the final bills that came in from Dresser and put pressure on them to justify all costs. Out of the blue Dresser told me that they were not planning to pay $1,700,000 of our invoices and presented me with a ten page detailed list of items where we had cost the project money.

Once a client questions pricing after the fact, neither side is going to be happy. Our teams were fully integrated and knew each other well. Finger pointing at this stage of the project was very tough.

PERCEIVED INEFFICIENCY

We went back and forth for about four weeks with lists and clarifications. We thought that our clarifications helped Dresser work their negotiations with Maraven. Finally, we were in the office of the Dresser project manager and the list had been worked down to $165,000. We did not agree that we owed any money and asked what the list consisted of for this amount.

He said there was no list. This amount was for "Perceived Inefficiencies". The saying "perception is reality" had never been more real to me.

By being integrated into our team we had short lines of communication and were able to do the impossible...but it was at times a "sausage making operation" that is best left behind closed doors. The final product was fantastic but getting there was definitely tough. We accepted this bill, but neither side was very happy with the result.

ARCO

I had wanted to work for Greg Sills of Arco since I had first met him in Houston in the early 1980s. He was in charge of half of the Gulf when we met and we had some great talks about project management. He brought the Villano project in Ecuador to Mustang with a mandate to redo the conceptual design and develop a project that could be approved.

Villano would be a 20,000 bpd heavy oil stand-alone facility in a remote part of Ecuador along with a departing pipeline to a main trunk line. Arco had done conceptual work with another engineering firm, but the price tag was too high.

Arco management was also concerned about the conceptual plan to cut pipeline and facility construction right-of-way into the rain forest. Indigenous people would always migrate into freshly cut right-of-way to expand their villages and farming areas. Arco had gas stations with hamburger stands all over California. The quote was that if they cut right-of-way and the rain forest was damaged, aerial pictures would get out and they would not be able to sell hamburgers in California... seems like people were paying attention to their consumers!

Arco gave us all of the data from the concept work they had done. Through kickoff meetings we were able to learn why the project failed to get approved. This work set us up with clear criteria to work toward.

The first area we attacked was the process design. The previous design had used huge distillation towers to treat the heavy crude. It was clear that the engineers had more of a refinery background than an oilfield one. These towers had to be hauled in over roads and required large cranes to erect.

We changed these towers to horizontal heater-treaters that could be air-lifted into sites that were cleared like forward bases in Vietnam...with no roads.

Then we developed a method to pull the pipeline through the rain forest without cutting a right-of-way.

Once we were about 60% of the way through our concept design, we brought in some of our top people from other projects to hear the plan, risks and methods for mitigation. Then we split into small groups and had these people brainstorm possible alternatives. Finally everyone reported out and the group selected the ideas that should be actioned to complete the concept work.

We had cut about 18% out of the budget through our work in process changes and modularization of equipment.

The new ideas generated significant layout and logistics changes that knocked another 20% out of the cost. This final cost reduction had taken us down to 65% of the original budget, which gave us room for a good contingency while still meeting Arco's approval targets.

The project was approved and we took it from concept through start-up in a reimbursable contract style with a fully integrated team of Arco and Mustangers in our office. Arco only put four people into our office instead of their normal 20 because we had defined the project so well. Arco received their best-in-class performance benchmark and new execution strategy on a tough international project.

While in Ecuador working for Arco we met people from Maxus Oil, out of Dallas, Texas. They were doing concept work for a similar remote production facility with a higher flowrate of 30,000 barrels of oil per day. After hearing how we had optimized the design for Villano, they gave us their facility to do in similar fashion! Gotta love it...when good project execution finds new work.

48: MOBIL & BRITISH GAS

We had been working for Mobil Producing Nigeria for some time and they introduced us to the top people at their home office in Dallas, Texas. Dallas had been impressed with our performance and asked where we thought they could improve. We felt that their material standards were way out of date and costing huge sums on their projects. They asked if we could develop an example to show them what we meant.

CONTROL VALVES

We had pricing to the Mobil material standards from Bouygues and we had pricing on the exact same valves in the same time frame on an Oryx project. The valves purchased under the Mobil standards cost about 75% more. We brought the vendor in to explain to Mobil where the additional cost came from. They did a good job of breaking down the additional costs Mobil incurred due to their specifications and showed that the requirements were not value-adding. With the vendor's help, we had directly linked scope to dollars.

> **"We directly linked scope to dollars."**

We gave Mobil similar examples in their structural steel and electrical standards. Mobil then gave us a project to totally re-do their standards for use worldwide. This was a big undertaking that pulled us in closer to Mobil for projects outside of Africa.

BRITISH GAS

Gulf Coast Strategy

Opening an office in Houston was a strategic move by British Gas (BG) to change the way they executed projects. They were bidding a three platform complex offshore Tunisia, Africa called Miskar. The complex would consist of a 40 man quarters platform bridge connected to a 340mmscfd sour (H2S) gas production platform that was also connected by bridge to a wellhead platform. The platforms were in 220 feet of water in a seismic Zone 2, warm weather environment.

Proposal Themes

Our experience matched this project and their Gulf Coast build strategy. In addition we had done a number of large multi-platform complexes offshore Africa, we had high flow rate sour gas experience, and we had good structural experience in seismic areas. We knew how to do conceptual work and pick the installation method early in order to drive down costs offshore Africa. These would be our key "themes" for the proposal.

On the cover of the proposal we put a structural rendering of the complete three platform complex created from our library of past structures:

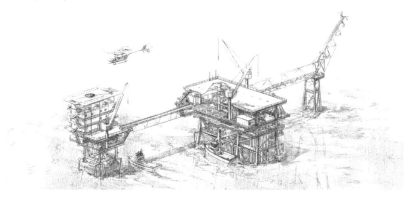

Innovation

Technically we tried to differentiate ourselves by working the installation problem offshore Tunisia. The lift barge would have to be mobilized from either the North Sea or the Gulf of Mexico. We evaluated the barges available and derived a concept that would increase the bid list from two barges to five, which would lower the installation cost significantly. We planned to design a module support frame instead of a deck. When the modules were installed on the frame and connected together they would form the deck. Our concept would reduce the "heavy lift" requirement by 70% with some increase in hook-up time after installation. We could show the smooth installation of the Dresser modules in Lake Maracaibo as the perfect example of our ability to work the details in this execution strategy and give BG a much less risky installation.

Miskar modules installed on support frame.

We won the project hands down and were going to embark on our first job working for a company with North Sea "DNA" wanting to become a hybrid with some Gulf of Mexico "DNA."

"The best way to predict the future is to invent it."
Alan Kay, TED Speaker

49: BENTON OIL AND GAS

Paul took an interesting call from Lloyd Benson one day. Lloyd was the project manager for Benton Oil and Gas, a small independent that was working to revive an old oil field they had acquired in Venezuela. He was working with Wilcrest Engineering, but was having trouble keeping the design team together. We had bought some of our drafting tables from Wilcrest in 1987 when they were in a tight spot financially. Wilcrest had been shrinking again and had been sold to Belmont Construction a year earlier.

CATS & DOGS

There is a natural animosity between engineers and construction people working on projects. Essentially, one wants to get it "right" while the other wants to get it "done." This animosity became evident when Belmont construction people bristled at carrying Wilcrest engineers on overhead between jobs. During the first downturn, it became obvious that Belmont only wanted Wilcrest so they could say they were an EPC company to enhance their value for a possible sale. The Wilcrest people were not valued as part of the core Belmont construction team. When they were out of work, they were let go to the detriment of the engineering team. Due to this treatment, key engineering folks were starting to leave on their own and Lloyd was concerned that his project was in jeopardy.

Lloyd wanted to know if Paul would hire the entire Wilcrest team. If he would, then Lloyd would move Benton's projects to Mustang. The kicker was that Benton was a "bootstrap" organization and wanted us to finance the engineering for six months until the oil production increased.

ABORTED ROLL-UP INITIAL PUBLIC OFFERING (IPO)

Belmont Contractors was one of the companies we had talked to about doing a roll-up IPO with. The idea was to put three or four companies together that would form the nucleus of an EPC (Engineer, Procure, and Construct) company with assets both domestically and internationally. Belmont was looking to purchase an engineering firm and was interested in Mustang. We had not seen good long term results from these combinations.

Construction projects are intensely engineering driven in the first quarter of the schedule, procurement driven in the second quarter and construction driven in the final half. The engineering side atrophies during the final three quarters of the project cycles. Generally during this time, the engineering group is supporting bid efforts. Engineering then becomes the scapegoat in management meetings that are concerned with profit during any downturn in work.

The most insidious part of the morphing of the engineering firm into a support role in a construction company is that they become non-competitive at what they used to do. When they try to flip back, they no longer have the right people and systems to be competitive. Their key people become tired of being second class citizens in the construction company and start moving to firms where engineering has more respect. A once strong independent engineering firm becomes a support group to construction requirements and loses its identity along with much of its capability.

We ended up not going forward with the roll-up IPO and Belmont decided to start building their EPC firm by buying Wilcrest Engineering. Events had played out just the way we had described and Wilcrest was in the engineering death spiral familiar to those in the industry.

A NEW TEAM

The offer from Lloyd Benson to move his team from Belmont was enticing. He had already talked to the Belmont leadership and they were supportive of him taking the Wilcrest team with him. Belmont was having trouble funding Lloyd's cash flow as the project started to grow and it no longer seemed like something they should support.

Paul met with Lloyd to nail down what the project entailed, current status and scope of work to finish. It was a nice on-shore heavy oil field development in Venezuela with proven reserves. Paul worked hard to make sure he understood the cash flow required from Mustang and the re-payment terms.

Then Paul and some of his best engineers met with the project team headed by Tom Davison. They dug into details on the engineering, procurement status and the scope of work to take the project all the way through startup with a team on the ground in Venezuela.

We could get some guarantees, but it would pretty much be a "handshake" deal because Hugo Chavez, the President of Venezuela, could mess with the project at any time. We could mitigate some of the risk of funding the team by having them do some other projects at the same time, where we knew we would get paid. We all liked the idea of getting a top-notch team and "heavy oil" experience.

We decided to take the offer...essentially acquiring Wilcrest Engineering at no cost and helping both Benton's and Belmont's cash flows. This was "Operation Horsethief" on steroids and something we had been doing for some time now... moving whole teams instead of buying companies...essentially we just picked up the payroll and had to get them billable. This team would become the nucleus of our onshore facilities engineering group.

Squeeze the handoff to create value.

50: SHARPENING THE SWORD

While times were a little slow in 1994, Paul put some people to work figuring out ways to improve our efficiency. Generally this was done on projects, but in some cases the initial effort was on overhead until he could see that the innovation was going to work.

STRUCTURAL

We developed software to take the structural computer model for a jacket or deck and roll it out into a stick figure drawing for bidding fabrication and installation.

Generally the engineers would work with the model for a few months to size all the members. Then a few months were spent sketching the joints and getting drawings prepared in drafting. By the time we had good drawings for bid, the design was within weeks of being ready for construction.

By developing the software to roll out the "stick figure" drawings early from the model, we moved right from early engineering into bidding. We could bid and get "cost-per-ton" quotes for the various structural components to be rolled into a lump sum with final drawing definition. We could also incorporate cost savings ideas from the bidders. Changing this contracting strategy allowed us to shorten the handoff time when drawings were ready for construction, because the contractor would already have trainloads of steel on its way to the yard.

This was a critical step in the growth of our thinking about how to reduce overall schedules and total installed costs on projects. No one was asking us to do this, but it was natural for us to think this way because of our determination to help the client get faster and more economical projects.

PIPING IN 3D

Through our pipeline group we bid and were awarded a facility modification for Arco Four Corners pipeline in California. The modification and upgrade was pretty simple but had  many hurdles to cross due to the regulatory environment in California. Once we understood that regulations would be a big challenge to the client and that they were trying to explain what they were doing to non-technical people it seemed like a picture would help.

Paul and David Sneed picked a team to do our first 3D piping design for a client, using techniques they had been developing. The 3D rendering of the design helped the client get technical approval of the design. The rendering also gave us a good sales tool to work on getting 3D into upstream offshore designs.

SALES ADVANCES

We were bidding for an onshore facility in Egypt for Phoenix Petroleum that had to bridge language, cultural and national barriers to win. Once we had written the scope of work and described what we were going to do for the client, it seemed like the best way to get this across would be to give them an example of the deliverables.

With very little effort we had a few people revise our "go-by" documents to actually reflect the real project including layouts and a first pass at the total project cost estimate. That way they could see the exact deliverable and level of detail we planned to provide. This was more effort than normal but would insure that we were communicating what we would provide. We won the project and essentially just fleshed out the bid documents to deliver the FEED. This was a very efficient project for operations because sales helped clarify exactly what needed to be done. This was a way that sales could help operations do more projects when times were busy.

PEOPLE ADVANCES

Design Coordinator

David Sneed started creating a cadre of design coordinators within the piping design group. These coordinators were very experienced pipers who also understood the coordination required with structural, electrical and instrument/controls designers on tight offshore platforms. He met separately with the coordinators to develop better design communication across the design disciplines. This effort would help us insure quality out the door and build our reputation.

Finder's fee

As things went crazy in 1995 we added a lot more meat to the Mustang skeleton and built more backbone. In May we started a finder's fee program for bringing in good talent that stayed a minimum of six months. If a person survived our pace for six months without the team running them off, then they had survived our "trial by fire" and would probably be a long term Mustanger. Imagine that...Horsethief for pay!

Going from make a project to being able to choose.

51: 1995 STARTED LIKE GANGBUSTERS

Things did not slow down at all from mid-October through the end of December in 1994, like they normally do. We didn't have to "store nuts" for the winter from August to October...we had to eat as many as we could because more were coming. Our bid load had also been staggering toward the end of the year and primarily on projects where we had positioned ourselves well.

BEEN THERE

We had experienced this before. We more than doubled in size from 1989 to 1990, going from 45 to 105 people. Then we doubled again from 1990 to 1991 in going to 200 people, despite the industry being in a downturn during 1991. Now, despite 1994 being a downturn year, we had grown from 250 to 305 and were poised to reach 450 by the end of 1995. Going from 250 to 450 seemed just as horrible and elating to us as going from 45 to 200 had been.

Yes, we loved pulling in more great people and challenging them. We enjoyed seeing our old hands step up to the new challenges. And we enjoyed the camaraderie developed on projects and at company activities. But, the infrastructure, organization and ability to handle hundreds of details flawlessly on a daily basis was creating huge cracks in what seemed to the outside world like a tight knit, homogeneous and smoothly run company.

The treadmill Paul and I had created with him executing and me selling enough to prevent layoffs just kept speeding up and Felix felt like he was the tread we were running on!

PEOPLE EVERYWHERE

During 1994 and 1995 we had teams in virtually every part of the globe - Singapore, Abu Dhabi, Egypt, Pakistan, Tunisia, Ecuador, Angola, Nigeria, Alaska, Equatorial Guinea, Spain, Russia, India, Algeria, Nova Scotia, Venezuela, Korea, Brazil, Indonesia and in Argentina. We also worked on more than 250 platforms in the Gulf doing modifications, revamps, full new platforms or subsea tiebacks. For onshore pipelines we had teams working in 15 different states in the USA in addition to Ecuador, Chile and Argentina.

We were doing everything from small offshore natural gas platforms to the world's largest multi-platform oil production complexes. We had pushed into FPSOs and had seven we were working to complete. We did 12 subsea completions as the industry started moving into deeper waters where a fixed platform was no longer economical. We were working on modularizing downstream (refinery and petrochemical) facilities in remote areas as well as east Houston. We were doing pipelines and pipeline related facilities across a broad range of clients. We were working for small Independent producers, the major oil companies and national oil companies. The breadth of our clientele and reach across the world was staggering when considering that it blossomed quickly in a two year period.

We were "selling while the shop is full" because our upbeat story was fun for clients. New projects were quickly knocked out because being busy increased our efficiency.

By January of 1995 we had 70% of our revenue coming from international projects. The oil companies had left the Gulf and we had successfully followed them either directly, or through contractors, vendors or national oil companies.

ADDING TO THE MIX IN 1995

Mobil Producing Nigeria Usari

In January we were awarded the Phase I front end design

Mobil Usari project, offshore Nigeria.

for a seven platform 250,000 barrels of oil per day complex for MPN and NNPC. This would be the largest front end we had ever done, but we had a good formula for doing these with the Mobil people in our office. Luckily, Daryl Rapp, was between projects for Oryx and took this project on with his team.

Command Petroleum's Raava Field through Hyundai

In January we were also awarded the Raava field in India, which was being developed by Command Petroleum, an Independent Australian oil company.

This project had onshore storage tanks, onshore pipelines, pipeline beach crossings and offshore pipelines. It had offshore platforms and tanker loading facilities. Mustang would manage the design and procurement in Houston with an in-house team from both Command and Hyundai. We would then follow the project through construction and startup in India.

This would be our first time working directly for Hyundai and had us very concerned about being paid due to the poor reputation Hyundai had with some of their vendors. We worked to get a reimbursable contract that would be paid in advance each month.

We took our budget estimate for doing the project reimbursable and split it into "mini monthly lump sums" that Hyundai could pay before the fifth of each month. To Mustang, it was a reimbursable contract and we tracked it and issued "invoices" each month even though we were paid the agreed amount. This was a $4.2 million dollar contract...lump sum to Hyundai and reimbursable to our thinking.

We staffed a Project Management Team (PMT) for Command Petroleum to run the entire effort. This PMT was over Hyundai. We had quite a balancing act since we were both over and under Hyundai.

Raava field development in India.

At the end of the project we were under our reimbursable budget by $190,000 and we took a check to our Houston representative...he was astonished!!! He now understood better how reimbursable contracting worked and how it helped push scope to the right places. He also understood how being reimbursable put engineering on the side of Hyundai to get the job done.

Ashland Nigeria's two small Platforms

We were also awarded two small platforms from concept through installation and start-up for Roger Benedict of Ashland, offshore Nigeria. Toyin had taken me to see Roger while I was in Lagos. Roger had a lifelike rattlesnake curled up on the floor next to his desk to get your attention and was happy to see a Texan walk in. They had minimal staff and he needed someone to do everything on this project so off we went.

Southern Natural Gas (SNG) compressor stations

The CEO of SNG (a West Pointer) called and wanted us to do some major compressor installations in Alabama. We had moved a very good onshore project engineer named Gary Neal into sales in 1994, but did not need sales work now. We moved Gary onto these fast paced compressor stations and told him to hurry up so he could go back into sales.

MPN Ekpe detailed design

Just when we thought it was safe and we were out of January, we won the Ekpe 180,000 barrel per day float-over platform design as a subcontractor to Bouygues. Now we really were staffing work out of thin air because contractors like Hyundai (Command Petroleum) and Bouygues (Mobil Ekpe) had based their bids on our execution strategy and we could not let them down.

MPN Qua-Ibo Terminal modifications

We were out of people so in April I did the site work data collection for this upgrade to the onshore facility where all of MPN's offshore oil came for processing at Ekit on the Nigerian coast. This project expanded into looking at the full MPN offshore development and helping them figure out some de-bottlenecking strategies.

Russian refinery move

We wanted to turn this project down in June of 1995 due to being totally overloaded. But Dick Westbrook wanted the experience of working in the former Soviet Union.

Dick flew into Moscow and then down to Chechnya where they took his passport at the airport and told him he would get it back when he returned. From there he went to a remote site to start putting a modular refinery back together. The only communication we had with him was once a week when a person would come by his location with a satellite phone, enabling him to call us. Shortly after he was there, the civil unrest grew into riots and insurgents overran the airport. Dick missed one week's phone call due to the satellite phone not showing up, but the next week he sounded fine and the civil unrest was far away from him. Dick completed another impossible project, but reinforced our concern with putting people on the ground in potentially hostile environments. Dick's potential problem totally consumed our small management team's efforts in trying to reach him and we felt powerless. That is why Toyin could never convince us to open an office in Lagos, despite there being plenty of work.

PROJECTS TO DIE FOR

These projects came fast and furious and were all projects to die for from almost any perspective in our past...we just couldn't help ourselves; we had to chase them hard. Paul, Felix and I wished we were just project managers running projects like these. Instead we were working like crazy to keep them all staffed correctly in a busy industry where companies were working every day to hire our people away. At the same time we were stretching everybody at Mustang to step up and take on more responsibility.

"Pride goeth before the fall."
Proverbs 16:19

52: DECISION TIME

We had been chasing some lump sum Engineer, Procure, Construct (EPC) projects with Foster Wheeler, USA (FWUSA) in Venezuela and Abu Dhabi. FWUSA chose to partner with us due to our contacts and heavy oil experience from the Benton Oil & Gas work in Venezuela. They were bringing the project management, procurement, in-country construction and financing to the bid effort. We met their project people in Houston and toured their offices as we worked to put proposals together. They had respect for our upstream project execution ability and we had a lot of respect for their project management systems and worldwide presence. In addition, they were willing to take on EPC lump sum work due to their strong construction group. We were bidding on jobs that would never pass our filters for eliminating risky projects. We did not win the initial projects we chased, but we did learn a lot about each other while putting together experience lists and calling out our respective strengths in the bids.

As a result of this work we received a call a few months later in December of 1995 from FWUSA headquarters in New Jersey saying that they wanted to make a serious run at purchasing Mustang.

TAKING STOCK

Administrative System Stress

Felix was way beyond the shoebox method of keeping track of monies in and out. Everything was huge and moving fast. We had to collect taxes for a number of states, and have registered professional engineers in some states to do work. Per-diems and travel had to be set up and arranged for teams of people. Contracting requirements many times were pretty ridiculous and took everyone's efforts to get straightened out.

By the end of 1995 I was still doing payroll and we were at 450 people. We had to get time sheets and expense reports from everyone on a weekly basis from all over the world in order to get invoices out on time (all manual using fax and hard copies).

Health insurance questions from employees and spouses were continuous. Threats of lawsuits would pop up regularly as we were caught in the net for having been involved in a particular project. Department managers and project managers tried to work a lot of the details in order to help Felix, but the weight of it all was squarely on him.

Project System Stress

Paul had created project management systems that matched our lean execution methods. They were modular and could be adjusted to the needs of a particular project. These systems for engineering and procurement were stretched for the large world class projects we were doing. Additionally we were managing full construction through start-up around the world. Our systems were inadequate and we were surviving through the brute force Herculean efforts of our people.

Paul was super wired within Mustang and in the industry. He knew that some of his best teams were feeling the stress as Mustang became stretched almost beyond the breaking point. He knew that three different groups were thinking that there was enough work in the industry for them to leave and start their own firm. He was doing everything he could to keep everyone together.

Gaps in every system and cracks in trust caused problems and friction within the project teams that fell squarely back on Paul.

Sales System Stress

I had Jim, Dennis and Gary in upstream sales and was also helping the two sales people in Pipeline. I had never worked in a sales team and had never seen what a sales manager does. I was creating the bare minimum of systems and reporting in order to not give sales people an excuse for being in the office instead of out in the real world meeting clients. When I was gone for two weeks on a worldwide sales trip (left going west and came back from the east) Paul jumped in and tried to organize sales reporting in his own meticulous manner. It was obvious when I got back that he had been very frustrated with my inability to predict sales, but I got the message that I needed more predictability.

The challenge with operations was that they always had someone or part of a team finishing up work or needing some short term work while they waited for a project to get going again. This could be one electrical engineer or a multi-discipline team needing anything from two days worth of work to needing a full scale project. Being able to match what we might win to the staffing needs that Paul and the department managers identified seemed close to impossible.

What they needed is depicted below:

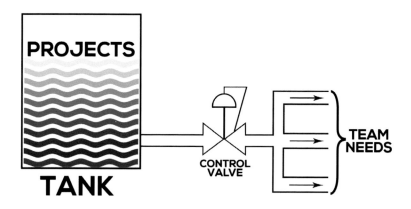

Essentially Paul and his managers wanted a control valve that they could open or close to give them the work they needed. My team's job was to keep the tank full of prospective projects that they could take or leave. The problem was that the bigger jobs could have many months between bid and award. We would not know if we were going to win or when the job would start until about two weeks before kick-off. Plus these bigger jobs were pitched based upon our execution strategy, meaning we would have some disgruntled clients if we backed out. The clients would rather have our "best available effort" than switch to another engineering firm.

All of this balancing between sales and operations, with a developing system that made sense, fell squarely back on me.

Stress between the owners

This day-to-day stress also manifested itself in stress between Paul, Felix and me. During the 1985 to 1987 preparation phase for starting Mustang we welded ourselves into a team with Paul as the lead and felt we could build a different company. Now we had that company and the wild success of the culture that was built upon our beliefs was stretching the bonds that held us together. We always tried to focus on the problem at hand and not let it get personal. The problems just kept coming so fast that the discussions felt personal and like we were not holding up our side of the original triangle based organization. Additionally, some of the problems just seemed too big and beyond our capability to break down and fix. Felix and Paul were continuously working contracts and determining where the company was financially. Paul and I were forever working the company organization, team organization and project execution strategies...sometimes from different directions because I was trying to take care of the client and he was trying to take care of Mustangers.

All three of us would have thoughts on which projects to take on and where Mustang was going. We had no strategic plan other than to keep our people and be what the clients needed. This plan...to have no plan...many times left us feeling like we were blowing in the wind...very uncomfortable for Paul, moderately uncomfortable for Felix and uncomfortable to me. Something needed to change before our bonds broke.

Outside Interest Stress

At the same time, we were all trying to get more time with our families and find a positive way to use our new-found wealth and experience. Paul and Kay were devoting more time to church and working at their kids' schools. Their house was getting smaller as the kids grew and they wanted to build a new home. Felix and Joyce were moving toward empty nesters and wanted to move to the country to raise horses and relax more. They liked finding specific needs in the community and anonymously helping. I was trying to give back to organizations that had helped me over the years. I contributed to MD Anderson Cancer Hospital because their cutting edge experimental chemotherapy had saved my life. I was on the West Point Board of Trustees Fundraising Committee. We raised private funds to provide the "margin of excellence" cadets needed. I was on the Board and in charge of Division II of the Sam Houston Area Council of the Boy Scouts of America, exposing 35,000 boys to a moral and ethical code. Ann and I were helping at our church and the kids' schools (Ann almost full time).

Each of us had other interests that we would like to explore. Felix, Joyce, Ann and I wanted to travel. Paul and Kay wanted to eventually have a ranch and Paul wanted to do some exotic game hunting around the world. Paul, Kay, Ann and I needed to get through/survive the teenage years with our kids and get them going in the right direction through college.

The tugs of family and other interests was a very real stress since we were making good money and had a successful business. We should have had the time for these other things but we were deathly afraid of taking our "eye off the ball" like we had seen other owners do and have it all fall apart. This stress fell on us, our spouses and our kids.

Selling Mustang Stress

> **"This met our feeling of, 'use us and abuse us... but don't buy us'."**

Adding into this mix was the fact that we were being queried regularly by companies wanting to purchase all or part of Mustang. Generally we turned these queries into alliances or teaming efforts to pursue specific projects. This met our feeling of, "use us and abuse us...but don't buy us." Just in the month of July 1995 we were seriously approached by a number of international companies:

- Kvaerner (Norway). They wanted to follow what Aker had done (in purchasing Omega) and buy an upstream engineering firm in Houston.
- Technip (France). They felt they needed a presence in Houston in order to get involved in the front end of projects.
- JP Kenny (UK). They were a world class offshore (underwater) pipeline company that wanted to get involved on the floating production and the subsea portions of projects.
- Inelectra (Venezuela). They wanted diversification in their client base and the ability to work on projects outside of Venezuela.

These serious inquiries were starting to make sense as a way to remove many of the stresses we were feeling.

If we could get with the right company, we could cash out part of Mustang and take our personal guarantees (we always said our houses and first born were committed) off of contracts. We could put some money and perhaps stock into the hands of our people and lock them in from leaving. We could immediately have great systems and support personnel to organize the hugely chaotic mess we had created. We would also be able to have time for our other interests.

WHERE DO WE GO FROM HERE?

We were not sure if we or our people could step up to the almost insurmountable challenges we saw in front of us. This revelation was very hard for us to admit. We decided that we needed to swallow our pride and seek the help that we needed through selling Mustang all or in part to a company that had everything we needed. Our clients, vendors, partners and Mustangers deserved better than we felt we were able to deliver.

We looked at our options of about 15 companies to determine who we felt could take us where we wanted to go and felt Foster Wheeler, USA (FWUSA) was the right company. We met with their management in Houston and provided information to see if their Board would be interested. If interested, we would go to their headquarters in Princeton, NJ. The cat was going to get out of the bag when the three of us left for a week to go to New Jersey, but we felt that we could explain why this would be a good move for everyone. 450 families were directly affected by our decisions and thousands more through our industry connections. This decision had to be pursued in a manner to take care of all the PEOPLE.

FOSTER WHEELER, USA

SWOT Analysis, end of 1995...
Unstoppable... Unique and... Fragile.

Strengths:
- Solid bottom line.
- Put out good work.
- Just-do-it mentality.
- 5% 401K contribution.
- Repeat work due to performance.
- No layoffs through two downturns.
- Doubled people while maintaining culture.
- Mid-level working leads (DMs & PMs) stepped up.
- Changed jobs and contracts from lump sum to reimbursable.

Weaknesses:
- Lack of a strategic plan.
- Little infrastructure for growth.
- Poor procedures for consistency.
- Lack of cross-fertilization of best practices.
- Little company and project management depth.
- Inability to benchmark performance against the industry.
- Working as a subcontractor (cannot take care of the client).

Opportunities:
- Diversify client base.
- Penetrate front end market better.
- Follow oil companies into deepwater.
- Paul & Bill move into Foster Wheeler management.
- Find more ways to push reimbursable contract strategy.

Threats:
- Oil price goes below $17 per barrel.
- Projects go bad and hurt reputation.
- Client pulls project due to poor staffing.
- Teams hired away or split off from Mustang.
- Big Boys could put best people on front ends.
- Low cost engineering centers take over the market.
- Paul & Bill leave gaping hole at Mustang when go to FWUSA.

"Why's" that were learned:
- Teams have personalities
- Clients have to compete for oil leases
- Pictures bridge language barriers
- Quality engineering is a game changer
- Don't build fat in the organization
- Stay competitive on small projects
- Your word is your reputation
- Planning is critical
- Re-planning is more critical

Mustang-isms:
- Modules 'R Us
- More than expected... Better than expected
- Making Heroes
- Let overload force the addition of overhead
- Innovate in everything
- Continuously change to match the industry
- People productive within two hours on first day
- Tracey Bayles can move mountains...and offices

Wants:
- Reimbursable direct to the client
- Better management structure
- More people pulling the load
- Better project controls
- Better procedures
- Family time

"Ands" that were learned:
- Innovate and meet schedule
- Take care of client and Mustang
- People Oriented and Project Driven™
- Subcontractor and drive the project
- Engineer and sell the next project
- Maintain rates and sell more work
- Growth and quality

Fast Facts:
- $45,000,000/year at the end of 1995
- 110,000 sq.ft of office space
- 450 people
- 2,000 people at the shrimp boil
- Top flowrate oil 250,000 bpd
- Top flowrate gas 150 mmscfd

Camaraderie:
- Bridge building contest
- Crazy hats at project status meetings

Sayings:
- All problems are communication problems
- Arrows in the quiver for sales
- Rubber ball management
- Buy a slice of Mustang
- Create a project

MUSTANG
End of 1992-1995
Need to Capitalize on our Uniqueness.

"Boom times are just as hard as the busts."

Paul Redmon
CEO, Mustang

PART 4: MUSTANG 1996-1998
STAYING POWER
Or... Execution Counts
The New Normal

At 450 people and over 150 clients, we were working domestic and international projects for vendors, contractors and oil companies...we were definitely hitting on all cylinders as we barreled down the road. Although the entire organization still relied heavily on Paul, Felix and me, it was working and putting out tons of great projects in the upstream, pipeline and related hydrocarbon industries.

Maybe we were feeling the "Seven Year Itch" in our union, but it felt like we needed to make a major change to allow Mustang to grow and prosper. We felt that our capabilities and resources were self-limiting. We also felt that we could sell our people on the greater security and opportunity available by becoming part of Foster Wheeler, USA (FWUSA).

We had stayed very busy in 1993 and 1994 despite the general industry being in a funk. We had taken managed risks in following clients overseas, by working in a reimbursable mode for them, vendors or construction and installation companies. We had proven that we were a strong player for front end engineering design. We had also honed our skid and module design skills in ever larger applications both onshore and offshore. We were competing and winning against the big boys...Fluor, Brown & Root, McDermott, Parsons, Bechtel, etc. And, we are positioned well for the new "Boom-Time" that had started fourth quarter of 1994.

We were getting better technically, better in selling the "Mustang difference" and better in our company organization. Riding the current crazy wave of work, we are looking forward to a sale that would smoothly transition everyone into FWUSA.

53: FOSTER WHEELER OFFER

FWUSA called to say that their Board had met towards the end of the year and had reviewed the discussions we had in December. They wanted to send a few people from headquarters to visit with us during the third week of January to perform some light due diligence reviews of Mustang to be sure that there would be no obvious deal breakers. This review would open the door to a meeting with the FWUSA management team at their headquarters toward the end of the month. The headquarters meeting would result in an offer of some type.

DAY ONE

Princeton, New Jersey

Preliminary due diligence had found no deal breakers and we were invited to meet with FWUSA Management for a detailed review. I flew separately from Paul and Felix to Princeton, New Jersey. Paul and Felix did not fully agree with my reasons to fly separately and joked that the survivor(s) would have the worst end of the deal due to having all of Mustang. I always refused to let the three of us fly together due to my "exposure-means-casualties" Army background and stories about other management teams that had met with disaster.

Feeling each other out

FWUSA briefed us on the breadth and depth of their worldwide capability. The company was definitely construction focused with engineering in a supporting role. We were very familiar with this type of company from working on engineer-procure-construct projects over the past two years with integrated full-service companies.

From our viewpoint, all we saw was opportunity every-where! FWUSA was unbelievable in their capacity and their straight-forward approach to projects of all descriptions. We could not have picked a better company to merge into and grow with. Each of us was drooling over what we saw that could make our life easier and provide plenty of room for our people to grow.

Paul saw procedures, standards and access to projects we would never even hear about. I saw seemingly endless capa-bility that I could probably never over-sell. Felix saw a legal team, an accounting team, a human resources team and a per-sonnel-recruiting team that could unload many of his activi-ties or streamline them. We all felt that being part of FWUSA would free us up in many respects to work on delivering better projects to our clients.

We did a presentation on Mustang and the significant changes we had gone through in the past two years. We em-phasized the culture we had developed and how maintaining our culture would be paramount to a successful sale into FWU-SA. The reality was that our people could easily leave the next day to go to another engineering firm in Houston.

We gave them a pro-forma Profit & Loss (P&L) statement along with a Balance Sheet. We felt that we could maintain our 450 people going forward, especially after seeing the po-tential synergies with FWUSA. We had minimal project-type overlap with their Houston office. We would nominally have $45,000,000 in revenue per year, generating about $7,000,000 in Net Profit before bonuses and 401K contribution; $5,500,000 after these were taken out. These were enough numbers for the big picture. We ended the meeting and went to lunch to swap some war stories. Then we split up in the afternoon for more detailed discussions.

FWUSA doesn't pull any punches

Felix met with a team to review our P&L calculations, our overheads, gross margins, cash flow, loan and bank balances. He helped the team rework the numbers into their formats to show what had happened in 1995 and then projecting 1996 at 450 people plus some growth. He reviewed the type of contracts we had and helped them evaluate possible contract risks. Felix was severely poked and prodded as they worked to footnote every number and develop a solid story.

I met with the sales and marketing people to review our bid procedures, client lists, current work, work we had identified to chase and potential for future work. We had very different experiences with some of our common clients due to FWUSA doing lump sum engineer-procure-construct (EPC) contracts and us doing reimbursable engineer-procure-construction manage (EPCM) contracts. However, their experiences were real and made it difficult for them to fully believe the win-win relationships I described. They also had a hard time believing our 40% success ratio in bidding for work.

Paul spent the afternoon reviewing engineering procedures and discussing project team management. He also met with top management on overall company organization and how we would fit into FWUSA.

That night Felix and I had a lot of homework to do with Paul's assistance. Felix had to crunch numbers to make sure that what FWUSA was putting into their spreadsheets was telling the right story. He explained to us that they were most interested in our revenue, gross margin, and earnings before interest and taxes (EBIT) and EBITDA-earnings after depreciation and allowances. EBIT and EBITDA were new terms to us, but made a lot of sense in a larger more complex construction-oriented company.

I had to get our bid logs from Houston and work an analysis into the FWUSA formats to tell the sales story in their language. They also did not believe we could win even 20% of the work I had projected and wanted me to put those possible new projects into their formats for analysis.

We were learning about some glaring holes in our systems as everything was being looked at very objectively and analyzed to see where we were weak. We knew we were good, but realized after the afternoon of explaining and defending, that we could be a whole lot better...but at what overhead cost?

DAY TWO

The next morning started with an early breakfast and interesting discussion after sleeping (sort of) on the challenges we would face. Each of us had ideas on how to plug some of the holes in our story and we worked on those after breakfast until the FWUSA people were ready to meet.

FWUSA worked with Felix to discuss their notes on the contracts they had reviewed. Since they did not do upstream offshore work or much for the pipeline clients we had, they wanted to get a firm understanding of the exposure we had beyond re-doing the engineering. They were familiar with doing front end conceptual work in a reimbursable mode but were not familiar with then taking the project all the way through construction in a reimbursable EPCM role. They targeted rolling from front end conceptual work into a lump sum EPC contract. Felix worked through explanations of how our contract was different from theirs and how the liabilities were much more limited, even though we were running what FWUSA would consider to be a large construction project.

No History of Planned versus Actual

My team was not convinced that our sales projections were valid. I had no history of showing that I could set sales targets and then meet them. This was the same problem Felix had faced the day before because we did not budget our P&L for the next year and then track how we did against the budget. Again, because we did not have this history, how could we reasonably project our profit for 1996?

Bootstrap Organization

Part of the reason we did not have historical data was that we were a bootstrap organization. We had "pulled ourselves up by the bootstraps" and had no debt or corporate taxes because we were a Sub Chapter S Corporation. Mustang's earnings were taxed through our personal tax filings. In terms of EBIT, we had no "IT" we just had a bottom line profit. Our "DA", depreciation and allowances, were minimal because we were an engineering firm with few hard assets. We did financials when a month was completed to show what happened, and what our bottom line profit was.

> "We had pulled ourselves up by our bootstraps."

We did not invest the effort to project sales, costs and profit and then compare to our actual performance...it did not seem like we could affect it anyway. We knew that we had built profit into our schedule of rates and if we stayed at a high percent of billable manhours, we would be profitable. Any projection and attempt to push things towards those numbers just seemed like it would make us put emphasis on the wrong things. We would fall into the trap of pushing for a bottom line instead of pushing to take care of the project and the client.

THE FWUSA OFFER

If FWUSA made a significant offer they would be risking a lot on their belief in Paul, Felix and me, because we were not a mature company whose value could be pinned down to a narrow range.

If they made a low offer they knew we would go back to what we had been doing and they would not get another chance to buy us.

They made an offer of $45,000,000 for the entire company. From our work with our consultant, we knew that typical values for top engineering firms were one third of annual revenue or in many cases 2.5-3.5 times net earnings. That would value us at $10-17 million based on 1995 or 15-30 million based on the 1996 projection of $45,000,000 revenue. Obviously they were factoring in growth in Mustang and in FWUSA due to the synergies they foresaw between the organizations. But still this was a phenomenal offer for a seven year old engineering firm in a relatively mundane industry and a super-competitive market. There it was, plain as day:

We thanked everyone for the significant amount of work and effort they had spent in understanding Mustang. We thanked the management team for the confidence they showed in us by making a very strong offer for the company. We told them that we would get back with them the next morning on how we wanted to proceed.

"All that glitters is not gold."
William Shakespeare, Poet and Playwright

54: READY FOR THIS?

What should we do?

We decided that we were too frazzled to talk about the offer as we headed back to the hotel. For three days we had been trying to run Mustang remotely, while at the same time being grilled about everything in the company. We split up to go to our rooms and catch up with our jobs at Mustang through email and phone calls, while letting the FWUSA opportunity settle in our minds. We would get back together for dinner and some discussion about the offer. We did have to smile though at the value that had been placed on the company we had helped create. The proverbial "Brass Ring" was firmly in our grasp and there for the taking.

DINNER

Dinner was fun as the discussion wandered everywhere from how we started to the people and projects we had pulled in, to where each of us wanted to go. Fun memories, but always a little scary looking into the future. Perhaps that was why we did not like to set targets for the company...they were like predicting the future. We were "driven to win" type guys and would beat ourselves up to get those numbers.

Being part of FWUSA would force us to start doing those projections and tracking our progress toward meeting them. We felt that we should work to set the bar low in projections in order to be able to meet or beat the goals while working in our normal fashion. This would be sort of like "gaming the game" but seemed like a possible way to move forward. We liked all of the people we had met and could see ourselves working with them long term. When the evening ended, we decided that we would sleep on the decision.

THE FIRST DECISION

Thoughts post-offer

Breakfast started out pretty quiet which was a little unusual for us. None of us had slept particularly well due to the fact that we needed to decide that morning how we wanted to proceed. No startup engineering firm in the offshore market had been offered one tenth the amount FWUSA was offering for Mustang, but we were all working in our minds to evaluate what the "soft cost" would be to us and to Mustangers.

We felt FWUSA would keep slicing at the Mustang amorphous blob until it was a cube and fit squarely into their organizational structure. The slicing would have to drive out some of our entrepreneurial spirit because that looked like risk to them. We also knew that during the next downturn it would be reasonable for FWUSA to require the two engineering houses (theirs and ours) in Houston to combine and reduce their overhead structures.

Paul felt that their Houston office was much stronger in terms of procedures and organizational structure than ours. We would be dealing from a position of weakness when the organizations might be combined, which would give him less input on how things would be set up and who would have key positions.

Felix felt that we would have to add a significant layer of overhead in order to fit properly into the FWUSA organization. This layer would negatively affect our ability to compete for EPCM type contracts.

Combine this new cost structure with our clients becoming uncomfortable that we were no longer "independent" of the construction contracting community and we might go into a downward spiral that we could not effectively reverse.

Gut feeling

This breakfast discussion was moving us away from the euphoria of the offer and into the mechanics of what being part of FWUSA would entail. This sale would probably not be good for the type of people we had hired. They wanted to be where engineering was king and not constrained by a construction group.

> "...this sale would probably not be good for the type of people we had hired."

Our gut feeling was that this looked more like a "sell-out" by Mustang's management team. Despite the fact that we would generously share this well-earned windfall, it would feel like we were buying people's loyalty instead of earning it.

Decision

We had tested the sales waters to knee deep and found that we were not prepared to go deeper due to our lack of business expertise.

We felt that there were too many ways for this sale to mess up the vision we had for Mustang. It would likely feel like we were sinking in quicksand as we watched our vision disappear in the FWUSA organization.

We met with the management team and thanked them sincerely for investing the time and effort they had expended in evaluating Mustang for possible acquisition. We told them that their appraisal was as good as they could do with the data and clarifications we had provided and that we were very impressed with the offer. Collectively, however, we felt that Mustang was not yet ready to be part of a larger organization and so we must decline the offer. Again we thanked them for working with us to this decisive decision point.

Lifted a load off of our shoulders

On the way to the airport we all breathed a sigh of relief. This was a path we had needed to explore. We had been like fish out of water at FWUSA and wanted to go back to our little pond. The discussions had been a good check that our philosophies were still very much aligned. We had also verbalized our principle concerns with the viability for Mustang going into 1996 and they generally centered on people. We decided to meet Sunday at Felix's home to decide a way forward. Strike while the iron of courage is hot and all the thoughts are fresh!

THE SECOND DECISION

Pick a direction

The primary concern from our FWUSA meetings was the potential to lose good people. We had been in a sustained "boom" since the fourth quarter of 1994. If we could prevent the loss of people, our jobs would be easier and Mustang would still be a fun, though tough, place for us to work. If we could solve this big problem, it would free us up to work on the other areas we had identified while at FWUSA.

The decision became obvious...we needed to give ownership to the people and get their 100% buy-in to the long term health of Mustang. Ownership would easily allow people to ignore queries from head hunters or their friends at other companies. Ownership would make it tougher for someone to decide to leave a company that was taking good care of them to go and start a new firm.

Through our meetings with FWUSA, we had determined a Fair Market Value for Mustang of $45,000,000. There were many ways to figure out the probable worth of a company, but this was about as concrete and up-to-the-minute as one could ever expect to have.

ESOP AND PHANTOM STOCK

Going back to our thoughts before we started Mustang, we decided to start an Employee Stock Ownership Plan (ESOP) that would put one third of the company into the hands of all the people. As a kicker to that plan we would set up a "Phantom stock" plan that would put additional stock ownership into the hands of 120 key people who would make our lives easier if they would stay long term. This Phantom stock would only become real if the company was sold or went public.

In many respects it felt like we could either push our people to move into the FWUSA organization or pull them in tighter to Mustang with an ESOP/Phantom stock program. Pulling our people in tighter felt better. We would be able to look our people in the eye and be proud of the decision we had made.

Joyce brought in milk and Toll House cookies for us to celebrate making the ESOP decision and resolving to stick with our decision not to pursue the offer from FWUSA. We would have nothing to hide concerning our meetings with FWUSA and we had a very positive plan for going forward. There would be no doubt that the caretakers of **MUSTANG** were focused on PEOPLE.

Image left : Mustang's owners standing, ESOP Custodians sitting.
Image Right: Paul Redmon signing the ESOP documents.

"Great leaders are great simplifiers."
General Colin Powell, U.S. Secretary of State

55: MAJORS VS. INDEPENDENTS

Industry wide benchmarking by the major oil companies pointed them all toward Mustang. Mustang projects were consistently "top-quartile" and the majors wanted to know why.

Our internal benchmarking showed that the same projects the majors liked were not top-quartile at Mustang. Our top projects had been done for the independent oil companies.

HOW TO GET TOP-QUARTILE

Contracting Strategy

Independents did not have "deep pockets" and could not afford for a project to have poor results. They did not want to reinvent the wheel or develop new technology...they wanted to "get 'er done". Our top projects had been done using the EPCM contracting strategy from concept through startup.

Stability of team

Independents would have the same 3-4 people on the project from concept through first year operations. They were accountable to deliver for the company. Independents would also "buy a slice" of Mustang by keeping a small team working for them. This gave them a voice to get more resources when needed.

Majors had a revolving door as the lead people "punched their ticket" with project work and then moved on to other management jobs. Each new leader would bring their background to the project and make changes. The new people would interrupt the flow of work to implement changes through their team of 30-40 folks.

Front End Engineering Design (FEED)

For the independents we pulled go-bys from past projects and quickly pieced the project definition together. In a few weeks we could show the owner what it would look like, how long it would take and what it would cost. The project at this point was aligned to the current industry capability. Then we did the project with weekly and monthly status meetings.

FEED for majors was a 4-6 month effort focused on getting internal agreement and Partner buy-in.

Design Criteria

We had standard criteria for every piece of equipment and every system required on a platform. It took about 30 systems to produce oil. Independents would expeditiously mark these up with input from operations and safety personnel.

For a major oil company the equipment and system definition was turned into a hundred small projects. There was a lot of scrutiny in terms of state-of-the-art solutions, long term operations costs and spare parts cost analysis. It took about 80 systems to produce oil.

Layout

We could generate a "paper doll" layout quickly from the layout criteria and equipment selections. This work was very subjective and generated from people's experience and check-lists. The layout had to consider drilling, quartering (safe area), oil production equipment, utility equipment and safety equipment. Similar to laying out a house, there are trade-offs everywhere.

Independents let us settle the layout easily, with comments limited to big picture things and very few people providing input. For majors it was just the opposite.

Organization

Independents put us in charge of the project with the owner team in a support role. The owner put an "umbrella" over the project to protect it from the owner organization, which could generate continuous input if left unbridled. Independents saw their job as insuring that we had what we needed in a timely manner. We needed timely input, firm decisions and funding (paying the bills) in line with the schedule.

Independents integrated with our team with a "best player plays" mentality. By integrating we became more aligned on get 'er done. Majors had more of an "us and them" feeling.

Schedule

Independents awarded engineering early to leave plenty of schedule for design, purchasing and construction. Majors would drag out the bid and award of engineering to the point where the schedule was in jeopardy from the time of the kick-off meeting.

Specifications

Independents used Mustang's general specifications and equipment specific specifications. They were simpler and more vendor oriented than the specifications used by the majors.

Freezing the design ...decisions that stick

Majors had the term "design freeze" because they had large teams of engineers, purchasers, operators, safety and maintenance personnel who would just continue to tweak things and "thaw" the design. This inability to freeze the design caused costly "work-arounds" and schedule slippage all the way through startup.

Purchasing

Majors had extensive bid lists. These clients had "Supply Chain Managers, Procurement Specialists and Program Buyers" whose job was to insure a fair and impartial bid process. Communication with the bidders was squashed, bid opening was a procedure and getting the bid evaluation approved was an iterative process.

Needless to say, these purchasing professionals scoffed at our "three bids and a buy" method of procurement using only proven vendors that could deliver vendor data in short order and robust equipment on time.

Our method kept us abreast of current proven industry technologies because we used good vendors. In their bids they would offer alternatives to what we specified if they thought there was a better solution that they had recently used.

Inspection

Independents let us use our inspectors in the field. The major's purchasing departments were concerned that our inspectors would allow us to "cover-up" problems. In the EPCM contract, the client was paying directly for the equipment with no mark-up by the engineer. There was no incentive for the engineer to do anything but competitively bid and get good equipment delivered on time.

TOP-QUARTILE

We knew that we could help the major oil companies benchmark better due to our experience with independents. It would take something dramatic, however, to push them to change. They told us they needed to improve their project metrics or they would not survive. If they sincerely wanted to change, we wanted to be there to help them.

"Leaders are those who empower others."
Bill Gates, CEO Microsoft

56: CONOCO TRIES IT

Conoco had been working to design their first-ever FPSO and their first-ever project offshore Nigeria called Ukpokiti. They had worked in-house for 15 months to design a facility around the use of one of their tankers and had a detailed cost estimate. They wanted us to review their design and prepare the International EPC bid document.

CHANGE THE GAME

At the kick off meeting we sat across the table from Conoco's project manager Joao De Olivera and his four person team. Joao described what they had done and related that the project was under enormous cost pressure. When he turned the meeting over to me, I told him that if he wanted to save cost, he should use Mustang's specifications instead of Conoco's.

Joao said that they had done some internal studies, after our benchmarking discussion, and felt that using Mustang's specifications could save them 20%. He wanted to use them if we were not charging too much for their use. I told him that they were free and that he would only be charged for any time we spent modifying them for the project. Then I told him that we would need all of their comments back in one week to meet schedule. He said, "The specifications are fine 'as is', you are free to proceed with them". Here was a small Conoco team, doing a high visibility project in a harsh Nigerian area and they seemed to have the autonomy to change how Conoco did projects. This project for a major oil company was definitely going to be different!!

> **"Using Mustang's specifications could save them 20%."**

THREE WEEKS IN

Using some new, but proven, technologies, we had a way to simplify the design and save 30% in both total project cost and schedule. We showed the Conoco team our findings and encouraged them to look seriously at what we were proposing, while we continued to develop the EPC bid package.

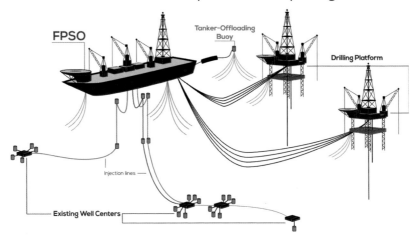

Proposed concept for Ukpokiti.

Joao's team came back a week later and said they wanted to do the project the way we proposed and forgo the EPC bid process. He had decided to jump right into detailed design with Mustang and do the project in our recommended EPCM manner with an integrated Conoco/Mustang team.

We had gained a lot of their team's trust in just a month!! We told Joao that we could staff up and do the project, but that we wanted to finish the FEED on the new concept while we started the detailed design and procurement. This would mean about four weeks of moving in two directions but would insure that we had a "Design Freeze" from the FEED documents. We wanted a solid basis in case the Conoco team wavered or their people were changed out.

RESULTS

During detailed design we sent our "Engineer Economist" Kurt Albaugh to Nigeria to figure out all of the logistics and costs to operate the FPSO. He developed a detailed spreadsheet that covered every operating cost Conoco would see through the life of the field.

All of the equipment was skid mounted along the USA Gulf Coast using our bid lists, bid packages and inspectors. We handled the logistics of export packing, shipping and receiving in Spain for delivery to the FPSO. Installation and startup of everything went smoothly offshore Nigeria and first year operating and production figures were right in line with Kurt's spreadsheet.

Ukpokiti FPSO tanker offloading crude to a shuttle tanker.

Conoco achieved the 30% savings in cost and schedule and Ukpokiti became Project of the Year within Conoco. Joao de Olivera was promoted to an Area Manager. Gotta love making heroes while being paid from a reimbursable contract by a client that truly wants you on their side of the table, helping to deliver their project in the best way possible.

ALLIANCING

What is it?

Alliancing was gaining ground as a way to shorten schedules by eliminating the bid cycles for engineering and construction. Conoco wanted to bid an alliance for offshore FEEDs worldwide. The alliance would cover fixed platforms, floating facilities and subsea developments. I met with the Conoco project manager and we both realized that we really did not understand how an alliance worked.

Junk Mail

I received a flyer for a three day seminar on alliancing. The seminar was going to define what alliancing was and walk through the steps required to develop one. The Conoco project manager and I went to the seminar. During breaks we discussed how to create a bid package that would give him good bids for evaluation. The seminar taught us the key steps to forming the Conoco alliance:

- Get to know the key players in both organizations.
- Brainstorm on the purpose: What could happen that would make this alliance very worthwhile?
- Examine the current business reality: What are the key issues for forming an alliance?
- Examine the predictable future: What will alliance results be two years from now (that you would bet your paycheck on)?
- Examine what is possible.
- Develop structures and practices for a way forward.
- Create a vivid demonstration of commitment.

Alliance Orange Juice Test

The CEO of your strongest competitor is in his jammies at breakfast. He has his orange juice glass in one hand when he picks up the newspaper and sees headlines about your alliance...the orange juice goes everywhere while some expletives are screamed and he wonders how we were ever able to get together!

CONOCO AKER MUSTANG (CAM) ALLIANCE

Aker-Omega had given us all of the Omega people and their projects. Aker just wanted assurances that if they needed facilities help to win a hull project we would support them. Aker had moved top subsea personnel from Norway to Houston in order to chase deepwater work. By having expertise in subsea and the layout of the seafloor for deepwater operations Aker had a leg up on getting in early on a project and being able to direct the hull their way.

We approached Aker about teaming up for the Conoco alliance. As a team we could handle any offshore project worldwide for Conoco, whether it was a shallow water platform, an FPSO, a semi-submersible or a pure subsea development and pipeline to shore.

Pictures of the CAM alliance signing ceremony were plastered all over the industry journals and I'm sure caused more than one "orange juice moment."

Signing Alliance documents.

57: ORYX SPAR

Oryx wanted a formal alliance. They explained that they were going to take a corporate risk and move into deepwater in a meaningful way. They were going to use North Sea spar technology to develop small fields in the Gulf. They wanted to develop the first spar oil and gas production platform in the world and felt they needed a tight relationship with their engineer due to the technological hurdles they would face. If everything worked as planned, then they would want to do a series of these "world class" spars. They wanted to use lessons learned and standardization going forward to reduce cost and schedule.

NEPTUNE

Concept

Oryx showed us the concept for the spar. It consisted of a 72 foot diameter cylindrical steel shell 705 feet long and weighing 12,000 tons with a production deck on top. The bottom of the spar shell would have a chamber filled with ballast material to lower the center of gravity and make the steel shell float vertically...like a cork with a weight on one end to tip it vertical. The cylinder would be anchored to the seabed with chain and wire cable...BIG chain and BIG cable!!

Millions of dollars had been spent by the oil companies and the large contractors to develop possible solutions for deepwater production. Concepts were tested with scale models in elaborate wave tanks in order to determine the motions wind, wave and currents would create in the structure or "vessel." Oryx decided that the spar gave them a conservative answer for producing their Neptune prospect in 1,930 feet of water.

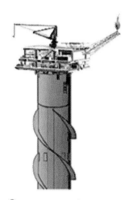

Spar concept.

Neptune spar installed.

Hull pieces in transport.

Spar assembled (ready to be uprighted).

The hull is an exotic piece of design work that had to withstand the severe currents and potential hurricane forces in the Gulf. It also had to protect the well risers and support the full production facility. In order to keep the hull size down and reduce complexity, Oryx did not design their first few spars to support a drilling rig. Drilling of wells was done by a separate deepwater drilling vessel.

Neptune contractors

The hull was built in Finland by Aker...justifying the Aker strategy of buying Omega for an entrée into the Houston market. Mustang designed the deck in an EPCM contracting mode. We had to develop tighter methods of controlling the deck center of gravity throughout design and controlling overall weight as the hull could only support 6,500 tons. We had to freeze critical design parameters early in the facility design. Similarly, the drilling, wellhead risers, mooring system and hull design groups had to freeze design parameters in order to progress the full design and get construction started in fabrication yards around the world.

Results

Neptune was considered a marginal field for deepwater and needed an economical solution. The world's first spar production development would cost Oryx (which was soon gobbled up by Kerr McGee in the ongoing consolidation of the oil patch) $300,000,000 which saved $90,000,000 over existing technology and the spar could be moved. Oryx planned to move the spar to the other edge of the reservoir when required to save drilling costs. Once the entire field was depleted, the spar could be moved to a new location.

Kerr McGee won the Offshore Technology Conference Distinguished Achievement Award in 2000 for the Neptune development.

Don Vardeman was our project sponsor at Oryx and helped implement the alliance with Paul Redmon as our sponsor. Don used our large Mustang wall calendars with the big blue horse on them, to track development stages on Neptune and took them to Board meetings and partner meetings to use in answering questions.

DEEPWATER CONCEPT SELECTION POSTER

Huge studies were being done worldwide by oil companies trying to figure out the best answer for their deepwater development. We were involved in 50% of them. Our deepwater concept selection poster helped them narrow the field quickly and put more effort into the "right" answer. Our poster was published in *Offshore Magazine* and had the big blue horse on it. We were the associated "expert" on deepwater developments.

Each time the Oryx (then Kerr McGee and then Anadarko due to more gobbling) alliance had a new deepwater prospect; Don Vardeman would mark on the latest Deepwater Concept Selection Poster where it fell in the various selection criteria graphs. If the concept landed in a yellow (caution) or red (not proven yet) area he would address the team's plan to mitigate the risk. Normally everything was green (proven and existing in the real world) which helped him with Board approval.

The Oryx deepwater alliance was built on six years of Mustang and Oryx working together and improving communication and trust. Steve Pyles (the original Sun Exploration phone call in Chapter 38), along with Daryl Rapp of Mustang were critical to the good communications and working through the rough spots. After the Kerr McGee purchase, management pushed to have another engineering firm do the topsides. We supplied all of our information to them, but the project did not go well. The alliance was re-instated and we did eight of the first nine spars in the world.

"Be on the cutting edge...not the bleeding edge."
General Dan Christman, Superintendent, USMA

58. CHEVRON COMPLIANT TOWER

John Ellis came to Paul and me with a vision he had for the structural engineering group. He wanted to hire top talent and go after the high-tech structural projects that were going to be needed as clients moved into deepwater. With his staff, he had come up with his wish-list of people and types of structures that they would like to position themselves to design.

WILL THE INDUSTRY BUY IT?

Paul and I had seen companies build a capability, figuring "if you build it they will come", only to find out that the investment was not seen to be of value by the industry. We told John that we liked his initiative in wanting to strengthen his group. We cautioned that there is no "Mother Mustang" to fund his hopes. His department would have to handle the overhead when these people were not billable.

John had worked the numbers and felt his group was large enough to handle the overhead and they were getting large structural budgets on the "now-normal" Mustang large projects. These budgets could support the people he wanted to get either as project managers or doing high-tech design.

John was also researching new PC based structural design programs. These were touted to be able to do the design work only McDermott and Earl & Wright could do with their in-house proprietary software on large main-frame computers. If he could develop and learn to use the new PC software along with getting the right talent, John felt that he could put together the "better mousetrap" for the industry as it moved into deeper water.

STEVE WILL

John Ellis hired Steve Will as his structural guru. Steve had worked on the Petronius Compliant Tower done for Chevron by McDermott. Petronius had set many records for structural height both offshore and onshore when compared to the tallest buildings in the world. Steve felt that the new twist on the design, called a Compliant Piled Tower (CPT) could be an economical alternative to tension leg platforms or spars for deepwater marginal fields in up to 3,000 feet of water.

Steve and John started experimenting with the software package for PCs that promised to do the calculations required for a complex "reed-type" structure. The structure would have the ability to flex and sway to dampen out the forces from wind, wave and current. It turned out that the programming was not ready for prime time, and they were going to have to work hand in hand with the software developer to correct the flaws. This was quite a setback for their plan to chase some marginal fields both domestically and internationally.

Petronius Compliant Tower done for Chevron by McDermott.

ELF AQUITAINE

Elf had been a participant in our deepwater tripod study some years earlier and trusted us in pushing technical boundaries in a safe and robust manner. They had a small field in the Gulf that was too deep for a conventional fixed platform but was not economical for a floating facility.

Elf paid for a CPT study. The study allowed us to test the software we had been helping to develop. This project did not proceed into detailed design but funded a strong structural group under Steve Will to prove that we could design a CPT.

EXXON

The possible Elf project gave us the leverage we needed to visit with Exxon, who had the patent for the CPT technology. We did a second CPT study for Exxon that proved our design capability to their experts. Then we were able to hammer out a royalty agreement and had the freedom to advertise our capability to offer CPT technology. The CPT matched the gray area in water depth between fixed platforms and floating production facilities...about 1,200-2,800 feet of water. We also proved the economics for marginal fields with high flow rates and low well counts.

Vision

Oryx had the vision to move into deeper water production with spar technology. They did not wait for the major oil companies to develop methods. John and Steve had the vision to fill a water depth gap with compliant piled tower technology. They wanted to create a better implementation of technology that was created by major oil companies. Both visions were successfully implemented by Mustang.

CHEVRON

Rhonda Redwine, Chevron Angola's project manager, conducted a design competition for the Benguela-Belize field in 1,280 feet of water. Our CPT won what would be the first compliant tower installed outside the Gulf of Mexico.

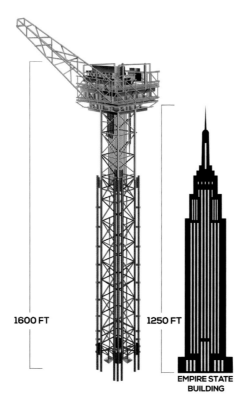

1600 FT

1250 FT

EMPIRE STATE
BUILDING

Benguela Belize CPT compared to the Empire State Building.

The project had Chevron's largest operating topsides at 43,500 tons and produced 220,000 bpd oil. It had housing for 157 people, included the first fully automated drilling rig offshore Angola and could re-inject 420,000 bpd of water back into the resevoir.

Our first CPT advertisement attempted to make it look simple.

CUTTING EDGE

In reality CPTs would be among the tallest free standing structures designed by mankind. By doing the first CPTs and production spars in the world, Mustang moved to the cutting edge of deepwater technology.

"America is another name for opportunity."
Ralph Waldo Emerson, Philosopher

59: DOWNSTREAM

Mary Needham called in June of 1996 to see if we were still interested in a strategic move into downstream process plants (refinery, chemical and petro-chemical) projects. This had been a topic of discussion when we hired Jim Vogt and again when we hired Dennis Frakes through her company. We had added about 100 people to Mustang in the past three months and had hit way more work than we had projected to FWUSA. Things were crazy, but diversification was always at the top of our list of things to work on.

LITWIN

Raytheon Purchase

Litwin had been sold to Raytheon Construction and Engineering in early 1996. Litwin was very stable and many of the engineers had been with them for 15-30 years. The key Litwin management personnel had signed a six month non-compete contract to insure continuity in capability as Litwin became part of Raytheon.

Immediately after the purchase, the Raytheon transition team started making numerous changes within Litwin in order to insure profitability. The net result early-on was a total lack of the personal touch. Due to the size of Raytheon, the Litwin people felt like they were just a number with no prospect of things changing. After three months, people without contracts started being snapped up by the competition and the survival of the "old" Litwin seemed untenable.

Mary wanted to talk about three top management people, Brent Colongne, Chick Houseman and Ron Jackson, who were within a few months of their contracts running out. She knew that they were planning to leave for slots in their competitor's organizations. These people had the personal relationships with the core Litwin people and core clients to be able to set up a downstream sector within Mustang. This sure sounded like the kind of team and resource (Litwin Engineers) that could move us profitably into downstream work.

First Meeting

We met Brent and Chick for dinner and spent a good portion of the evening discussing the cultures that had been developed at Mustang and Litwin. Interspersed in the dialogue were sprinkled thoughts on people, clients, project execution and the current state of the downstream industry.

One thing Brent and Chick liked about Mustang was the well-developed modular and skid design approach to control construction costs. The projected savings they had heard discussed at conferences were compelling but the war stories about modules having to be cut apart and re-worked in the field weighed heavily on the downstream industry moving in that direction. Mustang's proven modular experience would give them a distinct advantage in bidding.

They felt certain that they could make a significant contribution to both the bottom line and the stability of Mustang by providing diversification in clients and projects. All three turned in their notice and had a good story to tell the people still at Litwin, along with those that had left to other companies. They had found an engineering-oriented company with a good culture that would provide them with the support required to re-invent Litwin.

GETTING THE WORD OUT

Soon after arriving at Mustang, Brent, Chick, Ron and I attended an industry conference and had a Mustang flyer put under the hotel room door of every attendee. The next day, they were the talk of the conference and many questions were asked about this unknown company of "Mustangers" that they had joined. I told the Mustang story a hundred times, which helped Brent, Chick and Ron learn it.

I went with Ron and Brent on a number of the early sales calls in order to explain the history and capability of Mustang. Brent headed up the new sector, Chick ran the operation and Ron did the sales work. Soon the Process Plants sector was standing on its own and winning work without me.

An unbelievable win

Process plants had started pulling people out of the Raytheon-Litwin organization as they needed them for projects that had been won. One of their biggest clients approached Ron with the concern that he would pull people that their large refinery upgrade project needed. He wanted them to stay through project start-up. Ron acknowledged that many of the best people were on that project and that they would have to target getting them due to their knowledge of how Litwin had worked. Ron ended up negotiating a deal with the client and Raytheon to switch about 30 people to Mustang's payroll but leave them working at Raytheon-Litwin until the project was completed. This sales strategy blew my mind! On a Monday morning we signed up 30 people, said hello and then sent them back to work at Raytheon. The best part was that we now had their resumes to show that we had full service capability for the process plants industry in every discipline required.

LITWIN HELPS STIMULATE CHANGE

Procedures

Paul had found a new resource as the talent started to pour in from Litwin. Some of the people had been instrumental in developing Litwin's project and company administrative procedures. Paul pulled them together to prepare a complete set of procedures and to train the entire company. This was a huge undertaking that we had needed for a long time.

Automation

Much of the current work in downstream started with an automation upgrade project to reduce costs. The automation project then resulted in some other process and equipment modifications. The head of Litwin's 200 person automation group was Don Colchin. Don was the most "Mustangy" of all the people we had met, but had been with Litwin for 33 years, dating back to an internship in college. He told me later that he sat in his car for half an hour before coming in on the first day...wondering if he had made the right decision.

Don talked John Kealey into coming to Mustang a few months later to head up the instrument engineering department within the Process Plants sector. John was a bit intimidating due to his raw intelligence but a genuine and caring person who became a great Mustanger. The talent we were assembling in instrument and automation was staggering considering the short time frame.

The upstream industry was moving into much larger projects and was primed for figuring out how to automate these facilities. We were sure that the timing was going to be good for Don's department to work across upstream, pipelines and downstream.

PROCESS PLANTS CONNECTS THE DOTS

At the annual Engineering and Construction Contractor's (ECC) conference, Ed Merrow, the owner of IPA, gave a talk on contracting. Chick brought it to me because it matched our philosophy. Primary components were:

Client Project Execution Plan

EPCM Contracting

Integrated Team

Quality FEED

Stage Gate approvals

Stepwise freeze the design

Lump Sum Fabrication & Construction

All of Ed's recommendations paralleled the "win-win" contracting strategies we had been trying to convince Brent, Chick and Ron to try in downstream contracting. They were the basis that we had built Mustang around in upstream.

We were very interested in learning more about IPA and seeing if their findings could be applied to upstream projects... to help us move more clients toward EPCM contracting.

"If you can measure it, you can improve it."
Lord Kelvin, Engineer

60: INDEPENDENT PROJECT ANALYSIS

All major oil companies and national oil companies had both upstream and downstream assets. Upstream assets were close to the wellhead and provided initial separation of oil, natural gas (gas) and water and put the oil and gas into pipelines. Pipelines and tankers delivered the oil to refineries and petrochemical plants...downstream assets...as feedstock to be distilled into many products.

IPA BENCHMARKS THE INDUSTRY

Ed Merrow had started a company called Independent Project Analysis in 1987 (good year!) to analyze project performance in the downstream industry (refinery and chemical). He developed a systematic method of analyzing projects and an objective set of metrics with which to judge project success. He was allowed to gather detailed project information from the oil companies and boil it down to his metrics. His objective was to help companies understand their performance on their own projects and then let them see how their project metrics compared to their industry peers. He wanted to develop, and help clients understand, the common risk factors that resulted in poor performing projects. At the same time, he wanted to figure out what were the keys to best-in-class project performance. He wanted to help his clients improve their capital utilization.

Soon, Ed's clients were asking him to help them develop a better project execution strategy that would give them a better chance of benchmarking in the top-quartile of their peers. As his databases grew larger, they provided statistically significant evidence that supported a new project execution strategy.

IPA FINDINGS IN DOWNSTREAM

IPA was able to correlate good project definition with the ability to stay on track through successive phases of a project. Projects that were executed with good early project definition benchmarked "best-in-class." It became evident from the downstream projects studied; that a properly executed front end engineering design (FEED) was paramount to ultimate project success. IPA then took its findings and created a method to grade the quality of a FEED that could estimate how the project would turn out in terms of cost, schedule and first year operability. This was a huge step for the oil companies, essentially giving them a cookbook to work from in order to generate good projects.

IPA also documented what was needed during each stage of a project in order to keep it on track for cost and schedule. In order to not let the cost and schedule creep across time, IPA wanted certain things "frozen" at each stage.

Each stage had a "gate keeper" who had to approve the quality and completeness of the deliverables for a stage before the project could proceed to the next stage. This "Stage Gate" process was heralded as the best way to manage large complex projects and keep them in control.

The stage gate process was also designed to kill a project early if it was not technically or commercially viable. This was a good development because once started, projects tended to take on a life of their own and no one felt empowered to stop them...leading to poor results.

"Stage gate was designed to kill a project early."

Once IPA benchmarking and the resultant stage gate processes proved themselves in downstream, oil companies put IPA to work on upstream projects.

IPA MOVES TO UPSTREAM

Early on, in the '70s and '80s, offshore projects were not that large and poor performance was generally covered up by a rising oil and gas price. Due to advances in seismic and three-dimensional characterization of the reservoirs, upstream projects were increasing in size, and the oil companies needed better project management tools to deliver them. In 1994 and 1995, the IPA stage gate process started to take hold in upstream where we did most of our work.

Since our larger projects were being done for contractors and not for oil companies, we missed the early development of the stage gate process. Across time, Texaco, Mobil and BP started using the process. Each company had a name for their stage gate process, and they varied slightly in the deliverables for each stage.

STAGE GATE STAGES

Initiation Stage

The project was initiated by determining the project goals in terms of cost, schedule, quality, safety and first year revenue. With this information, the engineering firm could outline the various concepts that were applicable and help the client evaluate which was best for the project and their organization. Sometimes client experience with a certain concept outweighed other factors. Generally the teams wanted to limit deliverables (drawings, design criteria, etc.) at this stage and use experience to estimate concept cost and schedule to +/- 30% for comparison.

Serious attention was paid to determining project risk factors and understanding how to mitigate them.

Feasibility Stage

During the feasibility stage, the selected concept was developed in greater detail such that everyone could understand and look at it from their unique perspective. During this time, portions of other possible concepts may have been included in the preferred concept in order to mitigate certain risks. The cost and schedule estimates were moved to a +/- 15% accuracy.

Definition Stage

The preferred project concept was worked in more detail to nail down the scope, cost and schedule along with appropriate contingencies during this stage. The result of this stage was that the project was taken to the company Board for funding. This concludes what IPA termed Front End Loading (FEL) for a project... similar to FEED.

Execution Stage

Detailed engineering, procurement and construction are completed during this stage in accordance with the execution plan. Similar to going into battle, though, the plan rarely survives the first bullet.

Evaluation Stage

The final stage involved assessing the performance of the operating development and feedback gathering for future projects. Most companies called this feedback their "lessons learned" for future use. Oil companies had been using some type of process like this but without much discipline. By paying IPA to help collect the lessons learned, this activity became more indoctrinated and was more likely to get used in the future.

WE WERE STAGE GATE BELIEVERS

From the data, IPA concluded that an Engineer, Procure, Construction Manage (EPCM) contracting strategy provided the best results for cost, schedule, quality, safety and first year operations. The strategy would save 25% in cost and schedule over lump sum. EPCM was the strategy Mustang had been beating the drum for since 1987.

"EPCM is 25% cheaper than lump sum."

If IPA could get the industry to focus on quality FEED/FEL, it would play right into our strength that we had been developing since our CBS Engineering days. We had 17 strong years of developing methods to squeeze engineering and develop FEEDs with the "right" level of definition. We were primed and ready for anyone who wanted to implement IPAs findings.

"STAGE COACH®"

Doing our "horse-thing" we created our "Stage Coach®" process to tie in with the client's stage gate process. We wanted to show that our stage coach process would fit like well-made puzzle pieces into the client's stage gate process. Our process delineated what inputs we would need at each stage and what deliverables we would produce. Because we worked for so many clients on multiple projects, we quickly became stage gate experts and actually trained client teams on their own process as we helped them work through FEL.

For smaller independent oil companies we gave them a "Cookbook Stage Gate Process" and training in order to use it on their projects. It was a lean, diet version of what the big boys were using, but gave them the same amount of control.

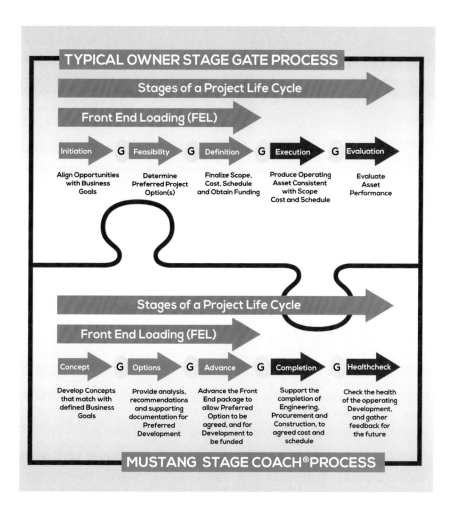

ORYX HIGH ISLAND 379

While stage gate was developing in the upstream industry, Daryl Rapp's team did a significant PDQ (Production/Drilling/Quarters) platform project for Oryx in eleven months...which was definitely PDQ (Pretty Damn Quick) for the industry! The fabrication yard in Corpus Christi, Texas brought every client they could think of to see the deck in their yard and discuss schedule, cost and safety benchmarks.

Oryx deck loaded on barge for transport.

Everything went well on this project. It was done in an EPCM fashion with an integrated team that had worked together on four previous projects. The cost of this project was materially significant to a company the size of Oryx and could cripple the company if it went out of control. This project was done with a Concept Selection Phase that was approved by management, a Definition Phase and an Execution Phase. Although not Stage Gate per se, the project had all of the elements and was a glowing success. It played right into the project execution strategy Ed Merrow was touting...to deliver best-in-class projects.

"BEST-IN-CLASS"

ORYX & MUSTANG

Infrastructure builds differentiation.

61: INFRASTRUCTURE 201

Jim Vogt and Dennis Frakes met with me for about four hours after work one day to dissuade me from the "entrepreneurial spirit of sales" at Mustang and get me to stop chasing smaller projects. Their rationale was good and the discussion evolved into a watershed discussion of all the problems they saw at Mustang from a professional sales perspective. I took a lot of good notes and used them as we started putting more overhead pieces into the sales organization in order to better support outside sales.

I could not, however, move us away from chasing any small project that old or new clients had. These small projects did a number of things for Mustang that helped us differentiate ourselves in the industry.

SMALL PROJECT DYNAMICS

Small projects provided about 60% of our billable hours and in tough times could flex up to 85% with more effort. These billable manhours filled in all the small gaps to keep our overall billability high. If we stopped chasing them, we would quickly lose the ability to bid them competitively because they take a different mindset than large projects. Once we lost this ability, we would not be able to flex into them as needed in downturns.

We staffed small projects with some very experienced leads along with some younger people to reduce the overall manhour cost average. This gave us an immediate mentoring system for training young people. On many of these projects the engineer also did the purchasing and field inspection, allowing them to see first-hand what worked and where problems came from.

Small projects normally lasted from six weeks to 18 months in duration (compared to three to six years on larger projects). The cycle from engineering, to bid, to award and construction was very short which allowed for good feedback. Our people could be on three of these projects in different phases and in two years have been involved in 10 to 12 projects.

Small projects were generally more profitable per man-hour due to the use of open contracts that had decent rate schedules for call-out work. Often we could also convert an overhead hour to a billable hour, and that really helped our bottom line.

Small projects allowed our people to develop tight relationships with clients on work that did not require a bid. Many times these tight relationships, developed over many small projects, gave us a leg up in winning much larger projects later when these clients moved up in their organizations. Mustangers could see how their efforts and relationships helped bring work in the door.

Jim and Dennis could understand my reasoning for continuing to chase everything, but felt their relationship building skills could be better used to bring in larger projects.

Operations develops their "sales bone"

> "We were always looking for someone with a sales bone."

Due to the discussion with Jim and Dennis, we put more follow-on sales responsibility on the shoulders of the small projects project engineers. They were doing the projects and keeping their heads up looking for other opportunities in similar fashion to what Paul, Felix and I did in the first few years of Mustang. We were always looking for someone with a "sales bone" somewhere in their body that we could help put some muscle around and many stepped up to the challenge.

SALES SUPPORT

Proposals
The quantity, quality and size of proposals were also increasing significantly so we brought in David Jackson to coordinate our proposal efforts. He was also a lay preacher who helped the quality of our Wednesday lunch Bible study group. David helped us work many large and small proposals at the same time and worked with me to develop standard pieces that could be tweaked quickly to seem custom for the project. We also started tracking our proposals and projections of manhours we felt we would win against the actual results. We were learning how to better support operations with good data and had the time to get operations more involved in the proposal effort.

Contracts
The Ex-Litwin management team introduced us to their lawyer, Don Cruver, who worked for them as outside council to help with contract negotiations. Contracts were much more complex in the downstream world and Don immediately impressed us with his ability work with client legal teams. Don only worked on the contractor side in working out contracts and had done so for many years with the largest engineering and construction companies in the world. In the industry it was generally felt that he "wrote the book" on fair contracting.

We asked Jim Vogt if he would move into running a contracting group for Mustang and he accepted. He paid attention to detail in contracts, and we knew that with Don Cruver's support we'd get good contracts going forward. We had Jim and Don teach contracts classes to our sales and project management people. These classes gave them the knowledge to help coach their clients in the early stages of a project. We felt that some early coaching on acceptable contract language could get us to a better starting point, and we had reasonable success with this effort. One of my favorite things they came up with were the "seven lies" the client contracts person will tell the contractor:

- You have to sign the document the way it is since we cannot change it.
- All the other contractors sign it without any changes.
- Your attorney is giving you bad advice.
- We would never really ever use that part of the contract against you.
- This is a new agreement we have to use. We cannot use the old agreement.
- We cannot pay you unless you sign our contract.
- We are the "deep pockets" for liability so you do not have to worry.

> **"There is never a good reason to sign a bad contract."**

Jim didn't like it when I said he was now heading up our "Order Prevention Group" because getting an acceptable contract was now a necessary hurdle to overcome. As Don liked to say, "There is never a good reason to sign a bad contract." To their credit, Jim and Don were always able to work something out with the client if they wanted to use Mustang.

Marketing

We needed a marketing person to help me with all the ideas I had for external and internal marketing of the brand and culture of Mustang. I had interviewed a number of people and had whittled my way down to a lady that could work three days a week until her children were a little older. I was pretty pumped up about her talent and capability to crystallize the messages we needed to get out.

Then Mike Farley... a new person Jim had hired to help in contracts...came to me and felt I should take the time to meet Dena Lee with whom he had worked at Brown & Root. He felt she was very capable, would love the Mustang spirit and would probably move due to some changes in her work environment. Once I met Dena, I was in a quandary as both women were a terrific match for what I needed. I ended up going with Dena primarily because Mike had been at Mustang long enough to know what it was like and he was confident the fast pace would not crush Dena.

Dena Lee

Within a week of Dena's starting I did not know how I had been surviving without her. Just unloading all of my thoughts on her was a relief as I knew they would get acted upon in some manner that I could adjust as we went forward. After three months I asked Dena how she liked working at Mustang. She said the change from Brown & Root was like stepping off of a super-tanker onto a speedboat, but she loved it and everything she was learning about Mustang.

PAUL'S DOUBLE-TEAM APPROACH

Paul had developed about nine core teams around project managers. These teams could take on any upstream project and be fleshed out with the required talent. We had been having trouble "coming out of the gates" on the larger projects in the same fashion we were used to on small to mid-sized projects. One of our key success factors was getting ahead on projects, getting engineering off of the critical path, and relieving schedule stress. On the larger projects there just seemed to be too many early priorities to set up this winning scenario. It seemed on large projects that one of the two critical areas suffered in the early going...either the technical development or the reporting and organization. This lack of progress would taint the client's feelings toward our team, and we would be put into a catch-up and defensive mode.

Sales helped some by working with clients to pick a start date that was two to three weeks after the project award. This gave us time to start shifting resources and set up for a quality kickoff meeting that could dig into the project and get alignment. With David Jackson's help we started creating some of the project status report documents in our proposals, such that the project teams could just use them immediately.

Paul started putting two of his core teams on the first six weeks of big projects. The primary team would immediately start working the technical details of the project in order to deliver quality products at the early milestones. The secondary team would work all of the "soft" issues like setting up project files, communications, detailing the scope of work, schedules, cost estimates, action item lists and meeting notes.

By doubling the strength of our team for the early phase of the project we could out-perform in the client's eyes.

Then the secondary team would move onto its own project and be supported in a similar fashion by another team. This took a lot of coordination from Paul and the project managers but helped solidify them as a team. It also helped Paul push common procedures as they were necessary for this type of support and execution.

"Luck is when preparation meets opportunity."
Seneca, Philosopher

62: EXXON VISIT

A crazy series of events occurred over a three month period. The major oil companies came to see Mustang for briefings on our FEED capability and full project execution through startup. Endless questions were asked and addressed about how we were able to execute so many medium to large projects both domestically and internationally with best-in-class metrics. We think our ability to do the Oryx 15,000 bpd oil platform for Steve Pyles in 11 months may have been a key stimulant for these meetings. IPA's findings, had also been an influence. Luckily we had been in "idea" meetings like these with Conoco, Arco and Unocal and had found that it did not hurt at all to speak freely and "give them both barrels" in our effort to help them change.

STAY ALIVE

Oil companies had continued to shrink and consolidate internally from 1989 through 1997. Each oil company stated that they needed to change how they did business or they would not survive the continued consolidations they foresaw in the industry. These statements surprised us as the companies were large international players (Texaco, Amoco, Mobil, Arco, etc.) and had been around forever. We were too far down in the food chain to understand what they were seeing in their future.

We did however know how to help them deliver projects for 25-35% less cost and schedule if they could trust us and to some extent get out of our way. They said that they wanted to learn how to execute and Mustang-ize their project delivery systems as much as possible and would look for a project to work together!!

IMPETUS TO CHANGE

The discussions were not about engineering cost and how to squeeze it. We were talking on a much higher plane about ideas and teaming and "best player plays" type of thinking. Where could the client bring value and where could Mustang? The majors vs. independents topics from Chapter 41 were covered in each meeting. We had worked for many of these clients (Conoco, BP, Texaco, Mobil, Mesa, Oryx), but had not worked for some (Unocal, Amoco, Exxon, Shell and Chevron).

Everything we presented derived from our core beliefs of setting up win-win strategies, getting the engineer on the same side of the table as the client and setting the vendors and contractors up for success. We knew that the engineer and the client's relationship with that engineer were the keys to driving project success in any way that the client defined success. We had talked the talk and walked the walk for so long that there were no holes in what we presented in the discussions. We could give concrete examples from past projects to clarify ideas we were presenting and objectively challenge the clients as to why they could not operate in a certain manner. Where they saw risk in our methods, we explained how that risk was mitigated by the way we implemented the idea.

These discussions were fun but stressful as we wanted to move these clients to a new place...into a Mustang-type space, but did not want to overwhelm them with too much at one time. Changing a client's "corporate spots" was not going to be easy, but it sounded like survival was at stake. Even if nothing ever came of these conversations, we had been discussing ideas on a semi-equal footing with top people from the strongest oil companies in the world. It felt like there was more potential for the industry to turn a little more in our direction if we would just stay-the-course.

EXXON COMES BACK

We're interested

We had no previous experience with Exxon and were surprised at how serious they seemed to be about improving their project execution methods. They did not give us data on their past projects because they did not want to taint our thinking. All of our discussions were very open - especially since we felt that we had nothing to lose. After all, what were the chances we would do a project for Exxon? From our discussions, however, Exxon pre-qualified us for their Diana natural gas… no oil…development offshore Louisiana in very deepwater of about 5,000 feet!

Diana bid

We were crazy busy and even had two full teams working at Mobil's offices in North Houston on Nigerian projects when the Exxon bid package arrived in a huge notebook. It looked like 30 people had worked on it for months and it was very detailed in exactly how they wanted everything presented back to them. We would have to reformat everything we had about Mustang's experience and prepare reams of spreadsheets that they could then slice and dice to numerically figure out who should win the contract. We ranked winning at 15%, and we could not spring 10-15 people for six weeks to work up the bid they requested. Everyone was 120% billable, so we needed to just turn this bid into part of a long term sales effort.

We decided to bid this single level purpose built floating gas facility as if we were doing it for Oryx or Arco or a get 'er done team from Mobil. The hull was going to be a four legged semi-submersible designed by others, so it was just a large 300 million standard cubic feet per day offshore gas facility that we knew how to do.

Typical semi-submersible.

We thanked Exxon for their interest in Mustang and said that we enjoyed the meetings to discuss how they would like to "Mustangize" their project execution methodologies. In line with those discussions, we were presenting how we would do this project for a large independent oil company. If they were serious about changing how they did projects, then this should be the starting point for both companies to work out how the project would be executed.

A little coaching on manpower

"It is in the trash can" were the first words out of Steve Byatt over the phone. Steve was BP's representative on Exxon's Diana project because BP owned a significant stake in the field. He said that our proposal was not thrown in the trash immediately, but that when they saw our manpower planning portion of the bid they felt that we could not handle the project and therefore discarded the proposal. He was calling as a courtesy just to make sure they understood the chart correctly, because BP was very interested in Mustang competing for the project. Steve said that he knew we had two very big projects and so his impression was that we were strapped for people. This was very interesting to have a "coach" on the inside that felt Mustang would be good for the project. We showed him that we did have the staff available to match their timing.

Systems and procedures

Eventually the evaluation boiled down to three bidders. Exxon expressed concern about our systems for engineering and project management. Frank Milburn was going to be the engineering manager for Exxon, and I put him with Paul.

Talking technical details about his passion for creating good systems in a one-on-one environment was like a duck going into the water for Paul. Paul knew all of the history behind creating the systems and the features he wanted to add. A few hours later I came back, and Frank had good confidence that our systems were sufficient for Diana.

Getting a contract

We found that Exxon is like a small country with a treasury department and legions of lawyers. Felix had been going back and forth trying to get a contract we could sign if this job came to us. The Exxon project people would not let our part-time lawyer Don Cruver talk directly with their lawyers to resolve the liability issues. Paper was just sent back and forth for a month with no movement from either side. Finally I called the project manager Ken Larson (who was a bit of a maverick in the Exxon organization) and told him that all we needed was to let Don Cruver talk to their head of legal and it would be resolved. Ken set up the call and twenty minutes later Don had agreed wording that worked for all parties.

Exxon said they were very serious about changing how they did projects and awarded us the Diana project. This result of our discussions was awesome but scary. This was way different from helping Oryx move to a new place after years of relationship building. Exxon wanted to change how they worked while executing a fairly large $500,000,000 project in a world record water depth and using some new technologies.

> "The only constant is change."
> Heraclitus of Ephesus, Philosopher

63: EXXON DIANA HOOVER

Paul and I saw Lynn Boyd, the head of Exxon Houston, coming down the hall at the hotel and we went to say hello. Our wives and the Exxon Diana project leadership team, with spouses, were all gathered in a wonderfully appointed hotel banquet room getting ready for a sit-down meal and fun activities to celebrate the kick-off of Diana. This was a big deal because Exxon and partner BP were planning the deepest drilling and production complex yet to be attempted in the world at 4,800 feet of water depth. Exxon had committed to an integrated teaming arrangement with Aker doing the semi-submersible hull and Mustang Engineering for the production facilities in an EPCM contracting strategy.

Exxon had assigned top talent to the project and were committed to changing how they did projects as they moved strongly into deepwater. They wanted this project to help them develop leaner project development practices. Then they planned to split the talent they had brought together into multiple teams to take those practices around the world. This dinner was part of a new beginning for Exxon's project development personnel...one that would have far reaching implications.

TIME FOR CHANGE

Lynn looked a little ashen-faced, and we asked if he felt ok. He said that he was ok, but had just taken a phone call that would significantly change the project we were about to kick off in the next room. He was formulating in his mind how he would address the probable impact of the call in his opening remarks for the evening. We went to our table and told our people that something was about to change on the project and we needed to listen closely to what Lynn had to say.

Lynn opened his remarks by welcoming everyone and thanking us for our hard work in bringing the Diana concept into focus over the past two months. Then he said that a few miles away from Diana, drilling had just discovered a mammoth oil reservoir. Combining the new Hoover reservoir with Diana would make sense due to the huge costs involved in putting a floating facility in 4,800 feet of water. Lynn said that everyone should enjoy the beginning of Diana and just be aware that over the next few weeks the team would have to figure out how to incorporate the Hoover oil reservoir.

Our team definitely enjoyed the evening and the time with Exxon/BP/Aker leadership personnel, but our minds were wandering. The Diana project becoming Diana Hoover would mean the project would significantly change. Oil production facilities with high flowrates were 20 times as complex as high flowrate gas facilities. Oil also produced much higher revenues and would significantly raise the stakes for good performance by Exxon. Diana was going to change from a relatively proven 500 million dollar natural gas concept to a probable 2.5 billion dollar combined oil and natural gas project. We were not sure if Exxon's conservative nature would demand that they switch to a much larger engineering firm and revert to their normal project processes. Could their desire to change withstand the pressure of this now HUGE project?

DIANA HOOVER

Artist rendering of
Diana Hoover.

How big is it?

Exxon stayed the course with Mustang and Aker. In combining the production of both Diana and Hoover reservoirs, we changed the concept from a semi-submersible to a Deep Draft Caisson Vessel (DDCV). This was a heavily modified spar-type concept. Unlike the Oryx Neptune spar, the DDCV would be a full-fledged Production, Drilling and Quarters (PDQ) facility with flow-rates of 100,000 barrels of oil and 325 million standard cubic feet of natural gas per day on a "can" twice the diameter of Neptune. The urgent questions were how big the deck would be and how much it would weigh...as these would be the driving criteria for design of the caisson vessel.

We had beaten the deck size around, but did not have enough information on the drilling rig, quartering requirements and equipment sizes to pick a firm answer. Caught in the middle and being a man of action, Ken Larson just picked a size from the information available and gave it to both teams! This was a bold move that upset everyone who was trying to figure out the problem. After a week or so the ripples died down and everyone was onboard with figuring out how to make the deck size work. Ken's leadership had moved the project forward.

Can we buy something?

In my sponsor meeting with Lynn Boyd, he asked how he might help. I showed him that we had boiled the purchasing system on the project down to 21 steps for each item. Per discussions we had on moving toward a Mustang execution method, I showed him that our system had six steps. He took the list and met with his team to see if they could streamline the purchasing. They were able to move it down to 11 steps. This was an improvement but did not seem like enough...until a number of Exxon people said that this was a HUGE movement for a company that changes glacially. ☺

Can we build something?

Paul and I were called into a meeting with Mike Flynn the project manager. We had failed to issue the first 75 of the 7,000 piping isometrics needed in construction.

Mike asked what our error percent in construction was with our isometric design process. We told him that the industry standard was 1.5-3.0% errors and we prided ourselves on being at less than 0.5%. A higher error rate seemed like a small price to pay to keep the schedule on track and he asked us to delete some steps in our process.

> "As the piping goes...so goes the project."

We could not fathom how to back off and knew that the real problem was that engineering had landed on the project critical path. We knew that a large error rate would give the fabrication yard easy excuses for slipping schedule. The piping errors would lead to much larger costs, since, "As the piping goes... so goes the project." We asked Mike to give us five days to get the initial isometrics out and ten days to get back on track. We hand-picked 20 designers out of 15 projects to flesh out the Diana Hoover team and got them ahead of the delivery curve.

Diana Hoover deck fabrication at
Brown & Root's Houston yard.

Brown & Root Yard

Things were totally crazy at the yard. B&R was qualifying and hiring craft people at a prodigious rate in order to flesh out the yard. These were the biggest decks ever built on the Gulf coast. Purchasing and supply systems for steel, pipe, electrical and instrument materials were being stretched along with receiving as trainloads and truckloads of material were arriving daily. Some valves were so large and heavy that only one could be delivered on an 18 wheeler tractor-trailer.

In the middle of this hubbub, our yard manager, Fred Nichols, developed a spreadsheet to track piping isometrics by area of the platform and processing system. He worked with B&R and Exxon's construction manager, Decie Autin to insure they had the right drawings ahead of time. Fred took us off of the project's critical path. Our motto was to "Make Brown and Root a Hero" and we did our part.

Make Brown & Root a Hero !

64: GROWING WITH EXXON

Paul Redmon and Dennis Frakes went on an around the world tour of oil companies, construction companies and some competitors. Dennis wanted to show Paul what was out there and Paul wanted to see how our message landed in other parts of the oil patch. They came back saying that our project execution methods, culture and track record were well received. In their words, "The world is our oyster and we just have to figure out how to eat it."

They met a Texan named Nick Bradshaw while in Perth, Australia. They were very impressed with his project management, construction management and client relationship skills. He was the type of person we needed NOW since we were working "change-how-we-do-business" world class projects for most of the major and large independent oil companies.

EUDC

I was the only contractor invited to a two day off-site meeting of Exxon's top management in Houston. The purpose of the meeting was to determine the vision, goals and organizational structure for Exxon's upstream business unit world wide. This was preparation for doing a number of projects the size of Diana Hoover or larger. The result was forming Exxon Upstream Development Company (EUDC). EUDC would use best practices that had been developed on Diana Hoover.

EUDC wanted to develop close relationships with critical suppliers in order to provide best-in-class project development worldwide. In visiting with top management at Exxon there was concern about our performance to date and whether or not we could step up to what they wanted.

MANAGE THE CLIENT'S PERCEPTION

The Diana Hoover project had expanded to add the Madison and Marshall reservoirs. Nick Bradshaw looked at all of the data we had and from his mega-project experience felt that at first-blush the entire project was a resounding success. He felt that our main problem was that we had not managed the client's perception of the project. Even the top people at Exxon were caught up in helping to solve some of the big challenges. Nick met with top people at both Exxon and BP to gather data and see if he could present the Diana Hoover performance in a way that would change their perception.

Mustang data

Nick went first to determine proven capability at Mustang. At 650 people in the upstream project sector, we were second only to Brown & Root. He then looked at the major upstream projects at Mustang and developed the following pie chart:

Major Projects in Mustang
March 1998 Snapshot

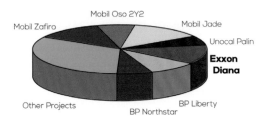

Nick then put Diana in perspective relative to all major projects being worked at Mustang. We had about 400 of our 1,000+ people working on major projects.

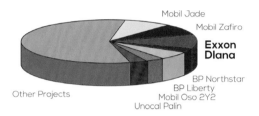

Major Projects Work off
(first half 1998)

Exxon data

Working with Exxon personnel, Nick was able to pull up data on recent major projects that he labeled A-G, leaving the key to their project names with Exxon for confidentiality. Some of these projects had BP as a partner. He included data from our Mobil Jade project for Equatorial Guinea that was done in our Gulf of Mexico fashion and benchmarked best-in-class from IPA. Jade was Mobil's "game-changing" project.

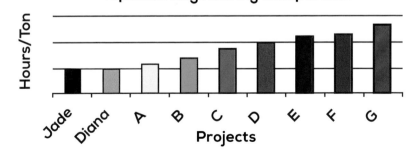

One of the true measures of how efficient the engineering is on a project is to look at the Engineering and Procurement (EP) budget...including the equipment cost. Nick found that on large projects like Diana, Exxon was used to equipment cost being 30-80% over the budgeted amount due to scope increase. Engineering that can control equipment cost will generally get that equipment delivered on time for ease of construction... saving additional dollars.

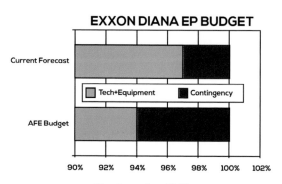

EXXON DIANA EP BUDGET

Engineering 75%+ complete.
Equipment 98% bought.

Scope growth

A critical issue Nick had to deal with was the perception that Mustang could not predict the size of the project, resulting in "surprises" in the manhour growth. Nick related the key historical context of the growth as follows:

- Diana started out as a gas facility to be done in typical Gulf of Mexico fashion – a paradigm shift for Exxon.
- Diana evolved to a major integrated deck on a DDCV; first of a kind for Exxon and Mustang, while taking the industry to a new level of complexity.
- Diana Hoover started detailed design after six weeks of concept work, when industry benchmarks would suggest four months being needed.

Nick provided some simple sketches for visual impact (the solid black lines are decks):

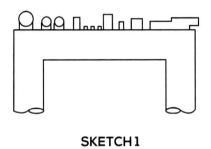

SKETCH 1

SKETCH 1
Diana Sketch - 1 Deck

SKETCH 2
Diana & Hoover Reservoirs
9 Deck Areas (Initially)

SKETCH 3 Diana, Hoover,
Madison, Marshall 19 Deck
Areas (Mezzanines Added)

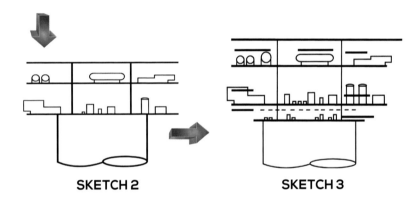

SKETCH 2   SKETCH 3

Service cost benchmarks

Nick put our major projects into the following chart to demonstrate repeatable industry leading engineering execution for major oil companies. The engineering cost as a % of Total Installed Cost was half of industry norms.

PROJECT	YEAR	MANHOURS	SERVICE COST AS % TIC
Exxon Diana	1998	350,000	8%
Mobil Jade	1998	210,000	6%
BP Northstar	1997	300,000	6%
Unocal Pailin	1997	230,000	7%
Mobil Usari	1996	175,000	7%
British Gas Miskar	1993	150,000	5%
Dresser - Venezuela	1991	300,000	6%

Summary and way forward

Nick's analysis showed that Exxon and Mustang had created a strong integrated team that delivered industry best-in-class performance for engineering and EP spend. Engineering and procurement quality was good and engineering was off the critical path quickly... no construction delays.

His analysis also enumerated project systems that needed to be upgraded for better control. He also suggested improvements in the project organization.

Once Nick had put the Diana Hoover project into context within the industry, we had an audience that was interested in listening to how we were addressing each area of weakness in order to be a good partner for EUDC going forward. We became EUDCs engineering firm and separately competed and won their Automation contract for worldwide upstream projects...MAJOR wins for Mustang!

"Alone, the Diana reservoir was an average-sized development. Overnight, all of that changed. The challenge was pulling all of the teams together and having them (the vendors) at the right place at the right time." Image and Caption: Kunkel, Bill "Selecting the Right Production System", ExxonMobil's Hoover/Diana A Deepwater Pioneer, March 2002; page 11

65: UNDERSTANDING MUSTANG

We had been doing a number of projects in Venezuela through Benton, Solar, Dresser Rand and others. We ended up using a number of local contractors and engineering firms in order to increase local content and save costs. One of these companies, named Tevinca, employed a technical engineer we had worked with at CBS named Tony Smith. Tony had been good friends with Don Leinweber and approached us with the idea of Mustang buying all or part of Tevinca. The idea was that through Mustang, Tevinca could do work outside of Venezuela and stabilize their workload. Tony brought the CEO of Tevinca to Houston for a visit.

CULTURE

During the course of Tevinca's visit we were talking about culture and how to win the hearts and minds of our people. The CEO told us about a program he had instituted that had a lasting effect with his people.

Once a month he would have the new hires come to the board room for a lunch prepared by his chef. He would informally have each person talk about their experience, where they had come from, hobbies and what they were hoping to find in their job at Tevinca. As the conversations developed, he would find opportune times to interject the company philosophy and encourage them to help him keep the positive culture.

These people generally had never been into a board room or even talked with a CEO. They became more receptive to understanding the culture and wanting to be a part of it. Stories from the day went home with them and were recounted to neighbors.

MUSTANG-IZE IT!

Seize the thought

The idea about lunch with the CEO struck my "inside-sales" nerve and resonated loudly. We had been working hard to push our culture through 1,000 people, two buildings, remote project teams, and projects all over the world. We had real concerns, as we brought in 20 new people a month, that our culture would become watered down to the point where we became just like any other engineering firm in Houston.

New hire breakfast is born

We picked the first Tuesday of the month and would hold off until we had 30-50 new hires. Tuesday because Mondays were always crazy! We picked breakfast so people would go to it first before going into the office. Perhaps the best thing we did was take it off-site to the Pine Forest Country Club.

People were greeted downstairs and directed up to the ballroom where they received a name tag and a Power Point presentation pamphlet. Then they went through a breakfast buffet. We had ten-person circular tables with 2-3 managers at each table. We started with a prayer, then time for eating and socializing. I would then pick a table and have a person stand up to say "who they were, what company they came from, what department they worked in and what project they were on." I would then say something about the project to make a point about Mustang's culture, vision or strategy.

At the end of this time, I would ask everyone to pick up the power point presentation and I would flip them to two or three slides to emphasize things we had not covered. I also encouraged them to go through the entire pamphlet with their spouse when they got home after work.

New hire breakfast topics:
- Just do it attitude in everything.
- ESOP to show where the owners were coming from.
- Continuous growth means things will change.
- People Oriented…Project Driven™.
- Everyone being in sales.
- Encouraged them to participate in activities.
- Plans for the future…be what the market needs.
- Cross-train to stay billable.
- Provide "arrows-in-the-quiver" to sales.
- Blue horse means quality and it starts with them.
- Operation Horsethief…it brought you…help us.
- Quick review of seven projects that had started in the past month for Texaco, Amoco, Exxon, BP, Tesoro, SF phosphates and Coastal Aruba.
- Thanks for choosing Mustang!

As people left, they were given a bag with special Mustang goodies for them and their families.

Adding a little spice to the new hire breakfast.

DESCRIBING MUSTANG

Mustang's uniqueness

Our flat organization enhanced our commitment to communication. Engineering and projects were the focus which helped us in hiring and keeping the best people. Our fit-for-purpose engineering, Gulf of Mexico efficiency, re-use of prior work and drafting room focus allowed us to set industry best-in-class benchmarks. We were definitely project driven with a just do it mentality.

Mustang's value add

The culture that resulted from our uniqueness created tangible value to clients. They weighed our culture heavily in their evaluations to pick an alliance partner that would help them deliver their stretch goals. They had seen us get engineering off of the critical path and understood the value in having an engineer pushing for that result. Being able to deliver Gulf of Mexico costs and schedules into the international market was also highly valued. By putting the right people together in a teaming environment and bringing in lessons learned from all of our projects, we were able to give clients added value.

Mustang's processes

We worked hard on the front end of a project to set it up for success as defined by the client. Our systems had been created by us to work for us and leverage our ability. Supply chain integration with engineering and construction set our projects up for a smoother than normal flow in the industry. Using our lessons learned and startup experience, our designs had innate constructability and safety designed in. Our modular design methods set projects up for better cost, schedule, quality and startup.

BUSINESS STRATEGY

Our uniqueness, value add and processes made us the number one partner for industry alliances, one-of-a-kind projects and projects where a client wanted a step-change in performance. In order to maintain our momentum on the cutting edge of the industries we served, we developed a list of our strategies to emphasize at our new hire breakfasts:

- Be profitable on all projects.
- Strict control of overhead.
- Attract and keep the best people.
- Focus on repeat business.
- Constantly improve efficiency.
- Continue to be competitive on small projects.
- Expand client/project base.
- Cross-train people.

BUSINESS TACTICS

In order to support our strategy we developed the following tactics to help our new hires and managers understand how to get there on a daily basis:

- Primarily rate based work = built in profit.
- Monthly financial statements = control overhead.
- Referral hiring, best projects, activities = best people.
- Project focus – takes care of the client = repeat work.
- Overload of work forces improvements = efficiency.
- Special Projects Group = small project competitiveness.
- Pipeline, Process Plants, Automation, etc. = broader base.
- Move people to hot projects = cross-train.

CROSS-FERTILIZATION

We now had twelve sales people between the upstream, downstream, pipeline and automation sectors. My weekly coordination meeting with all of them seemed disjointed because when we would talk about something in one sector, the other people's eyes would glaze over. Finally I had each sector brief their value proposition for discussion by everyone.

Then we pushed each person to come to the meeting with an opportunity for one of the other sectors. This was a tough "ask" because a sales person would be risking some of their "sales collateral" to set up another sector.

We started a cross-sector sales target list so everyone could see the opportunities being generated and then to celebrate the wins e.g. pipeline getting work due to an Exxon downstream contact, automation was getting work due to a Conoco pipeline contact, etc. This turned out to be a good way to leverage the best relationships of our sales people.

CONTROLLER

We hired a controller to help Felix get a better grip on financials and give us a steering wheel for Mustang. The controller came to me and said that he could not do his job because he did not have budgets to control against. He had a point, so I sat down with a pencil and on one page did a Pro Forma Profit & Loss (P&L) budget for 1999 for him to set up and control against. My P&L had headcount, manhours, billable manhours, billing rate, costs for big areas and ended up with a bottom line per month. Of course 1999 would probably not be as calm and orderly as it seemed in November of 1998 but I felt that I had taken a lot of things into account.

READY FOR 1999

We had come together as a team in 1998 and understood ourselves better. The industry had picked us for all of the major alliances and we had developed the systems required for the larger and more complex projects companies were developing. One of the new systems was interface management. We were learning that topsides facility engineering people knew how to coordinate suppliers and technical disciplines much better than hull or subsea or drilling people could. We were finding a new niche as not only topsides engineer, but also as the interface coordinator.

> **"One of the new systems was interface management."**

The bottom falls out!!

Right at the end of 1998 the bottom fell out of the oil price as OPEC opened the valves and the world was awash with oil. Overnight the price dropped from $35 to $11 per barrel.

$11.00 PER BARREL OF OIL

The oil companies had become pretty light on their feet and immediately shut down every project they could. The industry went into a resource shedding tailspin that was crazy-fast. The ability to go from competing for resources, to closing down and protecting the bottom line, was truly amazing to anyone that had been in the industry for over fifteen years.

This was a tremendous shock, but we had built a strong organization that was ready.

"NO FATE"

TIME TO PERFORM

SWOT Analysis, end of 1998...
Hitting our stride...ready to step up...

Strengths:
- Benchmarked best-in-class performance.
- Doubled people to 1,000+ while maintaining culture.
- Chosen for many industry alliances.
- Solid bottom line.
- ESOP implemented.
- Diversified into downstream and automation.
- Diversified out of the Gulf of Mexico.
- Cross-fertilization on many levels.
- Working directly for oil companies internationally.

Weaknesses:
- Lack of a strategic plan.
- Company and project management depth.
- Paul, Felix and Bill overloaded.

Opportunities:
- Penetrate front end market better.
- Continue to follow oil companies into deepwater.
- Find more ways to push reimbursable contract strategy.
- Continue to diversify client base.

Threats:
- Big Boys could decide to put best people on front ends.
- Teams hired away or split off from Mustang.
- Project goes bad and hurts reputation.
- Client pulls project due to poor staffing.
- Oil price stays below $17 per barrel.
- Low cost engineering centers take over the market.

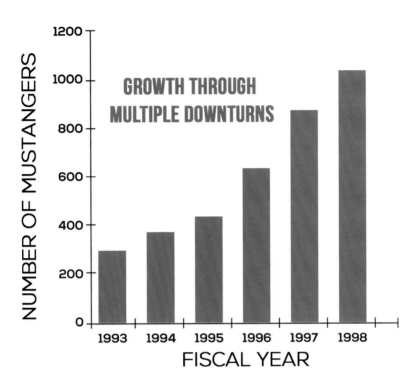

End of 1996-1998
The New Normal

"Déjà vu
all over again."

Yogi Berra,
baseball player

PART 5: MUSTANG 1999-2000+
MAKING HEROES
Culture is king.
Full Throttle with Joined Up Thinking.

We had developed a unique place in the industry now that we were 1,000 people doing $100,000,000 of revenue on reimbursable contracts...yes, we had even convinced downstream and pipeline clients of the advantages to our contracting philosophy. Our unique place in the industry resulted from being the engineer on the front end of projects.

We were positioned to help the client figure out how to deliver their entire project in the best way possible. We could adjust execution plans to match the current industry realities. Many times we were on teams comprised of multiple; oil companies, contractors, countries and cultures. Because we had the information on scope of work, schedules and cost, we were in position to facilitate the entire project. As long as everyone believed we had their best interest in mind, we could work the communications to deliver the results.

Our reimbursable contract allowed us to focus on the project. This unwavering focus pulled all of the other players into trusting Mustang to communicate and coordinate for the best outcome.

We had built a company that had tremendous trust and loyalty both internally and externally. We were confident in our ability to create "Heroic Space" within which companies and people could work. Teaming in that space would allow us to win more than our fare share of work as the industry would tighten due to the low oil price. We had to stay the course and continue "Making Heroes".

Find a language that communicates.

66: BRITISH PETROLEUM ALASKA

January 7, 1999 and the spot market pricing for oil was down to $9.00 per barrel. The oil companies were now very light on their feet and quickly shut projects down. The ripple effect through the industry was just as swift and dramatic. It was the 1984 through 1989 downturn squeezed into 5 weeks.

Thankfully our projects were at a stage and of enough importance that they continued. The shock of this collapse, however, and what it could have done to Mustang was a big concern to us. All we could do was to make sure we were innovative, efficient and the first choice of clients.

NORTHSTAR

Alliance

British Petroleum Alaska (BPA) had pulled together a "world class" alliance of four contractors and three engineering firms to do the Northstar project. It would be the first offshore oil production north of the Arctic Circle in the world. The project would entail building an island, drilling wells, installing modular production facilities and quarters and pipelining the oil to Prudhoe Bay. At Prudhoe Bay the oil would be injected into the Alyeska pipeline for use in the "Lower 48".

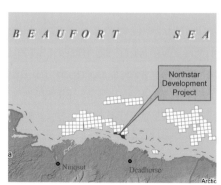

BPA was executing their "puddle jumping" strategy to develop smaller fields in a lean fashion. The next "puddle" for the alliance would be the Liberty prospect.

Seasonal weather windows

The alliance had to work around weather windows in Alaska. The island in 40 feet of water would be built in the winters using ice roads over the tundra to haul gravel and dirt. Module transport, installation and hookup could only be done in the summers after the icepack had broken up. The catch phrase in construction on the North Slope was to "Caveman" everything because at -20ºF to -40ºF things just stopped working.

Everything on the North Slope had been built in the lower 48 and barged from staging areas in Seattle, Washington. We believed that we could develop a layout of tighter modules that could be built in Anchorage, Alaska. Our experience working on integrated teams with fabricators would be severely tested as these would be the largest modules ever built in Alaska by an order of magnitude. Creating jobs in Alaska however, would be a feather in BPA's cap for community relations.

Squeeze Handoffs

In reviewing how the contractors would do their piping we found that they would redo our piping drawings into a software package called Acorn. Acorn generated all the details they needed to make the pieces of pipe and bar coded them for tracking through fabrication. Acorn also generated all of their material purchase orders. We bought Acorn and did our drawings in the fabricator's formats with their bar codes. This saved them having to hire piping designers, reduced errors from their re-drawing effort and delivered materials 8 weeks earlier to their yard.

Digital and Digestible™

We named this design method digital and digestible as one day of training in Acorn created significant project savings.

People had to get out of their comfort zones to take advantage of discoveries like digital and digestible. They had to trust their alliance partner across the normal division of engineering and construction being in silos. Between Northstar and Liberty we created short "handoff schedules" for each discipline i.e. structural, piping, and electrical, etc. The schedules showed only the design, purchasing and construction handoffs to get agreement between all parties. Then we worked together to squeeze the handoffs and make them more seamless.

Throw away 3D model

In order to help communication of timing and handoffs we created "throw away 3D models" of the modules as they would progress in fabrication. The model was generated quickly from go-bys we had in our libraries. It was just a picture with no "computer smarts". Everyone could "buy space" and the picture showed what was needed in the construction sequence.

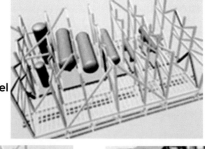

"Cartooned" steel and equipment.

Piping and second level added.

3rd level steel, equipment and piping added.

Alliance partners used these models to do fabrication yard layout planning, manpower planning and establish need dates for cranes or other equipment. The pictures gave construction confidence that the design and purchasing would deliver what they needed to efficiently fabricate.

These picture models cost 50-100 manhours to create and were thrown away when the real 3D design started. They had served their purpose to get team alignment and clarity of purpose across the alliance.

Megaphone approach

The contractors had tremendous Alaskan experience and wanted it all considered in the FEED since we were pushing the technology envelope in many areas. The constant flow of good ideas was spinning the design team out of control. We needed to take the concept and define it to start detailed design as shown below:

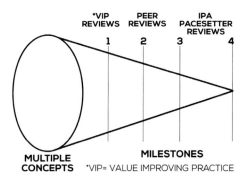

We needed "loose/tight" properties in this model. Between milestones (mini stage gate) things would loosen up to obtain creative ideas. The milestones were used to tighten up and force decisions.

In order to control manhours, we decided to take the new ideas that seemed promising offline.

We assigned a second technical team to develop the new ideas and see if they had merit. If they were good we plugged them back in. This allowed the main team to stay focused and deliver a well defined package like this:

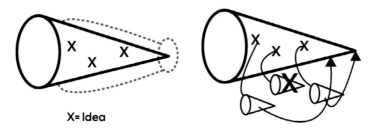

X= Idea

Old way... fuzzy result.   **New way... tight design.**

IPA rated Northstar best-in-class. Northstar then reduced the cost and schedule of Liberty significantly with lessons learned.

Northstar Island, Beaufort Sea Alaska in winter.

"The hand is the cutting edge of the mind."
Jacob Bronowski, Scientist

67: MOBIL

Oceaneering had us modify and upgrade the Ocean Producer FPSO for Mobil to use in proving the size of a field offshore Equatorial Guinea. Then Mobil bought it, renamed it the Zafiro Producer and had us add equipment to increase capacity to 80,000bopd. They discovered a new field called Jade and needed a conventional platform installed to produce the reservoir and send the oil over to Zafiro.

Mobil wanted to do this platform using IPA's stage gate process along with their recommendations for EPCM contracting with an integrated team.

JADE

3D Skid

Mobil knew we had good skid design capability from our Zafiro work. We split the Jade production facility into a number of production skids and on our own nickel designed one in 3D CAD. We stress tested the software by rolling typical changes into the design. Everything worked well and we were amazed that we could do it on a PC-based system...thank you Rod Canion and Compaq Computer!!

We showed the design to Mobil and did changes to line sizes and control valves as they watched. We could do the design in the same manhours as 2D and changes in half the time. Then we showed that the software could "dump out" a complete bill of material, weight and center of gravity for free! Mobil gave us the go-ahead to do all of the skids in 3D.

The structural deck was done in 3D as that was already our standard. Mobil authorized us to do the interconnecting piping between the skids in 3D after the skid success.

We sub-optimized steel design by adding skid steel, but to great advantage in cost and schedule. We did this drawing for Mobil to use in explaining the skid construction methodology:

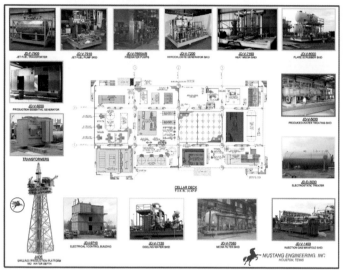

Breaking the Jade deck into skids.
Essentially a Work Breakdown Structure (WBS).

3D rendering of Jade in 550 feet of water.

The Jade jacket and deck were built a few hours from Houston and were visited by most of the industry. The yard used the 3D model to help in construction planning. A new use was in preparation for lifting the upper deck to set over the lower deck and equipment. They did a clash check and fixed interferences that are normally discovered when the deck is up in the air suspended from a number of cranes.

Here is a summary of Mobil's and IPA's analysis of this industry top-quartile best-in-class project:

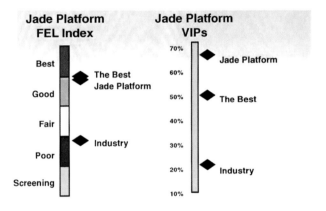

Mobil and IPA benchmarks.

Zafiro upgrade

While working Jade we upgraded Zafiro to receive Jade production. These projects helped carry us through until the oil price bounced back to $18 per barrel.

Mobil's learnings would soon be transferred to Exxon as they were acquired to form ExxonMobil. The major oil companies had been right about their concern over surviving. The large oil price fluctuation and the size of projects was forcing consolidation.

EXXON MOBIL

68: EL PASO

Deepwater technology development started following the same scenario that had been seen in shallower water. The major oil companies developed technology with large engineering and construction companies. Then the "fast followers" figured out how to translate that technology for producing "marginal" fields with tighter budgets.

PRINCE

El Paso did the world's first Mini-TLP using a MODEC design in 1,450 feet of water. A Tension Leg Platform is a buoyant production facility vertically moored to the seafloor by tendons. We did the 50,000 bopd production facility on this new type of hull that had four legs supporting the deck. MODEC did the project lump sum with us reimbursable for the facilities.

World's first Mini-TLP in 1,450 feet of water.

NEW NICHE

The industry used our floating experience as the hull design varied and topsides grew larger

10 December 1999   UPSTREAM NEWS   Page 7

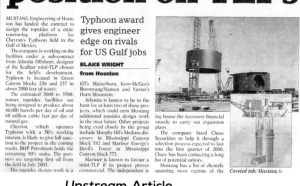

Aker study on how to play Horn

VASTAR Resources has selected Aker Maritime to conduct conceptual engineering studies for its Horn Mountain discovery in Mississippi Canyon blocks 126 and 127 of the deep-water Gulf of Mexico, *writes Blake Wright.*

Aker is examining three separate potential development scenarios for the field, respectively centred around a subsea spread, a tension-leg platform and a spar. The operator has also engaged Alliance Engineering to conduct topsides design studies for potential host structures.

The operator recently completed its appraisal drilling programme and is confident that the field contains its predrill estimate of roughly 125 million barrels of recoverable reserves.

Given the scope of reserves and the field's 5400-foot water depth, the company is understood to be leaning towards a floating solution for the field.

"We do feel there is enough oil there to justify a standalone development," said a Vastar spokesman.

Vastar has confirmed that

Mustang in pole position on TLPs

MUSTANG Engineering of Houston has landed the contract to design the topsides of a mini-tension-leg platform for Chevron's Typhoon field in the Gulf of Mexico.

The company is working on the facilities under a sub-contract from Atlantia Offshore, designer of the SeaStar mini-TLP chosen for the field's development. Typhoon is located in Green Canyon blocks 236 and 237 in about 2000 feet of water.

The estimated 3000 to 3500-tonnes topsides facilities are being designed to produce about 40,000 barrels per day of oil and 60 million cubic feet per day of natural gas.

Chevron, which operates Typhoon with a 50% working interest, is likely to give full sanction to the project in the coming weeks. BHP Petroleum holds the remaining 50% stake. The partners are targeting first oil from the field in July 2001.

The topsides design work is a

Typhoon award gives engineer edge on rivals for US Gulf jobs

BLAKE WRIGHT
from Houston

Elf's Matterhorn, Kerr-McGee's Boomvang/Nansen and Vastar's Horn Mountain.

Atlantia is known to be in the hunt for at least two of these projects, which could earn Mustang additional topsides design work in the near future. Other projects being eyed closely by the group include Murphy Oil's Medusa discovery in Mississippi Canyon block 582 and Mariner Energy's Devil's Tower in Mississippi Canyon block 773.

Mariner is known to favour a mini-TLP if its project proves commercial. The independent is

ing house the necessary financial muscle to carry out expansion plans.

The company hired Chase Securities to help it through a selection process expected to last into the first quarter of 2000. Chase has been contacting a long list of potential suitors.

Mustang has a list of clientele spanning most regions of the

Coveted job: Mustang is

Upstream Article

Mustang designed topsides for Anadarko's Marco-Polo field. The world's deepest Mini-TLP.

"Now we need to morph Mustang."
Paul, Felix, Bill 1999

69: ADOPT A PARENT

We had survived the first quarter of 1999 with a small blip down in people. This had allowed us to "high-grade" by moving some people out to open up slots. We did some "sharpening the sword" activities like developing a workbook for skid design and subsea pipeline tie-ins. This was business as usual for us during downturns but at 1,000 people it was too much stress for our low overhead operation. We needed to get out of the feeling of direct ownership in order to do the right things to set Mustang up for the long term.

UNCONVENTIONAL

Chase

In July we set up a meeting with Chase Bank to discuss selling Mustang in a professional manner. Chase had familiarity with Mustang from setting up our ESOP in 1996. All three of us were fully committed to take this action through to a conclusion. We wanted Felix to fully retire. We wanted to monetize the ESOP for our people so they could invest the monies outside of Mustang. And, we wanted Paul and me to not lose the value we had created in Mustang.

No poker face

We told Chase that we needed to come clean with our people on the sale process. Mustangers had noticed us meeting more than normal and asked what was going on. We were not good at having a poker face, but could justify some meetings as working to set up 5 international projects with multiple company participants.

> **"They had seen companies lose 50% of their value overnight when rumors of a sale were confirmed."**

Chase strongly recommended against letting our people know the plan. They had seen companies lose 50% of their value overnight when rumors of a sale were confirmed. Companies lost value because key people left and clients would not award new work until they were comfortable the dust had settled after the sale.

We discussed at each meeting how culture was everything at Mustang. Culture allowed us to attract the best people, made our systems efficient and created loyalty throughout the industry. Open communication was the ethos underpinning our superior project execution abilities. Selling like Chase wanted would take the shine off of our culture and, in the long term, we would be losing something special.

We felt that the loyalty we had in the industry required that everyone be brought into our plans to sell. We wanted transparency in the sale process. Chase begrudgingly agreed and we came up with a term for our approach to the sale:

ADOPT A PARENT

This phrase let everyone on the Chase team know that we were a very strong young adult company that needed a quality parent to facilitate growth into adulthood. We were not selling because we had to or because the industry demanded us to sell. We were voluntarily selling a very strong company that was poised for continued double digit growth. When executed correctly, we felt that this sale would provide a stronger industry partner for clients and contractors.

SOUNDS LIKE SALES

Concept

Paul and Felix said it sounded like a sales job to get all Mustangers, clients and vendors aligned with our philosophy for adopting a parent. They tasked me with figuring this out while they worked with the Chase team on a pamphlet to send out to potential buyers.

We wanted to paint the picture of "Adopt a Parent" in sufficient detail that everyone could understand why and how we would sell...whether they agreed or not. We wanted to show where we had come from, our current status and where we were headed. Then Mustangers, vendors and clients could evaluate how the Mustang sale strategy would or would not work for them.

The message was that Mustang had built a winning team with a unique strategy that was transparent and helped all players. When they would buy into this premise, getting them to trust us in the sale process would not be a huge leap of faith.

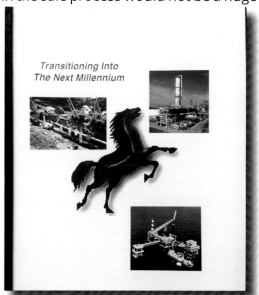

Pamphlet presenting the "how and why" of the sale.

Transitioning into the Next Millennium 10/4/99

We prepared a pamphlet with a bit of a multi-media effect to keep it interesting. It started with a memo from us and then had a little philosophy about life being about change. We then gave some history on Mustang and where we were at present. We wanted people convinced that Mustang had developed a winning team and culture that extended broadly through the industry. Then we addressed why we needed to transition and the process we would use to identify our parent. Finally we wrapped up with anticipated questions and answers.

Typical pages showing current projects.

Rollout to management

Monday morning October 11, 1999 we had boxes of pamphlets in the conference room for the management meeting. I introduced the 25 people to my pastor, Steve Peace, and said that we were going to spend the next few hours discussing a transition plan for Mustang. We planned to do this in an unconventional manner and felt we should start with some time spent in prayer and reflection. After the prayer for strength and understanding, we handed out pamphlets to everyone. We read through it out loud, stopping to discuss or answer questions as appropriate.

Most of our 1,000 people had been through one or more sales of engineering firms due to the topsy-turvy nature of the industry in Houston. Significant concerns were voiced.

There was considerable appreciation expressed for how this transition was being handled from the start. The fact that we were leading with the management team, then Mustangers and then announcing to the industry would carry a lot of weight and engender trust.

Mustangers

Managers handed out pamphlets to their people and read through them. One question we did not anticipate was what people could say about this outside of Mustang. We told them that if they thought the plan was good for them and clients, they were free after the meeting to call and talk to anyone. If they felt it was all malarkey and spelled the end of Mustang then they should wait. We recommended they take the pamphlet home and discuss it with their spouse. Come in tomorrow and ask any questions of their manager. If, after doing this, they still felt it was a horrible idea, then they were free to express those feelings to anyone without repercussion. A few jaws dropped but we were transparent and committed.

Clients

The next morning coincided with the monthly Mica project meeting in one of our conference rooms. Mica was the world's deepest and longest subsea well tie-back to an existing platform and required new state of the art technology. This was the first project BP and Amoco personnel had been part of since their merger and we had helped them combine their design methods. The project meeting also included Exxon and Mobil people who had just met each other a few months earlier after their merger.

We handed out pamphlets and walked through them in summary form. There were a few questions but everyone seemed to understand what we were doing and why. Then one of the Mobil folks said he sure wished management had done a pamphlet like this explaining the merger with Exxon. That got everyone laughing as the BP, Amoco and Exxon people agreed.

Emails had gone out to all of our clients, vendors and contractors late Monday presenting our transition plan. We spent Tuesday and Wednesday visiting with as many clients and contractors as possible.

Non-issue

By Thursday our "big news" was a non-issue throughout the industry. The response coming back was "Mustang has a good transition plan...please do not mess it up". *Upstream*, the weekly "industry rag" presented their take on Mustang and noted that Mustang would be a great acquisition for a company wanting a Houston presence. Of course they opined about who might be interested in buying Mustang.

Mustangers just went back to work and we were free to work openly with Chase, who now had a good story to tell potential buyers

"Pushing through your comfort zone can pay handsomely."
Douglas McGehee, Author

70: BP NORTH SEA

Judy Wagner called from Aberdeen, Scotland to ask if we would do the conceptual work to modify their Pompano platform design in the Gulf for use in the North Sea. They had done a FEED for their Clair field in the North Sea with an engineering firm out of London and it did not meet the stage gate economic hurdles of partners Shell, ChevronTexaco and ConocoPhillips. They wanted to redo the FEED from a different starting point.

CATALOG ENGINEERS

We set up our first teleconferencing room to conduct weekly meetings with Judy's team overseas. BP had costs for Pompano from 1985 and had factored them to 1999 costs. They felt they could get to a better cost for Clair by starting with Pompano and adding North Sea requirements rather than trying to skinny down the North Sea FEED they had just done. They wanted to reduce Clair cost by 30%

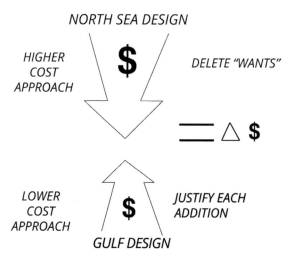

"Adds" easier to limit than deleting "Wants."

The BP UK team felt we were "catalog engineers", meaning we just picked equipment out of a catalog with no customization. This was how they felt we were able to do production facilities so cheaply. We sent them examples of our equipment bid packages and bid evaluations. They said the equipment was definitely customized and were amazed at the few hours it took us to do the work. In order to change their mindset we used the mantra of "Clair will be different" on all correspondence. Clair had been around since 1977 and was only viable now due to new drilling technology. The project would die again if we could not change it.

ANALOG

We proposed they change from Pompano to our Jade platform for the go-by or what they called the analog. They did not want to start with a "blank sheet of paper" for Clair:

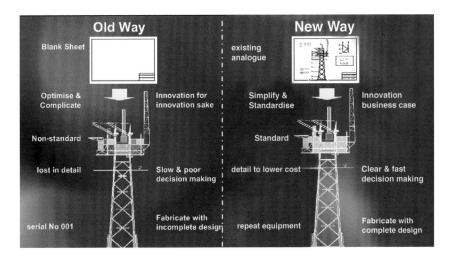

Slide BP North Sea used to describe their concept.

Having an analog was a big change for BP UK. Jade was an IPA best-in-class project which would help them stick with the design and not go back to a blank sheet. Jade's structure and facility were in 3D to help people see the differences between Gulf of Mexico and North Sea design. It also matched the flowrate, water depth and quartering requirements closer than Pompano. Jade was in the final stages of construction so we could walk people through it to discuss differences.

Jade demonstrated how we had moved 40% of the man-hours and 60% of the purchasing out of the deck assembly yard and into small skid shops. This would help employ people more broadly across the UK, help with safety in the deck yard and significantly reduce cost.

RESISTANCE

The BP Clair team continued to feel that we were "light weight" engineering for the demands of the North Sea. They did not like us being reimbursable as it felt like a blank check. They did not like spreading skids to vendors they had not used in this way before. They did not like our removal of 90% of the walls they used for containment of spills. They did not like our integration of drilling and production to reduce equipment. And the list went on and on.

Judy enlisted the help of top BP management out of London to push the North Sea team to "find ways" to make what Mustang was proposing work in the UK regulatory environment. They made it clear that the project would not go forward without these major changes. Together we developed a 40% cost reduction and the project was approved.

"Clair will be different"

MUSTANG NOT A MATCH

The BP Clair Team wanted us to proceed with the project using IPA's recommended strategy of EPCM with a reimbursable contract. We had significant reservations about being the engineer on Clair and gave a summary presentation of our history to their team.

In the Gulf we had helped move BP from EPC contracts to EPCM with best-in-class results on three significant projects. For BP/Exxon Diana we helped deliver a step change in cost and schedule compared to BP and Exxon benchmarks. In Alaska for BP we had done three step change projects that cut projected costs in half on aggressive schedules and with significantly more Alaskan content.

BP had helped build Mustang into a world class firm, but was also very tough to please. We felt that Clair would add another layer of complexity in that we would have to deliver decisions from the UK government. With BP's normal change out of people on projects we would probably find ourselves in a bind between their team and the government. We showed them this spin on an old joke:

GOVERNMENTAL ACCURACY
- Measure with a micrometer
- Mark it with a piece of chalk
- Cut it with an axe

OIL COMPANY ACCURACY
- Reservoir ± 40%
- Production Flowrate ± 20%
- Flow Stream Analysis ± 1%

Then we made our pitch asking them to get commitment from the people they would assign to the project on two things. First they would work on Mustang's behalf to get regulatory approval by the government. Second, they would stay on the project through the first year of production.

DELIVER THE DIFFERENCE!

Clair possessed the largest undeveloped resource on the UK Continental Shelf. We would be putting the first fixed platform in the West of Shetland area exposed to the full force of the North Sea storms. The BP team under Graham Ferguson signed up to take the project through first year of production and worked to deliver a Mustang Gulf design.

Clair BP/Mustang team at our Chili Cook-off.

The Clair team had a Nordic theme at our annual chili cook-off. That is Graham wearing a mop on his head. He said that he would wear a mop every day to save $300,000,000!!

Sir Ian Wood of Wood Group, top BP management and representatives from the UK Government came to the christening party. They all congratulated the Clair team for:

Delivering the Difference!

Clair set a new benchmark for cost and schedule in the North Sea. It was delivered for 35% under the original FEED and developed a new segment of the industry by spreading work out to skid shops across the UK.

Rendering of Clair.

Clair deck being installed.

71: DEEPWATER TSUNAMI IN 2000

Mustang had been making a name for itself in deepwater worldwide. The industry was bracing for what had been termed the "Tsunami of deepwater work" that was about to hit. The new combined oil companies wanted to start these 3-5 year projects despite the low oil price. Industry rumors were that a number of the deepwater studies would kick off as projects in 2000.

DEEPWATER DARLINGS

Integrated teams

We had been involved with 70% of the deepwater studies done for the Gulf, West Africa, Indonesia and Brazil due to our alliances with owners and key contractors. We brought production facility, subsea flowline and riser experience along with project integration experience to the studies.

Clients wanted their studies done by the "A" team, resulting in our being associated with the same strong industry players time after time. Many of these combined teams were housed in our offices because we were coordinating the entire effort with the client. The teams always had contractors for:

- Subsea manifolds, flowlines and flow assurance.
- Pipelines (Intec or JP Kenny).
- Hull, mooring and risers (two types of hull normally).
- Drilling unit.
- Topsides and project integrator (Mustang).
- Client

Sometimes the hull contractors (Aker, Technip, MODEC, Atlantia, Spars Inc., etc.) would pull us into a study due to our flexibility in getting to a good topsides solution for their hull design and our reputation with deepwater clients.

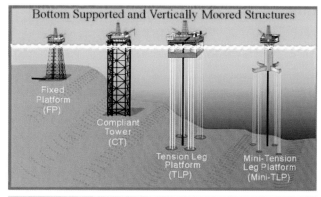

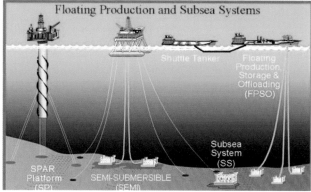

Deepwater Development Systems

BP TAKES THE LEAD

Beat the Tsunami

BP wanted to get out in front of the predicted deepwater tsunami that promised to cause worldwide shortages in everything from engineering to large chain and flowline riser material. They were pre-qualifying contractors for a series of deepwater developments and we sent in ours with Fluor. These were going to be the biggest and deepest floating projects... pushing industry technologies in every area. We felt that we needed Fluor's top-rated project management systems in order to compete for the topsides design and project integrator scopes of work.

Coaching

BP visited with us during pre-qualification and gave us some coaching. They had interviewed Fluor, who had also submitted alone--without Mustang. BP understood why we felt the Fluor systems might help with project control. They felt however, that the systems were too restrictive for the freedom that would be needed to push the technology envelope in so many directions. They encouraged us to bid alone and we cancelled our teaming arrangement with Fluor.

HIVE

BP had a new purpose-built room called the HIVE where 15 people could view a reservoir in 3D. The team would actually feel like they were inside the geologic structure and could plan drilling requirements to drain the reservoir. With multiple experts able to collaborate in real time, BP was able to reduce the number of wells and the cost per well. Cost spreadsheets were projected up on the wall and reflected cost changes in real time as a well was moved... amazing!

We asked if we could bring the Mobil Jade 3D model over and review it with them in the HIVE. BP heartily agreed and wanted to see what the benefits might be. We showed in detail how operations, safety, maintenance and design engineers from multiple disciplines could "walk through" the model. They would be able to discuss details in a collaborative manner. Since all interested parties would be present, we felt that this should help the team get to decisions that would stick.

While in the HIVE, we showed how the model calculated the weight and center of gravity (CG) in real time. These numbers and locations are important in floating facilities. For Jade we were off by 14.6 tons for the 8,250 ton deck and the CG was right on when weighed prior to load out.

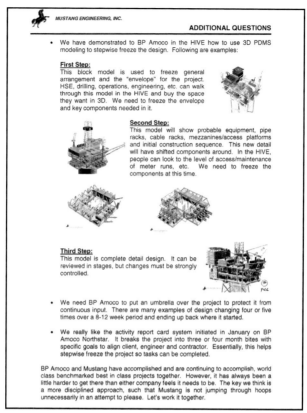

Page from our bid showing how we design in 3D.

Silo busting

BP had learned from its' experience on Exxon Diana that there were significant savings to be earned if they could have more design integration between drilling, production facilities, the hull and the subsurface teams. Each of these teams operated more like a silo on Diana because they were pushing technical envelopes and had to focus on their own budgets and schedules. By developing a program over 5-10 years, BP felt that they could push more integration as the technical challenges became more manageable. BP wanted a program of projects that would allow each successive project to build on the new technologies of the ones that came before it.

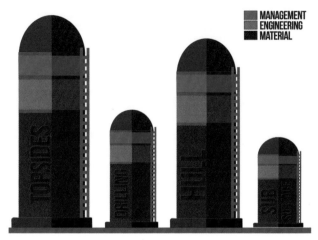

"Silo" philosophy in deepwater due to pushing new technology in all areas.

BP takes control

BP would have multiple partners on each project in order to spread the risk. Major partners were Shell, Exxon, Chevron and BHP Billington. During the bid process it became evident that BP would be the best at program management to deliver on promises as they would have to get agreement from the partners. Some of these partners were used to being in charge and could slow down decisions on capital expenditures if they did not agree with the solution.

BP would have to deliver new technical solutions for drilling the deepest wells ever done in deepwater and creating the largest deepwater floating production facilities along with the most complex seafloor drilling/completion and manifold/flowline systems yet devised in the industry. This would be space-age type development on the seafloor and innovative floating cities that would produce the fields. BP needed to stay close to the action in order to deliver safety, quality, cost and schedule targets.

29 Questions

We had pre-qualified by showing Tom Gauthey's team coming off of a Mobil Producing Nigeria project going onto the first project, Holstein. This project would also set the standards for the following projects. Six months later AJ Cortez's team would come off of a Mobil Zafiro/Jade project to go onto the second project, Thunderhorse.

Twelve months after the first project, Phil Schneider's team would come off of the Madison/Marshall addition to Diana for Exxon and move onto the third project, Mad Dog.

We proposed separate strong talent under Scott Worthington to help BP with interface management between the normal silos in deepwater projects. BP would be pulling in their resources from around the world and absorbing technical people from their partners to cobble together a significant management team for this effort. Our interface team would have to help align the management team with the silos and the execution plan...hundreds of people on each project.

From our pre-qualification, the BP team developed 29 questions for us to answer as our proposal...all very specific to Mustang. Critical concern was staffing and we noted that the talent in the industry would come running toward these projects so it would be more a matter of assimilating and getting the talent producing.

For a "quick start" to Holstein we suggested just upgrading the Exxon Diana project to the higher flowrate. BP was a partner to Exxon on that project and would have access to the design. We also had flowcharts showing input and deliverables time-phased for everything above the seafloor in deepwater. These had been honed over the industry's premier deepwater studies completed by integrated teams at Mustang.

For "status of the sale of Mustang" we noted that it had been five months since the announcement. We had added 240 people and new projects during that time. We said that if we were in consideration, we could meet with a few top decision makers at BP to discuss the probable buyer.

For "does Exxon have first priority on staffing at Mustang" we noted that we would only take on work we could staff. We gave the example of Exxon wanting to award Diana to us but we could not staff it immediately. We worked an agreement between Mobil and Exxon to staff Diana as a Mobil project ramped down.

For "have you improved your management processes" we noted success on four world class projects. These were Mobil Usari offshore Africa, Unocal Palin offshore Thailand, Exxon Diana in the Gulf and BP Northstar in Alaska.

After reviewing the answers BP had us do a series of interviews with individuals and groups. One interview was just ex-Amoco personnel and very open-ended.

Upstream felt that Brown & Root, McDermott, ABB and Fluor were in strong positions for topsides and interface management. We would find out later that this series of projects was the strategic goal of Fluor and B&R for the year 2000. They could "zipper" BP and their partners from the CEO to the design engineer in pushing to win the contract.

"Culture eats strategy for breakfast."
Peter F. Drucker, Educator

72: BP DEEPWATER

We took the call and Paul sent me over to BP Plaza to sign the biggest contract ever awarded in the Gulf. As I walked from one building to another with one of the top decision makers, I asked him what turned the tide for us to be awarded the project. He said that he really could not say as he had voted against us...oops, that was a little awkward. 😊

CONTRACT

Signing

I went into a conference room with about 20 BP key players and was seated next to the program manager. He said that we should each say a few words before signing the contract.

I thanked them for choosing Mustang and said that we had the right teams lined up for each project to match their technical strengths. We felt that BP was a year in front of the "deepwater tsunami" of projects and would actually develop the technologies needed by other oil companies. We had one question, what tipped the scales toward picking Mustang?

The manager expressed total confidence in the choice of Mustang for a prime role in their program. They felt all companies would have to hire significantly for these projects and our culture readily assimilated new people and created strong teams better than anyone else. This was the most vivid demonstration of "culture eats strategy for breakfast" that I would ever see.

> "They felt all companies would have to hire significantly for these projects and our culture readily assimilated new people and created strong teams."

Change in staffing

The manager went on to say that instead of starting just Holstein in three weeks, they were also going to start Thunderhorse. Due to this change, they needed the standardization team to start concurrently such that equipment for the program could be selected for both projects.

As we were signing the contract I said a little prayer, wondering if I was signing the death warrant for Mustang's culture. We would have to go on a hiring binge to staff these teams plus assist BP in program management and interface coordination.

I used to joke that I would go hunting and poke a bear in the eye and run into Paul's cabin with it chasing me. Then I'd run out the back door and slam it, trusting Paul and his teams could skin it. This would be one BIG bear!

Upstream seems to know before us.

KICK OFF MEETING BIG SURPRISE

Mad Dog?

Paul had pulled about a hundred rabbits out of a well-worn hat to staff teams for the kickoff meeting. We had the project managers from the MPN and Mobil projects there with key members of their teams to start Holstein and Thunderhorse.

Holstein spar.

Thunderhorse semi-submersible.

We had our project manager from BP Liberty there to start the standardization team with some strong talent. We also brought some of our department managers so they would understand the staffing needs firsthand.

Mad Dog Truss Spar.

We noticed that BP's core team for Mad Dog was there and went over to say hello. We told them it was great for them to be present and see how things were being set up. They said that they were actually there because BP had decided to kick their project off at the same time to lower costs. This change in strategy would also insure first oil for BP from whichever project finished first. Each project had to contend with different schedule risks.

Staffing challenge

We needed to staff teams for three of the biggest and most challenging deepwater projects in the world. We also had to staff integration teams to break the deepwater silos. Additionally we had to staff a project team that would be doing the standardization. Talk about dead men walking...this would be 300 people out of our 1,000 person company that had everyone currently billable on projects!! The 300 would grow to 1,100 in 26 months.

Our saving grace was that BP and their partners were not prepared for this change in direction either and it would take time for them to staff with people from around the world. BP had to develop all the other parts of the project, e.g. drilling rigs, hulls, mooring, drilling programs, risers, subsurface manifolds and flowlines, worldwide sourcing of materials, etc.

Atlantis

After 18 months the standardization team lead by William Chumchal rolled onto the fourth project named Atlantis under Greg Sills of BP Arco. It was a semi-submersible that received all the benefit of the other projects. Silos were firmly busted on Atlantis (shown below) with significant savings.

"Choose well. The choice is but brief, yet endless."
Johann Wolfgang von Goethe, Writer

73: ADOPT THAT PARENT!

Both of the final contenders understood the importance of Mustang maintaining its culture in order to dominate the niche it had developed in the hydrocarbon industry. Mustang was poised to double in size in all sectors over the next 12 months due to project awards while up for sale. They knew this amazing result was due to reputation and culture. Both suitors were focused on the upstream sector and winning the world's most sought after deepwater contract from BP reinforced their choice to pursue Mustang.

CHOOSING

Final two

Paul was leaning toward Kiewit, a large family owned industrial construction company headquartered in the USA. They had moved into offshore construction with the purchase of 49% of the Aker Gulf Marine fabrication facility in Corpus Christi, Texas. Paul worked hard on some bids with Aker Gulf Marine to show Kiewit how strong we were in the upstream industry.

I was leaning toward Wood Group, a family owned engineering and offshore services company out of Aberdeen, Scotland. My feelings were based on seeing the demise of so many engineering firms when they were purchased by a construction oriented company. Being "services" oriented, Wood Group would understand the "people and culture" component better. Culturally, Wood Group felt that they were the "Mustang" of the North Sea.

Mustang goes into a huddle to weigh bids

US engineering house to sift suitors' offers over weekend

BLAKE WRIGHT and ERIK MEANS

from Houston

MUSTANG Engineering has kicked off a fast-track evaluation of bids that landed last Friday from four would-be suiters of the Houston-based outfit.

The company, which put itself on the market last October, is set to review the offers with a decision on a firm course of action targeted for the end of the month.

US-based construction company Peter Kiewitt & Sons, which already owns 49% of Texas ship-

Evaluation: Bill Higgs of Mustang Photo: AD KOEN

tang's asking price at approximately $100 million.

Mustang's stock has gone up in recent months due to a number of high-profile jobs landing on its

onslaught of new work from the supermajor both domestically and in the international arena.

Mustang was recently involved in a cost-reduction study for the development of BP Amoco's Clair field in the North Sea and is well-placed to receive any additional work that may come forth in light of renewed interest in the development.

The company has also been attached to such headline developments as Chevron's Typhoon in the deep-water US Gulf, and Texaco's Agbami and Shell's Ea fields off west Africa.

Conference calls with the respective bidders are understood to be lined up for this weekend. Mustang intends to choose a winner and a runner-up, and immediately begin hammering out a deal.

Another option for the company could be to remain an inde-

Upstream article May 5th 2000.

JP Kenny tips the scales

Wood Group had purchased JP Kenny about four years prior and set up a meeting for us to find out how it had gone since then. Kenny had been the top engineering firm for subsea and pipeline work worldwide based out of Houston and the UK. Wood Group had put people into a number of top positions in Kenny and pushed on bidding and salaries to be more in line with Wood Group. Kenny started losing projects they should have won and their people started leaving to follow those projects. This helped their competitors like Intec grow stronger. In the second year they started missing revenue and profit targets and were feeling somewhat helpless to stop the downward spiral. They had some tough meetings with Wood Group management where they demonstrated that Kenny had to be run in a much different manner than Wood Group Engineering in Aberdeen if it was going to be successful. To their credit, Wood Group changed how they were working with Kenny and they resumed their leadership role in the industry.

WOOD GROUP

The Company

We felt Wood Group more readily understood the importance of culture, compensation and capability in a Houston based engineering firm after their experience with Kenny. We would work primarily with their engineering arm out of Aberdeen that did modification and revamp work in the North Sea. We would also work with JP Kenny as we had on a number of deepwater projects already. We decided on Wood Group.

Rollout the decision

Now that we knew who we wanted for a parent, we needed to get the word out so we would be free to work final due diligence analysis. We did a pamphlet similar to the one dated 10/4/99, but this one was dated 7/20/00...the 13th anniversary of starting Mustang...it felt like another moon shot!!

The story was very positive since we had added 270 people and 115,000 sq. ft. of space since 10/4/99.

Our key criteria for picking Wood Group were:
- Cultural fit and good home for Mustangers.
- Significant value to shareholders.
- Opportunity to grow Mustang and become a leading worldwide engineering company.
- Ownership in Mustang and Wood Group for 650 ESOP members.

My favorite possible Q&A in the pamphlet was:

Q: Will you be mad if I'm a chicken-hearted wimp and leave Mustang because of possible changes?

A: Yes...but we'll get over it. ☺

CELEBRATE

The owners

Felix set up a celebratory dinner for us and wives at the very upscale four star restaurant Tony's near River Oaks in Houston. Toward the end of dinner we were all given two boxes to open. In the large box was a picture of Felix on a showroom floor with three silver Jaguar XKRs arranged around him.

Felix with his babies.

They were "Silverstone" limited edition...only 200 were made. Then we opened the small box and there were the keys!! This was way over the top...Felix and Joyce had bought the cars in the photo and were ready to show them to us. We all went outside and lined up side by side were the three convertibles with the tops down, looking totally amazing!! We all got in and started them up with huge smiles on our faces. We could easily talk back and forth on a beautiful evening outside of Tony's... unbelievable. What a great thing for Felix and Joyce to do as a thank you for helping him retire...you could feel the love and respect we had for each other...and the sense of accomplishment in saying "job well done."

Sir Ian Wood

The office was abuzz because Sir Ian Wood was coming to visit and meet people now that the sale was complete. It is not often in America that you get to meet someone that was Knighted by the Queen of England. Plus he now owned a big piece of Mustang and everyone wanted to know what type of a person he was. We set up for him to meet the extended management team and then had a party in the reception area with cake for anyone that could make it.

Paul Redmon and Sir Ian Wood.

Everyone found Sir Ian to be very personable and inquisitive about their daily tasks or some new thing he had heard about Mustang.

Eggshells

The Wood Group Board came to visit and we were all seated in our conference room. Sir Ian and his team were explaining why they felt the purchase was good for Wood Group and how well positioned Mustang was in its primary industries.

Everyone in the room was a little on edge and it felt like people were walking on eggshells. We had not had a boss in 13 years and wanted to be careful in how we came across. The Wood Group people had been cautioned by Sir Ian to not mess with Mustang as we knew our business.

Chief Financial Officer (CFO)

In order to stimulate some constructive conversation we said that we had been needing a CFO for over a year but wanted to wait until after the sale to hire one. We knew that acquiring companies generally want to put one of their own people in this position to insure no financial surprises.

Sir Ian Wood and Alan Semple (the Wood Group CFO) looked knowingly at each other and then Sir Ian broached the subject. He said that all members of the Board also felt that Mustang had outgrown a Controller and needed a CFO as its first priority. They felt that the CFO should be hired by Mustang and report to Paul with a dotted line to Alan.

Wow. Paul and I looked at each other and chills went up my spine. There was no better answer to this question. We really were going to have good autonomy as long as we delivered our plan and kept the boss informed.

While looking at the recent financials one of the new board members questioned what he thought was an error in that the number for interest was positive instead of negative. Alan Semple took that question and explained that this was just one indicator of how different Mustang was. Mustang was debt free and earned interest from money in the bank...instead of paying interest on loans--unusual!

Sir Ian's philosophy

Sir Ian used a phrase "joined up thinking" to describe how he wanted the sixty companies he owned to work. He wanted the leadership teams of companies to figure out how to work with each other for organic and/or acquisition growth.

He also used the term "through-cycle growth" to describe what he wanted the leadership teams to deliver. He knew there were industry ups and downs, but wanted teams that could not lose in downturns, and take advantage of upturns.

BEDDING DOWN

We had a lot on our plates now that the sale had been completed and our new bosses had expressed total confidence in our ability to take Mustang forward. There were things we needed to fix organizationally:

- Succession planning to insure there were leaders ready to step up and to eventually transition Paul and me out.
- Strategic plan for good communication between us and Wood Group and with our people.
- Leadership training to pull the management team together as a unit.
- Accountability training to get every Mustanger aligned and pulling the load.
- Implementing a business development process for better communication between sales and operations.
- Developing more project managers into project sponsors to pull that burden off of Paul and me.

In addition to these Mustang areas, we had to staff and figure out the BP deepwater program along with 200 other open projects. Over 30 projects were pushing the technical limits in upstream, downstream, automation and pipeline and had a lot of visibility.

Paul came up with the European term "bedding down" to describe what he wanted the company doing for the next year. He wanted to calm things down as much as possible, organize and start executing at a high level in all of these areas.

Individuals not companies create excellence.

74: DEVELOPING THE 2ND GENERATION

We could not control the start of the BP deepwater program once the decision had been made to start all three projects and standardization at the same time. In addition we had to staff program management positions to help BP with interface management across the silos inherent in deepwater projects. In order to meet this need, Paul and all of the department managers essentially moved onto the projects over the summer of 2000. Our thinking was that most of the hiring would be for deepwater and the world class project management systems we would be creating would become our latest and greatest, so we needed our department managers directly involved. This put me pretty much running the rest of upstream and the rest of the sectors. Paul also took on working with our new CFO and transitioning everything that Felix had been doing to someone else...seemed like it took 23 people to replace Felix.

LEADERSHIP TRAINING

Retirement goal

Leadership styles varied significantly due to being developed in different parts of the industry, at different types of companies and with a variety of mentors. Paul and I needed to build a good leadership foundation for better communications within the management team. This would be the basis for us to fully develop the 2nd generation of leadership we would need for us to step back from daily operations. We had set the goal of being able to retire from Mustang by the fall of 2002 and this was the first step in preparing the team.

Common language

We enrolled our management team in a 12 week leadership and management course that would be taught on-site by Charles Wilds. The course started with basic psychology to have a common language and then moved through understanding yourself as a leader through tests such as Transactional Analysis, Parent-Adult-Child, and Myers Briggs®. Once we understood ourselves and how we could better relate with each other, the course walked us through developing Mustang's vision, values and strategy and how to lead the organization to deliver what we outlined.

> **"...the strategic plan and budget would align our team to deliver our vision while maintaining our core values."**

We liked the idea of having a strategic plan that could move us toward retirement in 2002. The strategic plan would also provide us with specific spending requirements to put into the budget we were creating.

The budget would help us control spending during the prodigious growth that was occurring in all of our sectors. Our budget was being set up to be reactive to what would happen in 2001, however, not to get out ahead and move that growth toward an end state that we wanted.

When worked in concert, the strategic plan and budget would align our team to deliver our vision while maintaining our core values. By creating a one, three and five year strategic plan we could insure that we were moving toward a sustainable organization with 2nd generation leadership in charge. It was not going to just happen...we had to design it.

VISION, VALUES, ETC.

Each week we spent some class time writing down thoughts on the company vision and what we felt were our core values. On 2/2/01 the team was again reviewing wording for the vision when a lightbulb went off in Steve Knowles brain and he quickly wrote down his thought and said "I've got it." And he did...we now had the Mustang corporate vision statement:

VISION

Our quest is to embody a culture
that inspires super-motivated
people to make heroes of
Clients, Partners, Vendors
and Mustangers!

In another week we finally worked to agreeing our core values. From about 27 words we decided on the following:

VALUES

Safety

Integrity	Customers
Mustangers	Quality
Teamwork	Profitability

Innovation

BP had taught us to do a "Safety Minute" before every meeting to raise awareness. We put safety as an over-arching core value. Only about 30% of the team supported innovation as a core value, but Paul and I pushed that one as being a critical habit to create our differentiation. Similar to safety we put it as the underpinning to our values.

SLOGANS
People Oriented...Project Driven™
Steady work for steady people
Mustang will satisfy you!!
Engineer down the hall
Digital and Digestible™
Fit for purpose
Mustangers

MOTTO
Just do it!

The vision, values, slogans, motto and blue horse made us feel confident that we had a great basis to start working on our corporate strategy. Paul and I were very proud of what the team had put together to codify our culture and insure Mustang's destiny.

Strategic plan

Dena Lee had recommended a consultant named Mark Payton to help Mustang with market analysis for strategic direction in 1999. Mark became instrumental in helping develop the Mustang story for the sale and now we wanted to have him help Don Leinweber and me pull together our first strategic plan. We decided to break the plan into five critical areas: people, projects, management, strategy, and business development. Below these critical areas we developed 2-4 goals that would address the needs that had been identified through corporate culture surveys and client feedback surveys gathered through Mark's efforts. For each goal (the "what") we stated the rewards if achieved, the consequences if not achieved, the affirmations to be gained from achievement and the core values that the goal supported.

We wanted people to understand the "why" behind the goals presented. Then it was up to each sector, department and project to develop their own tactical action plans to achieve the goals "the how" in light of their reality. Each goal and tactical action plan had a "who" assigned to report out regularly on accomplishment by the agreed upon dates "the when". We made sure that our goals were SMART; specific, measurable, achievable, resource and time based.

Strategic objective

We wanted the team doing the right things to insure we could weather the next downturn in work. We knew that Mustang was going to create its own downturn independent of the industry when the BP deepwater program would de-staff in 2002…it would be too big of a hole in the backlog to fill. We wanted the leadership team to handle the next downturn no matter where or how it originated.

This was the one true real world test for the team. When a company starts to spiral down, can they turn it around and get it spiraling back up. Like in the Terminator movie, we believed in "no fate", believing that we did not have to spiral down with the industry. Getting the management team to believe in this concept would require a "trial by fire" in the future.

Blow up the myths

In order to hand off Mustang, we had to "blow up the myths" that had developed around us. Paul seemed to magically be able to put good teams together and help line out projects for success. I seemed to magically be able to deliver all of the work Mustang needed and stay upbeat even when things were tough. People called stepping into my office stepping into "Bill's world" where everything works to your favor and clients take care of you!

"Let's set them up for success."
Paul Redmon, CEO Mustang

75: PAUL'S EXIT STRATEGY

The reality was that Paul and I had all of the Mustang history to pull from in making things work and it could look like magic. I called it the "Noble House effect" after James Clavell's novel. The novel takes 1,000 pages to cover 7 days because the leader of the Noble House can pull from so much history in moving countries and people to do his will. We did it in a seemingly effortless manner, creating myths that would make it hard for people to believe we could be replaced. We knew that processes and systems combined with good leadership could replace what we were doing and spread the load to many hands.

WITH SUSTAINABILITY

Manage the project managers

Paul continued to reduce the number of people who reported to him. He elevated four upstream project managers to group managers with three to four project managers reporting to each. This let Paul keep his finger on all upstream projects through weekly meetings with the "four horsemen", whose job it was to develop best practices and insure their implementation.

Hire an experienced HR professional

We hired Sharon Paul to head up HR and she changed many things we were doing and started things we did not know we needed. We should have pulled in a talent like Sharon seven years earlier.

Sharon knew how to negotiate benefits and implement them much better than anyone we had. She knew how to set up a very responsive HR organization that could keep pace with our hiring 40-90 people per month while working to keep our culture. She recommended consultants to help us with leadership training, started a business book of the month club to foster communication and helped develop succession planning. She implemented 360 degree reviews for the leadership team, resulting in Paul and me getting meaningful feedback on how we were perceived in the organization. Once we had Sharon, we knew that we would never slight the HR function again.

Use the CFO to keep score

Our first CFO did not last very long primarily because he spent too much time working with Wood Group and not enough time working on Mustang. He seemed to feel that his career path was with Wood Group and we could not get his attention.

Our second CFO was Meg Lassarat...a super-intelligent powerhouse that was totally focused on figuring out Mustang. She definitely wanted to develop the tools for sector and department managers to run their business. She worked hard to insure that she understood the assumptions and basis for budgets and ran a very tight system.

We had to calm her down a bit on pushing the leaders when she saw them getting a little off track. Paul's philosophy was that he wanted the CFO to work with the leadership to develop the budgets and plans...but then the job was to "keep score." By knowing the score in close to real time, the leadership team was then tasked with figuring out how to win. He did not want the CFO directing the leadership team on action they needed to take. Once Meg was comfortable with this role, it took some pressure off of her and she excelled.

Develop an heir apparent...or two

Steve Knowles had come into Mustang working on the Mobil Zafiro FPSO under AJ Cortez. Paul had worked intensely over the years with both of them and felt that either could take the reins from him.

We continued to work with leadership consultants after completing the leadership course as they knew how to help us open up communication and get into the right conversations to move the organization. With one consultant we took the Myers Briggs Type Indicator® test and then discussed how each of us perceived people, things, ideas, etc. and how we judged those same things due to our personality type.

With another consultant we took the DiSC® assessment which helped us learn each other's leadership style. With each assessment we made adjustments to the organization and jobs people held as we learned more. Paul and his leadership team were getting much better at working with each other and within the company.

The leadership teams in all sectors and departments were doing the same testing activities as we worked to build their confidence in taking Mustang forward. We pushed this type of assessment and conversation two more levels down into the organization as that was where the leadership would be coming from in 5-10 years.

At one of our top level offsite meetings with a consultant, all of the sector managers came to the conclusion that they would definitely be in favor of Steve becoming President of Mustang and we were free to implement that change when we felt ready. AJ would take over the Upstream sector.

We then met offsite with our department managers and they also agreed that Steve had all the skills and heart to lead Mustang's 2nd generation.

Elevate department managers

Department managers now had 200-300 people in their groups and had developed leaders under them to split up the workload. I remember visiting with a lead electrical designer on one of the BP deepwater projects. He was managing a 120,000 manhour budget on a 24 month schedule...this was three times the size of the biggest jobs Paul and I had managed. We had incredible talent that had come into Mustang in all of our sectors.

The department managers were now running small companies with project managers as their prime client. Paul had department managers developing best practices and supported pushing these into all projects for consistency.

Emphasize system development and training

System development and training was a critical goal in our strategy to free us out of day-to-day action. State of the art systems were being developed on BP deepwater and department managers were implementing a Mustang slimmed-down version of them across all projects. Young Guns with four to six years at Mustang were being used to help with the training and tweaking of the systems to help bring the 3rd generation along. Paul had a passion for this area and instilled this passion deep into the organization.

Get an "owner" for each new initiative

We insured that we had a champion for each new initiative. Sharon took on recruiting. Chick Houseman took responsibility for making the California office profitable. Scott Worthington started our midstream group developing LNG technology and regasification of LNG to move it from tankers to pipelines. There were over 30 key initiatives in support of the strategic plan and all had someone other than Paul or me in charge.

Go hunting in October

It turned out that BP deepwater was still expanding in 2002. By 2004, however, we were ready for the transition to 2nd generation but Paul and I were like tar-babies...it seemed like things kept sticking to us.

Paul took three weeks off in the beginning of October for a hunting trip. In the middle of the third week Paul called me to say he was enjoying the time off and wondered if I could handle two more weeks without him. I told him that some things had come up, but that I was pushing the team to just handle them...so yes, enjoy a few more weeks.

It was interesting to see some faces at the staff meeting when I let everyone know that Paul would be gone until the 10th of November. People were uncomfortable not having Paul available. By the 6th of November I could feel that people were waiting with a barrage of things for Paul's return.

I called Paul and asked if he could keep himself busy until after Thanksgiving and he said no problem, he would be back December 3rd. Shortly after Thanksgiving I called and asked Paul to not come back until January 7th. He was ecstatic and said no problem. By the 10th of December the dam started to break and everyone started making decisions that just could not wait any longer. I was encouraging them to make decisions and then adjust as they saw results.

We finally had the 2nd generation in charge of operations by mid 2005. Steve Knowles and Don Leinweber took charge of pulling the 2006 strategic plan and budget together. In December 2005, we told them to take over and implement both.

On President's Day of 2006 we promoted Steve to President of Mustang and we pulled totally out of day-to-day operations with no ripples in the organization.

76: BILL'S EXIT STRATEGY

One of the reasons I wanted to help drive the first few strategic plans was to get better alignment between sales and operations.

WITH SUSTAINABILITY

Strategic plan to align sales and operations

Many of the large international projects we were chasing would take 6-18 months from identification to award. We needed the whole team onboard to stretch to do a project if it happened to land at a poor time due to our workload. Each time this had happened in the past, we had stretched to take on a project that we had chased. We felt pretty comfortable turning down work that "found us" when we were busy, but were not comfortable turning down work that we had chased and aligned to our execution strategy.

NEEDS	STRATEGY (WHAT)	TECHNICAL ACTION PLAN (TAP) NOW	CRITICAL AREA: PEOPLE STRATEGIC GOAL (PATH): #2 KEEP THE MORALE AND CULTURE AS DIFFERENTIATOR		ACTIONER	PRIORITY	TAP DONE (MO/YR)	FINAL (MO/YR)	COMME
REWARDS:			People will come to Mustang and stay with Mustang because it is different than other Engineering firms.	**AFFIRMATIONS:**			We are proud to be Mustangers and we set the standard.		
CONSEQUENCES:			Become like other Engineering firms and have to compete for everything based mainly on price.	**CORE VALUES EFFECTED:**			Integrity, Customers, Employees, Quality, T Profitability, Innovation		
NEED TO DEFINE THE CULTURE									
			Establish a Culture Team		L. Buckner			Jun-01	
			Define the Culture		Higgs				Working
			Emphasize Culture at New Hire Breakfast		Higgs				Ongoing
			Conduct Benchmark Survey of Culture and Morale		M. Kunz				
			Implement Culture Training		L. Buckner				
NEED MAINTAIN ENERGY IN ACTIVITIES									
			Plan and Execute Yearly Mustang Activities		L. Buckner		N/A		Ongoing
			Plan Project and Department Activities - Make a Need		L. Buckner				Ongoing
			Build Activity Enthusiasm Through Bulletin Boards and Newsletter		D. Lee				Ongoing
NEED TO GET NEW PEOPLE CONNECTED									
			Provide New Hire Sponsor Program		Kunz				
			Provide New Hire Briefing by HR		Kunz				Ongoing
			Provide New Hire Breakfast		Lamkin				Ongoing
NEED TO KNOW WHEN WHY PEOPLE LEAVE									
			Implement Formal Process for Feedback on why People Leave and Communicate to Leaders		Kunz				Ongoing
NEW EMPLOYEE DEVELOPMENT									

Format for the strategic plan.

Some plans didn't work

The first strategic plan tasked upstream sales with replacing BP deepwater in the fall of 2002 when it would ramp down significantly. We would need to replace 1,000,000 manhours of work per year in order to avoid a layoff of hundreds of people.

Our solution was pretty audacious. We had worked with Hyundai on a number of projects and felt that they were being treated poorly by the large American engineering and construction companies. None of the American oil companies would hire Hyundai direct, but needed their capability in shipbuilding for the mammoth floating structures in deepwater. The American oil companies seemed to be more comfortable with Hyundai and other Korean contractors (such as Daewoo) being used as a subcontractor to the American E&C firms. This contracting strategy created a poor execution strategy that cost significant dollars and schedule. We had helped Hyundai win projects where we were their interface with the client and the FEED engineer providing a defined project into their fabrication yard in Korea. We wanted to work with Exxon to approve this contracting strategy for some large FPSO projects that fit well into Hyundai's yard.

By August of 2002 we had everything in place for this contracting strategy. All the right parts of the Exxon organization had done their due diligence and had agreed to the strategy. I went to Korea for final negotiations of our contract since the first bidder's meeting with Exxon would be in September.

Just before I left, Paul told me that we might not be able to take on the project because the BP deepwater suite of projects was not projecting any reduction in staffing for the next nine months and this project should start in six months.

We received a good contract from Hyundai with rates that would allow us to go get people if we needed to. Our staffing projections however showed that we could not take on the Exxon FPSO project. We recommended another firm to Hyundai and they won the work direct to Exxon. They then did three of the world's largest FPSOs back-to-back over the next six years. This was a great win for Hyundai and our strategy, but showed how we needed better communication internally.

Miller Heiman®

Mark Payton did research to identify an existing sales system that used our philosophy of selling with a win-win attitude. We also wanted the system to engage operations people in a collaborative manner in order to develop better "team sales." Part of the solution would be to use a common language in sales such that all members of the team would understand the terms we used. The Miller Heiman® process fit the bill as it was designed to handle everything from simple to complex sales situations, had collaborative tools and provided a clear lexicon of terms for a common language.

One of the things we wanted to achieve with a sales process was better transparency into what our sales people were doing to advance a prospect toward becoming real work. With more transparency our operations people would be able to engage better and help the sales person close the sale. I could also get involved at the right time as I was considered to be one of the best closers in the industry...but I needed to have the right timing.

Paul and I wanted predictable sales. We wanted a sales process that would move a sales prospect through stages just like our stage gate process moved projects along. As the prospect moved through successive stages it became firmer and our backlog projections became better.

The primary tool for collaboration was the Miller Heiman Bluesheet®. On it the sales person fills in all the data they know about the prospect. Then, along with the operations and management team, possible actions are brainstormed and an action plan is agreed. As those actions are completed, the group gets back together to determine the best next actions. This was a big step toward getting people comfortable that they could produce the "Higgs magic" of booking projects.

Full Throttle

We developed the Full Throttle campaign around the Miller Heiman sales process to identify and energize sales teams around each sales person. Just like in NASCAR we needed a talented driver, a coach directing and a pit crew making sure the car was in tip top shape.

For our pit crews we assigned a project manager to each sales person along with proposal support, a probable future coach and two Young Guns for legwork and learning. We now had a team that would work part time to support the sales person. This team had a strong desire to develop an efficient process that would deliver projects into Mustang.

SECTOR MANAGER

ADMIN ASSISTANT   BD PERSON   PROJECT MANAGER

YOUNG GUN   YOUNG GUN

PROPOSAL SUPPORT   OPERATIONS PERSON

Full Throttle – "Driving Your Destiny"

Full Throttle was a critical part of my exit strategy as it demystified the Higgs sales process and gave technical managers confidence that they could direct sales with predictable results. Operations could drive sales to meet their needs.

Oz® Principle Accountability

As a company we now had a strategic plan, budgets, sales plans and project plans. We had good methods to measure progress and understood the key performance indicators (KPIs) to insure we stayed on track on each plan. As we grew, however, it seemed like we were continuously re-planning due to missing intermediate milestones in the plans and budgets. As we evaluated how we had incremented ourselves into not executing to the level we expected, it just seemed like management was "pushing a rope" in trying to get people to do what was required. We felt that we needed better personal accountability from our people to deliver these plans.

> "If you are pointing your finger at someone concerning a problem, there are three fingers pointing back at you."

The old saying was that if you are pointing your finger at someone concerning a problem, there are three fingers pointing back at you. When we looked at ourselves and asked some probing questions to some of our "old hands" it appeared that we had not communicated what we wanted people to do in an effective manner. Our people felt that their sense of accountability to making Mustang great had not changed but there were many conflicting demands coming at them from various directions. They felt that they needed clearer direction on how they could be part of the solution instead of being considered part of the problem.

Mark Payton suggested we try the Oz® Principle Accountability process as taught by Partners in Leadership, Inc. Once we understood the tenants of the program it sounded like it could have been written by Mustang.

In a very simple manner the program worked down from the strategic goals to the tactical action plans to the individual's goals. Each individual then understood how their manageable and achievable goals would roll up to deliver the company's goals. Now we had one of my objectives of "all eyes are informed eyes" to insure we were doing the right things.

At each level in the company the Oz® program wanted people to be able to see a problem, own that problem, solve it at their level and then do the action required. We also wanted people to communicate to management what they had done in case the same problem in a slightly different form was in another area of the company. All of this set up well for people to line out and progress through the use of their Planner Pads®.

Higgs Boson

Many people got a kick out of physicists discovering the Higgs Boson which had been predicted but not yet identified in an atom smasher. The announcement of its discovery described the particle as being all energy with no mass. They felt this described me! We needed to cultivate ways to duplicate my team building energy. I put the onus onto the marketing team as their inside marketing job. They along with the Rabble Rousers pushing team building activities would continuously rejuvenate the Mustang culture. All of this was tied into what became known as the "Heart of Mustang" program.

By 2004 I was out of day to day activity. President's Day 2006 we turned the company over to Steve Knowles and I moved to Charlotte in order to limit my availability. Paul was involved in creating an exotic game ranch west of Houston and the 2nd generation was in charge!!

"Legacy is etched into the minds of others and the stories they share."

Shannon L. Alder, Author

77: LEGACY

Paul, Felix and I had started Mustang with the vision of creating a company that took care of people in an industry that seemed to put everyone into win-lose scenarios. We loved doing the very challenging offshore oil and gas projects available in the Houston market and felt they would be more fun in a win-win environment.

CULTURE

The industry summed things up for us.

PROJECTS

Wood Group Mustang has stayed at the forefront of deepwater development by providing topsides and system integration support on world class projects. Generally the silos on deepwater projects have a blue layer where Mustang's interface coordinators reside.

Silos with the Mustang blue coordinator layer.

In 2016, *Offshore Magazine* provided awards for the industry's top five projects of 2015. Wood Group Mustang worked on two of them:

Chevron Jack/St. Malo semi-submersible.

The Jack/St. Malo field consists of subsea completions flowing to a semi-submersible floating production unit. It is the largest of its kind in the Gulf and can produce 170,000bpd of oil. The field is located in about 7,000 feet of water. Wood Group Mustang did the FEED and then the detailed design of the topsides. Wood Group provided the planning, managing and field execution of the commissioning.

JP Kenny did the pipeline design. The combination of extreme water depths, large diameter, high-pressure design and pipeline structures set new milestones for the Gulf.

Anadarko Lucius spar.

Mustang did the first production spar for Oryx in the 1990s when they took the risk to develop Neptune. Subsequently Oryx was acquired by Kerr McGee who was acquired by Anadarko. Aker's yard in Finland for spar hulls was acquired by Technip. The Oryx-Mustang-Aker legacy is pictured above. Lucius is the largest and most technically advanced spar. It is moored in 7,100 feet of water and will produce from multiple fields at a rate of 80,000 bpd oil.

Anadarko does not believe in re-inventing the wheel and has a philosophy of "design one, build two." It feels like Anadarko and WG Mustang are a perfectly matched best-in-class team in terms of philosophy. The second spar will be installed at the Heidelberg location in 2016.

PEOPLE

In 2015 the 2nd generation handed off to the 3rd generation at Wood Group Mustang. Michele McNichol took over as CEO from Steve Knowles. She came to Mustang on the BP Thunderhorse project when we were absorbing amazing talent from throughout the industry.

Although the culture and the "Heart of Mustang" have evolved, they are still a differentiator that can be felt.

Heart of Mustang logo.

In the final analysis, Mustang has always been about making heroes and people taking care of PEOPLE.

Wood Group Mustang logo.

SWOT Analysis, end of 2000+ ...
Full Throttle with Joined Up Thinking

Strengths
- People – Mustangers.
- Culture – environment.
- Client focused.
- Integrity/reputation.
- Dedication to work quality.

Weaknesses
- Training at all levels.
- Saying no to work.
- Promoting culture at all levels.
- Strategy for systems, procedures and processes.

Opportunities
- Strategic acquisitions.
- Synergies with Wood Group (Joined Up Thinking).
- Expansion in international markets.
- Developing standards learned on BP deepwater.
- Potential technology alignments.
- Development of low cost engineering.
- Move into program management.

Threats
- Inability to make BP a hero.
- Losing people damages culture.
- Increased competition through mergers.
- Industry perception of overload.
- Shortage of skilled people.

EPILOGUE

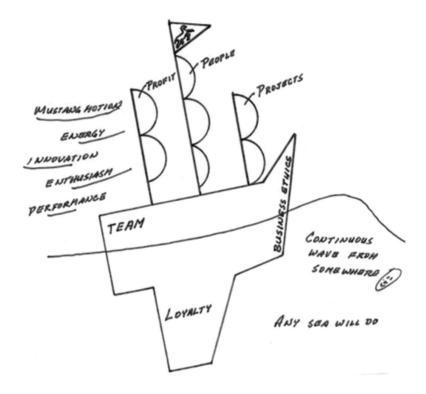

Everyone at an off-site meeting was asked to draw their concept of Mustang as a ship. I drew this and had the following explanation:

"Naturally Powered"
MUSTANG Ship designed by Paul, Felix & Bill

It is a squatty, plain sailing ship shaped more like an unsinkable cork...nothing fancy, but indomitable. The ship is leaning to imply that it is always moving...similar to the *MUSTANG ENGINEERING* letters and the blue horse on one hoof.

We wanted this ship to be "naturally powered" by our team's performance, innovation and enthusiasm. Pay us market rate for above-market performance. No worries about protecting ourselves. More than expected, better that expected.

We built with a strong deep keel of loyalty for stability in any storm. The keel let us pull more wind to go faster in good weather. We helped build in loyalty between Mustangers, vendors and clients toward a strong Mustang, based upon performance. Steady work for steady people. Buy a slice (team) of Mustang.

We named the ship "Team" as team building and team execution would be our focus in every facet of the business, from projects to administration to philanthropy.

The main or "Royal Sail" in ship vernacular, is People. People would be the main force pulling the ship along, due to their reputations, attitudes and desires. Projects are out front pulling, where we can see them and concentrate on getting them right the first time. People Oriented...Project Driven™.

Profits are also critical to pulling the ship, but are in the background of our attention. They are actually pulled along to some extent by the people and projects.

The ship is assisted by riding a "continuous wave from somewhere." This wave is generated by philosophies of; sell while the shop is full, continuous recruitment, and taking on all types of work...a "no one cares if we survive mentality." Our feeling in building this ship was that "any sea will do" as this team could rise to any occasion and would deal with the "current industry realities."

Proudly waving above everything is the Blue Horse which represents all we stand for in the world. It is there to remind us of our desire to live above the common level of life and deliver on our commitments.

The ship I drew only looks to the future in the aspect that the ship is prepared for anything that comes.

Bill Higgs

MUSTANG KNOWLEDGE [THE INDEX]

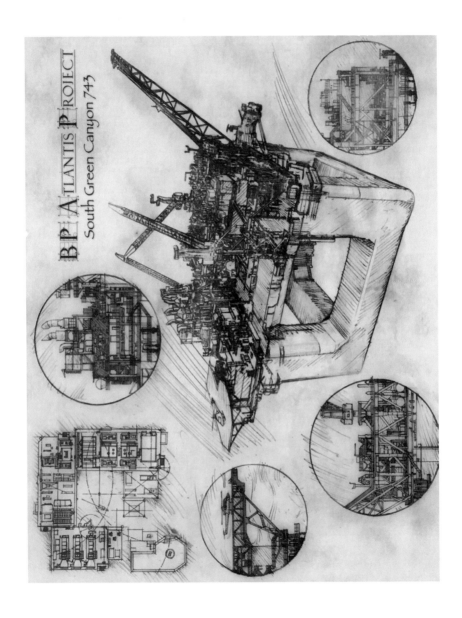